DATE DUE

9·5·68			
OCT 1 '83			
MAY 0 3 2003			
GAYLORD			PRINTED IN U.S.A.

FAMOUS AMERICAN DUELS

ALEXANDER HAMILTON

FAMOUS AMERICAN DUELS

WITH SOME ACCOUNT OF THE CAUSES THAT LED UP TO THEM AND THE MEN ENGAGED

BY

DON C. SEITZ, Lit.D.

Essay Index Reprint Series

BOOKS FOR LIBRARIES PRESS, INC.

FREEPORT, NEW YORK

First published 1929
Reprinted 1966

To

WILLIAM O. TAYLOR

FOREWORD

The narratives I have here gathered are filled with thrills and foolishness. In spite of the progress of civilization, the duel survived well up into the latter part of the last century in the United States. Happily human sensitiveness has become sufficiently dilute not to demand satisfaction for affront on what was once called "the field of honor." There proceedings took place under a code of rules modified to fit circumstances sustained by a public opinion that did not permit a jury to convict in the case of fatal outcome, if, indeed, it ever came before one. Distinguished statesmen fought to defend their fair fame. One man who became President, and another who was Vice-President at the moment, reddened their hands. Four of the encounters listed ranked as national tragedies. So great became the evil that legislatures were compelled to enact statutes for its suppression.

Certain students of society have argued that the duel was a decorous influence, in making men careful in their conduct toward each other through personal accountability. The claim is hardly borne out by the facts. All too often the wrong man died. The best excuse was that the duel prevented informal brawls and gave personal encounters an atmosphere of gentility, safeguarding rights at least as far as the pistol mouth. The free fight between Andrew Jackson and the Benton brothers, detailed in the pages that follow,

vii

is given as an example of the wrong thing from the
duelling standpoint.

If, in a few instances, the critical will conceive that
the incidents are rather heavily documented, the reason
may be found in a desire to portray the extreme meticu-
lousness observed in order to make trifles appear important enough to fight about. The volume is written
to reward the curious and to make more accessible
strange chapters in American history.

Thanks are due to Robert Hunt Lyman, Charles H.
Taylor, Clarence S. Brigham, Curator of the American
Antiquarian Society; Charles E. Goodspeed and Miss
Alice R. Flynn, for valuable assistance.

D. C. S.

Authors Club, New York,
January, 1929

CONTENTS

LIST OF PORTRAITS

FAMOUS AMERICAN DUELS

CHAPTER I

THE DUELLO

WE get the word "duel" from *bellum* and *duo,* Latin terms for "war" and "two"—the combination and contraction of which are made to mean "war between two." Probably the custom had its origin in the rule which the German tribes brought when they invaded Europe, of compelling men to fight out their differences with one another. Buckle, in his *History of Civilization in England,* lays the practice to chivalry, reaching its polite perfection in the pleasant land of France. He finds no evidence of any single private duel being fought earlier than the sixteenth century in England, and even then not many until the latter half of Queen Elizabeth's reign. In France duelling was common early in the fifteenth century, and in the sixteenth so spirited were the Gallic gamecocks that seconds fought each other on the side.

Chivalry departed with armor and Don Quixote. When mail was the fashion, knights jousted on horseback, in the splendid style described in *Ivanhoe.* The accidental killing of King Francis II, of France, husband of Mary, Queen of Scots, in an encounter with one Montgomery, a Scotch knight in his service, spoiled the pastime. When coats of mail disappeared, gentlemen fought as a rule with rapiers. The French nobility became as sensitive as fighting birds; a look or a chance jostle were deemed enough to warrant an encounter. From the days of Charles IX on, the record reeks with blood. Prosper Mérimée's *Chronicle* of the reign of that King gives a lively picture of the *raffinés*. Nor does Dumas exaggerate in *The Three Musketeers,* who flourished at a date but little later. It is asserted that during the first decade of the seventeenth century not less than two thousand French nobles fell by the sword in defense of their egregious honor.

Italy, too, took kindly to duelling, but the bravo killed the habit among gentlemen in that sunny land. It persists in mild form in France to this day, where, thanks to custom and poor marksmanship, it has assumed a comic form. Mark Twain really laughed the seriousness out of it in his burlesque of an imaginary encounter with M. Leon Gambetta, the humor of which, while pretty deep for the Parisian mind, nevertheless made itself felt.

Up to the outbreak of the World War duelling was practically compulsory in the German Army. The Kaiser endorsed it, and officers who failed to accept challenges lost their commissions; that is, pressure from above made them resign. In the German universities duelling was a function that took the place of hazing in American colleges. The combatants were so heavily swathed that cheeks and chins were the only parts left vulnerable. The scars thus secured were highly prized. Recently, civil courts have checked these affairs, which were formerly regulated by the faculties. Heidelberg was famous for its duels, all solemnly conducted under a most meticulous code. Bismarck, when a student at Göttingen, fought twenty-eight duels, escaping with a single scratch. He evaded a twenty-ninth encounter by explaining that in calling the challenger "a silly youngster" he did not mean to be insulting but used the offending phrase "merely to express my conviction."

Spain was the first of the nations to forbid the practice, for there, as in Italy, the hired ruffian, hiding a dagger beneath his cloak, had become the minister of revenge. It was in the second decade of the eighteenth century that the King proclaimed the prohibition of duelling under a heading reading, *Pragmatica que su Majestad ha mandado promulgar, 1716, par la que prohibe los Duelos, Retos y Desafios baxo de gravas penas.*

In England the hot-Scots, who followed King James to Westminster, seem to have imported a superior sensitiveness along with short Spanish swords, dirks, and pistols. His Majesty had to warn them by proclamation. The duel, however, flourished under Charles, his son. One notable case was the encounter between Jeffrey Hudson, Queen Henrietta's pet dwarf, and Mr. Crofts. The pygmy had been the ward of George Villiers, the famous Buckingham of *The Three Musketeers,* who caused him to pop out of a pie at a dinner given in honor of their majesties. He was dressed in complete armor, and waved a sword bravely. The Queen, much charmed, begged the dwarf of the Duke, and thereafter he amused royalty. Indeed, Hudson did more. He captained a troop of Horse against the Roundheads and made a record for reckless valor. Henrietta took him to France when she left England in exile. Before this a London wit had written a verse describing a fight between the mite and a turkey cock, in which the dwarf saved himself by flight. Crofts, a young officer in the Queen's suite, taunted the little fellow with this and received a challenge. This he accepted, but appeared on the ground armed with a squirt gun. In a mighty rage Hudson insisted on a duel with pistols from horseback. It followed, and Crofts was shot through the heart.

Duels grew in frequency after the Restoration. Grim Cromwell would not tolerate such nonsense, but Charles II and his successors did. In King William's time Lord Townshend, Minister of Ordnance, fought a duel but only slightly wounded his antagonist. "It was lucky for me," said the latter, "that Lord Townshend used Government gunpowder; but for its bad quality the shot might have killed me."

A "Joe Miller" jest had to do with two would-be combatants, who compromised on the field. When one second suggested that they shake hands, the other said the ceremony was superfluous—their hands had been shaking ever since they arrived at the scene!

One Hyde Park encounter was called off at early dawn by the wit of a second who halted a passing hearse with the suggestion that if the driver would wait he might gain some custom. The principals laughed and made up.

Queen Anne's era saw much fighting. Charles

Mohun, a peer of Devon—"My Lord Mohun" of Thackeray's *Henry Esmond*—had a red record. He finally fought the Duke of Hamilton in Hyde Park in the early morning of November 15, 1712. Both were killed.

Duels were fought in strange and desperate ways—across tables, in locked rooms, and in the dark. The mild Ralph Waldo Emerson relates a tale of a fight between an Englishman and a Frenchman in London, where the seconds put out the lights and left. The Englishman, not wishing to hurt his antagonist, fired up the chimney—and brought down the Frenchman!

Much could be written about duels for silly causes. For example, Lieutenant Sterne, father of the Reverend Laurence Sterne of *Tristram Shandy* fame, was run through by Captain Philips, of Handyside's Regiment, in a row that began over a goose. Lord Byron's father killed Mr. Chaworth, at the Star and Garter, when they disagreed over the extent of their respective land holdings. Colonel Montgomery of the army was killed by Captain McNamara of the navy, because the latter objected to the tone of the former's "Call off your dog, sir!" when their two canines fell afoul of each other in Hyde Park.

John Wilkes, the famous agitator, was colonel of the Bucks militia as well as publisher of the *North Briton*. Some caustic things in this journal of reform roused Lord Talbot into a passion. He raged at Wilkes in person, demanding that he either disavow or accept responsibility for an article printed on August 21, 1762. Wilkes declined to do either. They fought at once, using horse pistols of huge caliber. The day was October 5, 1762; the place the Garden of the Red Lion Inn at Bagshot; the time seven o'clock in the evening. Although there was a bright moon, both fired without effect. Then Wilkes walked over to his lordship and avowed responsibility for the offending article. "His Lordship," said Wilkes, in his recital of the occurrence, "paid me the highest encomiums upon my courage and said he would declare everywhere that I was the noblest fellow God ever made. He then desired that we might be good friends and retire to the inn to drink a bottle of claret together, which we did with great good humor and much laughter." Both were no doubt relieved, though Wilkes averred his belief that Talbot fought with a king's pardon in his pocket, and he with a halter around his neck.

The great Dr. Samuel Johnson, in deploring the decadence of prizefighting, endorsed the duel—illogically. Indeed, most of his utterances were didactic and not logical. Boswell had raised the question in a company that included Oliver Goldsmith and General James Oglethorpe, founder of Georgia, who was then very old. Boswell wanted to know whether duelling was consistent with moral duty.

"Undoubtedly a man has a right to defend his honor," replied Oglethorpe, with a lofty air.

The humorous Goldsmith asked Boswell what he himself would do if affronted.

"Fight," was Bozzy's prompt reply.

"That solves the question," countered the creator of "The Deserted Village."

This set Johnson to observing. He held that what a man might elect to do did not prove it to be right;

but he went on: "As men become to a high degree
refined, various causes of offense arise which are considered to be of such importance that life must be
staked to atone for them, though in reality they are
not so. A body that has received a very fine polish
may be easily hurt. Before men arrive at this artificial
refinement, if one tells his neighbor he lies, if one gives
his neighbor a blow, his neighbor gives him a blow;
but in a state of highly polished society, an affront
is held to be a serious injury. It, therefore, must be
resented, or rather a duel must be fought upon it; as
men have agreed to banish from their society one who
puts up with an affront without fighting a duel. Now,
sir, it is never unlawful to fight in self-defense. He,
then, who fights a duel, does not fight from passion
against his antagonist but out of self-defense, to avert
the stigma of the world and to prevent his being
driven out of society."

This brought out a rare tale from Oglethorpe.
When but a lad of sixteen he was a cadet under the
great Duke of Marlborough, serving in the Low
Countries. Sitting in company with the eminent Prince
Eugene of Savoy, at the table of the Prince of Witt-
emberg, Eugene, evidently trying to test the spirit of
the Scottish youth, gave his wine glass a fillip in such
a way that the drops bespattered Oglethorpe. The
latter, with amazing coolness, fixed his eyes on Eugene, and smiling, said, "My Prince, that is a good
jest, but we do it much better in England." With that
he emptied his glass in Eugene's face. The words were
uttered in French, as Eugene knew no English. The
response had been much more than he had expected,

but before his temper could express itself an old general, sitting by, smoothed the situation with, "Il a bien fait, mon Prince, vous l'avez commence." The result was that the daring boy became Eugene's secretary and aide-de-camp.

On another occasion Johnson again discussed the topic, arguing that if public war could be justified, private war was equally to be tolerated. Later, when a kinsman of Boswell, Mr. Cunningham of the Scots Grays, on April 21, 1783, had fought a fatal duel with Mr. Riddell of the Guards, Boswell, much concerned, found Dr. Johnson far from being consolatory. "I do not see, sir," he remarked sententiously, "that fighting is absolutely forbidden in Scripture. I can see revenge forbidden, but not self-defense. . . . A man may shoot the man who invades his character as he may shoot him who attempts to break into his house." He argued further, rather lamely, that "a man is sufficiently punished by being called out and subjected to risk." At this Boswell shrewdly pointed out that the aggressor did not always fall, to which the pundit could only grunt assent.

In this instance Johnson condoned circumstances that were peculiarly atrocious. Riddell had formerly served in the Scots Grays. He quarreled with Cunningham over a game of cards and challenged him. Cunningham declined. Riddell left the regiment, but Cunningham's fellow officers nagged him to such an extent over his refusal that he sent Riddell a challenge. The latter saw no reason for reviving the dispute. Then Cunningham, meeting Riddell by chance, spat in his face. The duel followed. Cunningham fell at the first fire, badly wounded. Riddell was unhurt. Cunningham refused to leave the field without another shot, and staggering to his feet took such good aim as to kill his opponent. He himself recovered.

It was fated that Boswell's son, Sir Alexander Boswell, was to meet with death in a duel. Soon after the Cunningham-Riddell meeting, the Colonel the Hon. Cosmo Gordon and Lieutenant Colonel Thomas settled a dispute with pistols in Hyde Park, September 3, 1783. Gordon missed, and Thomas's pistol failed to fire. He gained a shot, but only "contused" Gordon. The second fire was futile. On the third Thomas was mortally hurt.

Editor Bate of the *Morning Post,* having refused to give the name of a letter writer, was called out by Captain Stoney. Bate was a parson as well as a penman. He stipulated fighting in a room without seconds. They both missed in pistol-fire, and went at it with swords. Someone broke open the door just as Bate had bent his blade on Stoney's breastbone. The fight ended there, and the Captain married the lady upon whom the letter in question seemed to reflect.

The celebrated Charles James Fox had to back up his hot criticism of Lord North's blundering policy in dealing with the revolting American colonies in 1779. William Adams, a supporter of the minister, challenged Fox, who was wounded in the affray. William Pitt and George Tinney fought over their opinions in 1796. Neither was harmed.

English noblemen who took part in duels or kindred affrays with fatal results could and did gain immunity when tried—as they were by their peers—by claiming the privileges of their station. Ordinary gentlemen went into hiding or sought safety in Europe when death ended a quarrel. Not all of them fought in the face of an affront. The great Lord Erskine once laughed an antagonist off the field who complained of his diminutive size, while the challenger was of gigantic proportions. Erskine blandly expressed a willingness to have an outline of himself chalked on the body of his opponent, shots taking effect outside of which were not to count.

There was an epidemic of duels in the British Army during the Napoleonic period, so much so that it had to be dealt with sternly by the war office. The Duke of Wellington was inclined to be lenient, seeing no great harm in one Hussar shooting another. The Government thought differently. In 1807 two squadrons of the Nineteenth Hussars were stationed in Athlone to protect a certain Captain Boycott, ancestor of one who was later to be in similar trouble with his tenantry—adding a new word to our language. There was assigned to the command Major Alexander Campbell, a veteran of the Black Watch, belonging at that time to the Twenty-first Fusileers. The squadrons had been under a brevet lieutenant-colonel, named Twentyman, whose real rank was that of captain. He was naturally superseded under seniority by Campbell, whose company was much resented by the Hussars. On June 23, 1807, General Kerr, in charge of the Athlone district, inspected the two battalions. When it was over Boyd, a Hussar captain, picked a quarrel over an alleged error of Campbell's in giving a word of command. Out of this trifle came a challenge

from Boyd. The men met immediately with the result that Boyd was shot through the stomach. They
had fought in a room seven paces apart. Boyd died
and Campbell foolishly fled. He returned after hiding
a short time, was tried, convicted of murder, and
sentenced to death. The jury recommended Campbell's pardon to George III, who gave no sign, and
the unfortunate major was duly hanged. One other
duelling officer also fed the rope.

In 1813, at the height of the struggle with France,
one Lieutenant Blundell was slain in a duel. The other
principal and all the seconds were convicted of murder. The king pardoned them, but they were dismissed
from the service.

The army view was well expressed by the lieutenant in Fielding's *Tom Jones,* who thus advised the
hero who had invoked "Thou shalt not kill" as a reason for refusing a challenge.

"Why, I believe there is such a command, but a
man of honor can't keep it; and you must be a man
of honor if you will be in the army. I remember I once
put the case to our chaplain over a bowl of punch,
and he confessed there was much difficulty in it; but
he said he hoped there might be a latitude granted to
soldiers in this one instance; and to be sure it is our
duty to hope so; for who would bear to live without
his honor? No, no, my dear, dear boy, be a good
Christian as long as you live; but be a man of honor,
too, and never put up with an affront; not all the books
nor all the parsons in the world shall ever persuade
me to that."

During the long reign of George III it is recorded

that one hundred and seventy-two known duels were fought, involving sixty-nine fatalities. In three cases both combatants lost their lives. One of the most notable of these affairs was between the Duke of York and Lieutenant-Colonel Lennox, of the Coldstream Guards, of which his Royal Highness was colonel. The Duke and George, Prince of Wales, were loitering in Vauxhall Gardens, when they were approached by two men and a woman, all of whom were masked. The three roysterers were very offensive, especially the woman and one of the men, who for some reason the Duke assumed to be his lieutenant colonel. The Duke called the man by name and demanded that he unmask, saying that he would apologize if wrong. The masker refused to show his face. It was believed the three were Colonel Lennox, the Duke of Gordon, and Lady Charlotte.

The next day at regimental inspection the Duke remarked that Lennox had "heard words spoken to him at Daubigny's Club, to which no gentleman ought to have submitted." The lieutenant-colonel, though on parade, then and there asked what the words were and who had uttered them. To this the Duke made no reply, and ordered Lennox back to his post; but after the parade was over sent for him and said he would not stand on his position if Lennox desired satisfaction. Lennox wrote to every member of Daubigny's to ask if they had ever known him to submit to insult, but got no replies. He so informed the Duke and again asked for the offensive words and the name of the man who spoke them. The Duke declined to answer. The duel followed, Lord Rawdon seconding the Duke and the Earl of Winchelsea Lennox. Lennox fired. The Duke did not. A curl was seen to shiver from behind his Royal Highness's ear, who was not harmed. There is more than a suspicion that Lennox's pistol was not loaded and that the curl had been previously disarranged. The Duke declined his turn. Lennox was a dead shot, so the theory of a bulletless weapon seems sound. The lieutenant-colonel called for a court inquiry, which found his courage all right but his judgment bad. He became Duke of Richmond and was one of the few popular viceroys in Ireland. It is related that here he was once bested in a drinking duel with a curate who held one jorum of brandy too many for him.

Prime Minister George Canning found it needful to "go out" with Lord Castlereagh, September 11, 1809. He receives a "tedious wound," as Creevey puts it. John Scott, editor of the *London Magazine,* was killed by an aggrieved Mr. Christie in 1821.

The Duke of Wellington's complaisance concerning duelling reacted on him in 1829. When he was serving as Prime Minister under George IV, his favorable attitude on the Catholic Relief Bill caused the Earl of Winchelsea to write a caustic letter to the Secretary of the Committee for Establishing King's College, London, in which he severely impugned the motives of his Grace for his part in founding that institution.

The letter was given out to the *Standard* and published. Old Arthur came to scratch at once, asking

Winchelsea if he really wrote the letter. He replied affirmatively. At that Sir Henry Hardinge bore back this missive:

London, March 19

MY LORD,—

I have had the honor of receiving your Lordship's letter of the 18th inst. Your Lordship is certainly the best judge of the mode to be adopted of withdrawing your name from the list of subscribers to the King's College. In doing so, however, it does not appear necessary to impute to me, in no measured terms, disgraceful and criminal motives for my conduct in the part which I took in the establishment of the College. No man has a right, whether in public or in private, by speech, or in writing, or in print, to insult another by attributing to him motives for his conduct, public or private, which disgrace or criminate him. If a gentleman commits such an act indiscreetly, in the heat of debate or in a moment of party violence, he is always ready to make reparation to him whom he may thus have injured. I am convinced that your Lordship will, upon reflection, be anxious to relieve yourself from the pain of having thus insulted a man who never injured or offended you.

I have, etc.,

WELLINGTON

Winchelsea referred the Duke to Lord Falmouth. Wellington wrote again:

MY LORD,—

Sir Henry Hardinge has communicated to me a memorandum signed by your Lordship, dated 1 P. M., and a note from Lord Falmouth, dated 3 P. M. Since the insult, unprovoked on my part, and not denied by your Lordship, I have done everything in my power to induce your Lordship to make me reparation, but in vain. Instead of apologizing for your own conduct, your Lordship has called upon me to explain mine. The question for me now to decide is this: Is a gentleman, who happens to be the King's Minister, to submit to be insulted by any gentleman who thinks proper to attribute to him disgraceful or criminal motives for his conduct as an individual? I cannot doubt of the decision which I ought to make on this question. Your Lordship is alone responsible for the consequences. I now call upon your Lordship to give me that satisfaction for your conduct which a gentleman has a right to require, and which a gentleman never refuses to give.

> I have, etc.,
> WELLINGTON

Winchelsea found it "impossible" to decline giving the required satisfaction. They met on Saturday, March 21, 1829, in Battersea Park. Winchelsea received Wellington's fire, which appeared to have been one of courtesy, as he was not hit, and then aimed at the atmosphere. The formality over, he proffered a written explanation to Wellington through Hardinge. It did not include the word "apology," so the Iron Duke said it would not do. Winchelsea then supplied the omission and His Grace departed. According to the Earl of Sefton, His Gracious Majesty George IV, now too fat and lazy to do much more than breathe, though still deeming himself the First Gentleman of Europe, "was delighted with the duel and said he should have done the same thing himself—that gentlemen should not stand upon their privileges."

Charles C. F. Greville thought the Duke had suffered indignity by meeting Winchelsea. The public knew nothing about the duel until it was over. Popular opinion sided with Wellington.

Black, the editor of the *Morning Chronicle*, had to

fight Mr. Roebuck in 1835, and Daniel O'Connell's son fought Lord Alvenley about the same time. The Earl of Cardigan wounded Captain Tuckett in 1840. For this he was tried by his noble peers and acquitted.

Sir Walter Scott relates the incident of a Laird of Culrossie who fought a duel for the honor of Aberdeen butter! The Scotch and Irish were always more touchy than the English.

The eminent Henry Grattan fought the Marquis of Londonderry, January 15, 1839, as the outcome of Daniel O'Connell's efforts to loosen the shackles on Ireland, in which Grattan joined. O'Connell had quoted Grattan, in a Dublin speech, as saying that Queen Victoria's life would not be safe if the Tories came into power. His lordship interpreted this as meaning that the Tories would murder Her Majesty, and considered the remarks "base" and "infamous." To this Grattan rejoined that he was not responsible for O'Connell's speech and, as he had made no allusions himself to Lord Londonderry, he demanded to know whether "base" and "infamous" applied to himself personally. In the absence of a disavowel of the murder suggestion, Londonderry declined to recall "base" and "infamous." They met on Wimbledon Common. Londonderry received Grattan's fire unhurt and emptied his own pistol in the air. Mr. Grattan expressed himself satisfied, as he should have been!

January 16, 1840, two members of the British Parliament exchanged shots. These were Messrs. Bradshaw and Horsman. Bradshaw, a radical, had descended to say scurrilous things anent Queen Victoria, then young on her throne. Bradshaw was the challenger, Horsman having declared in a speech at Cockermouth that Bradshaw "had the tongue of a traitor and the heart of a coward." After the pistols had popped petulantly, but without doing any damage, Bradshaw apologized for slurring the Queen and Horsman swallowed his heated verbiage.

The duel survived in Great Britain long enough to shock Queen Victoria and her Consort, Prince Albert. In 1843, Lieutenant Monro killed his brother-in-law, Colonel Fawcett. The Colonel had been challenged and accepted with great reluctance, but as an army officer he could not decline without losing caste. Public sense was deeply stirred. The Prince Consort and the Queen took a hand in putting the stamp of disapproval on such affairs of honor and they disappeared from the annals of the army thereafter. Albert wished to establish Courts of Honor after the German fashion, but Parliament went further and amended the articles of war so as to cashier both participants and all officers possessing knowledge of a duel who failed to attempt its prevention. The rule is still in effect.

The formal duel had a vogue in America from colonial days to 1883. Some of the near-encounters were interesting. Israel Putnam, challenged by a British officer, placed a lighted candle in an open keg of gunpowder, and invited the latter to join him in sitting beside it to await the result. On another occasion he went to the field armed with a musket. The offended party, finding him blazing away in practice, decided the risk too great to carry on further.

It might be proved that a duel was responsible for creating the value of the highest priced autograph in

the world, that of Button Gwinnett, a signer of the
Declaration of Independence from Georgia, which has
reached a valuation of some $51,000. Gwinnett be-
came involved in a dispute with General Lachlan Mc-
Intosh that ended in a duel, fatal to himself. An official account of the affair was given by George Wells,
before Assistant Judge John Wereat, who held an inquest into the matter. This he put in writing as follows:

"Late on the Evening of Thursday the 15th May
Inst. a Written challenge was brought to Genl. Mc-
Intosh, Sign'd Button Gwinnett, wherein the Said Mr.
Gwinnett charg'd the General with calling him a Scoundrel in Public Convention, & desir'd he wou'd give
satisfaction for it as a Gentleman before Sunrise next
morning in Sr. James Wrights Pasture . . . to which
the General humourously sent in answer to Mr. Gwinnett, that the hour was rather earlier than his usual,
but wou'd assuredly meet him precisely at the place
& time appointed with a pair of Pistols only, . . .
Early the next morning Mr. Gwinnett & his second
found the General & his second waiting on the Ground
& after politely saluteing each other, the General
drew his Pistols, to shew he was loaded only with
single Balls . . . immediately each took his stand, &
agreed to fire as they cou'd, both Pistols went off
nearly at the same time, when Mr. Gwinnett
fell. . . ."

This happened in May, 1777. They fought at
twelve paces. Both men were wounded, Gwinnett mortally. He died of his injury May 27, at the age of forty-
four. The note detailing the meager facts was mar-

LACHLAN McINTOSH

keted at $2,600. Although Gwinnett was the challenger, McIntosh lost local standing by his fatal shot. He had been the principal military officer in Georgia, and was appointed brigadier general in the Continental Army, September 16, 1776. Gwinnett had been an aspirant for the position, and it was his failure that led to the quarrel and the duel. He had been given a subordinate position in the service, and ill-luck following an expedition to Florida added to his exasperation at the prowess of his rival. McIntosh seems to also have had a hand in defeating Gwinnett for Governor of Georgia in 1777.

After the duel McIntosh was sent North for the rest of the war. Returning to Georgia with the peace, he was elected to Congress and in 1785 was made one of the commissioners to deal with the Southern Indians.

When, in 1778, Horatio Gates took command of the American forces holding Boston, he antagonized John Hancock so much that they froze up in each other's presence, and the ladies of their households declined to meet socially. Hancock was not of a duelling mind, but John Carter, one of his supporters, was, and faced the doughty General on the field December 31, 1778. They met in a pasture near the Roxbury meeting-house. Gates won the first fire, but missed. Carter then refused to take his turn. The General and his entourage were quarrelsome and made so much trouble that the civil authorities were compelled to interfere. Gates was sent South soon so the friction was ended.

Readers of Captain Frederick Marryat's sea tales are often regaled with accounts of duels among the of-

ficers of the British Navy. Our own navy was not free
from savage examples in the days when the Mediterranean squadron was important. One of these is curtly
recorded on a tombstone, near Syracuse, in Sicily,
which bears this inscription: "In Memory of William
R. Nicholson, a midshipman in the Navy of the United
States, who was cut off from society in the bloom
of his youth and health, on the 18th day of September,
A. D., 1804, aged eighteen years."

The person responsible for his untimely demise
was another middy, Frederick C. De Kraft. There
is no record of the provocation that occasioned the
affair. Pretty girls were numerous in Syracuse, and
one may have been the cause. Both youngsters were
attached to the brig *Siren*. De Kraft was placed under
arrest and sent home on the U.S.S. *Scourge,* reaching
Hampton Roads on February 5, 1805. He was relieved
of arrest on his arrival, and on April 12 granted a
furlough to be spent in Europe, but he did not avail
himself of this. Instead, he was ordered to the U.S.S.
Hornet on July 29. On July 3, 1807, he was sent for
duty at Norfolk, under Captain Stephen Decatur. He
resigned from the service on May 14, 1808, and thereafter engaged in civil pursuits. His son, James C. P.
De Kraft, became a rear-admiral in the United States
Navy.

On September 25, 1808, there was a naval duel between Lieutenant William E. Finch, U.S.N., and Lieutenant Francis B. White of the Marine Corps. Both
officers were attached to the frigate *Independence*.
They fought on Noddle's Island, now embedded in
East Boston, near Border Street, standing between

two elm trees. White was killed instantly. Finch, born in England, was the son of an actress of that name and the Earl of Bolton. The bar sinister sent him overseas to find his fortune, and he entered our navy as a midshipman in 1806. Perhaps rude reflections on Finch's paternity led to the meeting. In 1833 he became heir to some property from his father, and being so recognized, he changed his name to William Compton Bolton. He died a Commodore, at Genoa, in 1849, while in command of the United States fleet in the Mediterranean. He sailed as a midshipman with David Porter on the famous cruise of the Essex, but being put in charge of a prize off Bermuda, was captured by the British and so did not see the South Seas.

An American duel which made a great stir was that between Colonel Thomas H. Cushing of the regular army and Congressman William I. Lewis of Virginia. Cushing's life was saved by the fact that the pistol ball sent by his antagonist struck his watch and so was made harmless. One of the jokes of the day was that it must have been a good watch to "keep time from eternity."

Andrew Jackson, of whom much will appear in the pages that follow, once challenged General Winfield Scott. The latter declined, telling "Old Hickory" to console himself with a few epithets, such as coward, and await the outcome of the next war to see if they were true. The Tennesseean took no further action, but was civil to Scott ever after.

The celebrated Sam Houston, liberator of Texas, while a member of Congress in 1823, fought a duel

with General William White of Nashville, an anti-
Jacksonian. Houston was a partisan of the spirited
General, under whom he had served in the Creek
War. The duel was fought across the Kentucky state
line. On Jackson's advice, Houston held a bullet between his teeth to steady his nerves and stress his
muscles when taking aim. White was wounded in the
hip. Houston, who escaped injury, stood in Kentucky
when he fired; consequently, that state indicted him.
The Governor of Tennessee ruled that Houston, as the
challenged party, had fought in self-defense and refused
to honor a requisition for his person.

One of the most fearsome fights in American annals
between individuals occurred on September 18, 1827,
on a sand-bank in the Mississippi River, opposite
Natchez, then one of the toughest towns in the south-
west. Dr. Thomas H. Maddox and Samuel L. Wells
had gone thither to settle a difference. They were accompanied by their seconds and a party of friends of
both sides which included Colonel James Bowie,
wielder of the celebrated knife which bears his name,
Richard Cuney, Alfred Blanchard, Colonel R. A.
Crain, Colonel Morris Wright, Carey Blanchard, and
Jefferson Wells. Wright, the two Blanchards, Crain,
and Dr. Denny, a surgeon, were seconds or followers
of Maddox. The others were in like relation to Wells.
After some disputing as to procedure, Maddox and
Wells exchanged two shots without damage. Wells,
the challenged party, then withdrew the language to
which Maddox had taken exception and the two shook
hands.

All seemed well, when suddenly Richard Cuney assailed Crain with violent language and demanded a settlement of some difference that existed between them. In this Cuney was supported by Bowie and Jefferson Wells. Crain at once took the aggressive and fired at Bowie who was equally quick on the trigger. Both missed. Then Crain blazed away at Cuney who fell mortally wounded though returning the fire. Bowie next attacked Crain with his knife, but Crain, who was a redoubtable person, knocked him down with the butt of one of his empty pistols. In the melée that followed, Wright was killed outright, Bowie severely wounded, and Alfred Blanchard scratched. Cuney bled to death on the field. Twelve men were involved in the fracas. Both sides had enough and shared quite evenly the casualties. Bowie and Crain met afterwards in New Orleans and became reconciled. The former perished in the defense of the Alamo. Dr. Maddox survived until 1895, reaching the ripe old age of ninety-six.

While the duels recorded in the narratives that follow were between mainly public men, meetings of other persons less well known were plentiful. The South had an appalling list of private encounters. There men fought upon as little provocation as did the French *raffinés*. It is impossible to list the many affairs between gentlemen. One of these developed singular ferocity. This was the outcome of a dispute over a boundary line between two Georgia estates, near which Fanny Kemble, at that time the wife of Pierce Butler, once sojourned. The two young gentlemen concerned agreed to a battle to the death. Describing "a charming wood ride," Mrs. Butler thus reveals the story:

"While going along this delightful boundary of these two neighboring estates, my mind not unnaturally dwelt upon the terms of a deadly feud in which the two families owning them are living with each other. A horrible quarrel has occurred quite lately upon the subject of the ownership of this very ground which I was skirting, between Dr. H—— and young Mr. W——. They have challenged each other, and what I am going to tell you is a good example of the sort of spirit that grows up among slaveholders. . . . The terms of the challenge that have passed between them have appeared like a sort of advertisement in the local paper, and are to the effect that they are to fight at a certain distance with certain weapons—firearms, of course. That there is to be on the person of each a white paper, or mark, immediately over the region of the heart, as a point to direct aim; and whoever kills the other is to have the privilege of cutting off his head and sticking it up on a pole on the piece of land which was the origin of the debate; so that some fine day, I might come hither as I did to-day, and find myself riding under the shadow of the gory locks of Dr. H—— or Mr. W——, my peaceful and pleasant neigbors."

Later she continues: "That horrid tragedy with which we have been threatened, and of which I was writing to you almost jestingly a few days ago, has been accomplished, and apparently without exciting anything but the most passing and superficial sensations in this community. The duel between Dr. H—— and Mr. W—— did not take place, but an accidental encounter in the hotel at Brunswick did, and the former shot the latter dead on the spot. He has been brought home and buried here by the little church on his mother's plantation; and the murderer, if he is even prosecuted, runs no risk of finding a jury in the whole length and breadth of Georgia who could convict him of anything."

On her next ride through the "charming wood" she looked for Mr. W——'s skull on the proposed pole. It was not there, the informality of the affair having presumably made void the stipulation.

In the rough political period during which Abraham Lincoln rode the Sangamon circuit, James Shields, a brilliant young Irishman, was auditor of the state of Illinois. He was a native of County Tyrone, in Ireland, and his Celtic conceit made him a good deal of a butt in Springfield, where there was plenty of humor, rude but appreciative. Shields was a Democrat, Lincoln a Whig. Shields had refused to accept the depreciated State Bank notes for taxes. Simeon Francis, editor of the *Journal,* held his columns wide open for Lincoln, who, August 27, 1842, wrote "A Letter from the Lost Townships." In it he burlesqued Shields and his party broadly, to say the least. The letter was signed "Rebecca." The auditor was furious. Lincoln was pursuing his courtship with Miss Mary Todd, and pleased at his prowess with the pen, he talked the "Rebecca" letter over with the lady and her chum, Miss Julia M. Jayne. The pair put their heads together and concocted more mischief, writing another "Rebecca" letter, which was published in the *Journal.* This letter followed in Lincoln's vein and made fun of Shields, who had been calling for satisfaction provided he could find the author of the flippant effusion. As to this desire to fight, "Rebecca" observed: "I hear the way of these fire-eaters is to give the challenged party the choice of weapons, which, being the case, I'll tell you in confidence that I never fight with anything but broomsticks or hot water or a shovelful of coals, the former of which, being somewhat like a shillalah, may not be objectionable to him."

Supplementing this, the mischievous maidens composed a poem making fun of the auditor's efforts at gallantry, which had caused much amusement in Springfield society. This was the last straw. Shields sent General James D. Whiteside to Editor Francis with a flat request to be given the name of the offender. Francis appealed to Lincoln, who directed him to give his name and say nothing about the girls. This Francis did. Shields then, through Whiteside, asked Lincoln for a written explanation. This Lincoln declined to give but wrote the auditor that he could not answer further as his (Shields') letter contained an assumption of facts and also a menace. Shields replied disavowing any menace but categorically asked Lincoln if he were the author of either of the "Rebecca" letters. To this Lincoln responded with a verbal statement "that there could be no further negotiation between them" until the first note was withdrawn.

He was distinctly in a "jam," as the saying goes. Shields followed up his advantage by designating General Whiteside as his friend to arrange for a duel. Lincoln selected Dr. E. H. Merryman. The two connived to prevent a meeting. They parted, agreeing to procrastinate. Whiteside was astonished a day later to receive a proposition from Dr. Merryman to meet in Missouri, at a point opposite Alton, with broadswords as weapons. Whiteside would make no arrangement in Illinois, as duelling was against the laws of that state. He took on General W. L. D. Ewing and Dr. T. M. Hope as friends of Shields, and proceeded to the appointed spot in Missouri. There they were joined by John J. Hardin and Dr. R. W. English, who posed as mutual friends, endeavoring to head off the encounter. Soon Dr. Merryman appeared, accompanied by Messrs. A. T. Bledso and Hardin, who were armed. Dr. English appealed to Whiteside for an adjustment. Shields, who was not on the ground, but near by, refused this, but Hope and Ewing accepted from Hardin and English "a full and satisfactory explanation," as Whiteside records, and compelled Shields to accept it. This was on September 22, 1842. Lincoln did not appear on the scene and was never proud of the episode. There have been published a variety of versions of this more or less ludicrous affair. In one account it is related that Lincoln proposed to Shields that they settle the question by means of a game of old sledge. Another version of the affair states that Lincoln, practicing with a broadsword, snipped off the branches of an oak high over his head. This achievement conveyed such a measure of his "reach" to Shields that he was the more readily appeased.

Springfield laughed at Shields—and probably at Lincoln. The combative Irishman fought valiantly in the Mexican War, became a Senator from Illinois, a major-general in the Union army during the Civil War, and afterwards served as United States Senator from Minnesota—a rather remarkable record. Lincoln married Mary Todd, and Julia Jayne was her bridesmaid.

People who recall the late August Belmont, New York banker, and his sons, August, Perry, and Oliver H. P., may be surprised to learn that this imported agent of the Rothschilds fought a duel on September 27, 1841, at Elkton, Maryland, with Edward Heyward, described by Philip Hone as "one of the exquisite sons of Mr. William Heyward of this city (New York.)" The quarrel had taken place at William Niblo's saloon, then the resort of the fashionable fast set. Belmont was shot in the thigh, and the surgeons had some difficulty in repairing the injury. That a German money-changer should take to arms was considered surprising. Mr. Belmont was valorous, however. He married a niece of Oliver Hazard Perry, hero of Lake Erie, daughter of Commodore Matthew Calbraith Perry, U.S.N., who opened up Japan to the world.

During the war between the states duels were not uncommon among Confederate officers. The most notable of these took place between General Lucien M. Walker, of Georgia, and General James S. Marmaduke, of Missouri, on August 6, 1863, near Little Rock, Arkansas. Marmaduke was a fire-eater. Walker was a West Point graduate who had left the service in 1852, and joined the Confederate army at the outbreak of the civil conflict. The Missourian had made remarks reflecting on the courage of the Georgian, who challenged. The weapons were revolvers, the distant twelve paces. They were to fire at the word and to blaze away until one or the other fell. Walker was killed.

Kentucky outlawed duelling in the Constitution of 1850. The governor, on taking office, had to swear: "I have not fought a duel with deadly weapons within this State or out of it with a citizen of this State." The revisers of the State's Constitution in 1890, State's rights having ceased to be precious, struck out "with a citizen of this State." So the inhibition still remains part of the oath.

Illinois, it might be remarked, appears to be the only state in the Union that ever hanged a duellist. This occurred when Alphonso Stewart, challenged by William Bennett, was killed. Bennett was tried for murder, convicted, and executed.

Tennessee ended duelling as the result of an exhibition of moral courage on the part of Captain William Rule, editor of the Knoxville *Journal*. In 1873 he assailed in his columns some of the actions of Mayor Moses J. Wicks, of Knoxville, to which the latter took angry exception and demanded a retraction. Captain Rule refused, though opening his columns freely to anything Wicks might care to say in rejoinder. Wicks then challenged Captain Rule to fight a duel. Captain Rule declined, saying boldly: "With such an affair I refuse to have any connection. I recognize no heathenish so-called code of honor. I am opposed to duelling for the reason that it is contrary to the laws of my country, the law of humanity, and the law of God. You might take my life or I might take yours and yet not a single feature of the publication complained of would be changed by the results. If that publication was false, it would be false still; if it were true, it remains true; hence nothing could be gained by either of us losing his life in the manner proposed."

Wicks responded with a statement in which he left the editor in such a place in the "public esteem or contempt as a just and enlightened people consign him."

"The just and enlightened people" lost no time in making plain the "place" Captain Rule held in their "esteem." Letters from all over the state and nation flowed in. The Federal Grand Jury then in session issued a statement commending his stand and the legislature at its next session passed a law making the practice of duelling a crime. Captain Rule lived to enter his ninetieth year, dying at Knoxville, July 26, 1928, high in the regard of his fellow citizens and brethren of the press.

One unique feature of the Tennessee inhibition is that gentlemen, on being admitted to the bar, must take oath that they will not engage in duelling, for it had been found that about ninety per cent of duels fought were between attorneys, therefore, special steps were taken to curb their combativeness.

A latter-day duel that made much noise and sent one of the principals into voluntary exile for the greater part of what remained of his life came off between James Gordon Bennett, the younger, and Frederick May, over the line between Maryland and Deleware, at Slaughter's Gap, on January 7, 1877. Bennett had been guilty of unbecoming conduct at the May residence in New York, on the preceding New Years' Day while calling on Miss Caroline May, who was looked upon as his affianced. He had been drinking and lost his sense of propriety. The duel followed a cow-hiding which Frederick May, administered in front of the Union Club on January 3, though contrary to what might have been expected, May was the challenger. Charles Longfellow, son of the Cambridge poet, represented Bennett in the preliminaries, but S. Howland Robbins, of New York, served as second. Dr. Frederick May, of Baltimore, a cousin, acted for May. May missed purposely and the agitated publisher fired wild. His was probably the only duel on record where a licensed clergyman came along to see fair play. The Rev. Dr. George H. Hepworth, pastor of a lively church in New York, who wrote a religious editorial each week for the *Herald,* was the man. He afterwards became editor of the paper.

Surprising as it may seem, the formal duel survived down to present-day memories in the state of Virginia whence came Henry A. Wise, so prominent in the Cilly-Graves affair. He had fought with Richard Coke whom he had defeated for Congress in the Accomack district in 1830. Coke was wounded in the right arm. In 1842 Wise was challenged by Edward Stanley, Congressman from North Carolina, with whom he had a dispute on the floor. Friends patched up a peace. His son, O. Jennings Wise, met Patrick Henry Aylett, grandson of Patrick Henry, at Milton, North Carolina, July 15, 1859. Neither fired at the first command. At the second call Aylett's shot went wild and Wise fired in the air. Peyton Wise, a nephew of Henry A. Wise, and Judge L. L. Lewis faced each other near Warrenton, September 20, 1881. Lewis missed and Wise aimed at the air. This meeting grew out of the

"Readjuster" movement, engineered by William A. Mahone, H. H. Riddleberger, and John S. Wise, son of H. A. Wise, which ended in quarrels with each other. Riddleberger and George D. Wise exchanged three rounds at Atlee's Station in 1881 without injury to either party. John S. Wise and John S. Crockett fought in 1882. The first fire was a miss. On the second Crockett missed and Wise's pistol failed to act. Peace followed. The meeting was on the road to Yellow Sulphur Springs.

Riddleberger was kept busy with challenges in the heated era. October 15, 1881, he met Richard F. Beirne, editor of the Richmond *State*. The pistols were left uncapped by the seconds and a laugh was the only result. Later Beirne had to meet Colonel William C. Elam, editor of the Richmond *Whig,* January 30, 1883. A previous encounter had been prevented by the police. The fight took place near Waynesboro. Both missed on first fire. On the second shot Elam was severely wounded in the hip. This appears to have been the last American duel of any note.

CHAPTER II

THE CODE

QUITE naturally, as with most social practices, the duello evolved codes in which its etiquette was strictly laid down. Governor John Lyde Wilson, of South Carolina, compiled one such under the title, "The Code of Honor; or Rules for the Government of Principals and Seconds in Duelling." This was first issued in 1838. There were a number of editions, one published as late as 1858. The pamphlet numbered sixteen pages, octavo. Wilson made a sort of apologia to the public for his effort, in which he said:

"To publish a Code of Honor to govern in cases of individual combat might seem to imply that the publisher was an advocate of duelling, and wished to introduce it as a proper mode of deciding all personal difficulties and misunderstandings. Such implication would do me great injustice. But if the question were to be directly put to me whether there are not cases where duels are right and proper, I would unhesitatingly answer, there are. If an oppressed nation has a right to appeal to arms in defense of liberty and the happiness of its people, there can be no argument used in support of such appeal that will not apply with equal force to individuals. How many cases there are that might be enumerated, where there is no tribunal

33

to do justice to an oppressed and deeply wronged individual. If he be subjected to a tame submission to insult and disgrace, where no power can save him from its effects, then it would seem that the first law of nature, self-preservation, points out the only remedy for his wrongs.

"The severest penal enactments cannot restrain the practice of duelling, and their extreme severity in this state (South Carolina), the more effectually shields the offenders. The teaching and preaching of an eloquent clergy may do some service, but is wholly inadequate to suppress it. Under these circumstances, the following rules are given to the public, and if I can save the life of one useful member of society, I will be compensated. I have restored to the bosoms of many, their sons, by my timely interference, who are ignorant of the misery I have averted from them. A book of authority, to which they can refer in matters where they are uninformed, will therefore be a desideration."

He then proceeds to lay down "Rules for Principals and Seconds in Duelling." Chapter I deals with "The Person Insulted before Challenge Sent." Herein the procedure advised is very precise: "Whenever you believe you have been insulted, if the insult be in public, and by words or behavior, never resent it there if you have self-command enough to avoid noticing it. If resented there you offer an indignity to the company, which you should not.

"In case of blows or personal indignity, this caution is withdrawn, for the insult to the company is held not to originate with the insulted one. Blows may be returned, but satisfaction must follow. Otherwise, be silent on the subject and deal with it through a friend. . . .

"Never send a challenge in the first instance, for that precludes all negotiation. Let your note be in the language of a gentleman, and, like the subject matter of complaint, be truly and fairly set forth, cautiously avoiding attributing to the adverse party any improper motive. When your second is in full possession of the facts, leave the whole matter to his judgment, and avoid consultations with him unless he seeks it. He has the custody of your honor, and by obeying him you cannot be compromised."

Reasonable time is also urged for arranging details, like domestic arrangements, will making, etc., while; "To a written communication you are entitled to a written reply, and it is the business of your friend to require it.

Much space is given to the important duties of the second. He is supposed to be "cool and collected" and to act only on his own judgment; he is to "use every effort to soothe and tranquilize the principal; extenuate the conduct of the adversary wherever an opportunity is visible."

Rule 5 was most important, as evidenced in the record of several of the duels that follow. It read:

"If the person to whom you deliver the note of your friend, declines meeting him on the ground of inequality, you are bound to tender yourself in his stead, by a note directed him from yourself; and if he refuses to meet you, you are to post him."

In all such cases, however, "the seconds should interfere and adjust the matter, if the party substituting avows he does not make the quarrel of his principal his own." Further, in guarding against nepotism, Rule 7, provides, "If the party to whom you present a note employ a son, father, or brother, as a second, you may decline acting with either on the ground of consanguinity." This was designed to fend off feuds, all too frequent in the southland of that day and later. Minors are not permitted to bear messages to adults, while: "If a stranger invites you to bear a note for him, be well satisfied before you do so that he is on an equality with you, and in presenting the note, state to the party the relationship you stand towards him, and what you know and believe about him; for strangers are entitled to redress for wrongs, as well as others, and the rules of honor and hospitality should protect him."

Much detail is given by Governor Wilson to the conduct of the party receiving a note before challenge, presumably asking for explanation; for example: "If the note received be in abusive terms, object to its reception and return it for that reason; but if it be respectful, return an answer of the same character, in which respond correctly and openly to all interrogatories fairly propounded, and hand it to your friend, who, it is presumed you have consulted, and who has advised the answer."

Reasonable time is to be allowed on receiving a note from a stranger "to ascertain his standing in society, unless he is fully vouched for by his friend." Then, "If a party delays calling on you for a week or more after the supposed insult, and assigns no cause for the delay, if you require it you may double the time before you respond to him; for the wrong cannot be considered aggravated if borne patiently for some days, and the time may have been used in preparation and practice.

"Upon the acceptance of the challenge, the seconds make the necessary arrangements for the meeting, in which each party is entitled to perfect equality. The old notion that the party challenged was authorized to name the time, place, distance, and weapon have long since been exploded; nor would a man of chivalric honor use such a right, if he possessed it. The time must be as soon as possible, the place such as had ordinarily been used where the parties are, the distance usual and the weapon that most generally used, which in this State (South Carolina) is the pistol."

"The usual distance" is prescribed as being "from ten to twenty paces," and "the seconds in measuring the ground usually step three feet." The seconds determine the giving of the word and selection of position by lot; he who gains has the choice of one or the other, but "he cannot have both." The "challengee has no option when negotiation has ceased, but to accept the challenge."

When all is ready: "Each second has a loaded pistol, in order to enforce a fair combat, according to the rules agreed on; and, if a principal fires before the word or the time agreed on, he is at liberty to fire at him, and if such second's principal fall, it is his duty to do so. If after a fire, either party be touched, the duel is to end; and no second is excusable who permits a wounded man to fight, and no second who knows his duty will permit his friend to fight a man already hit."

"I am aware," continues the Governor, in elaborating on this point, "of instances where a combat has continued, not only after slight but severe wounds had been received. In all such cases I think the seconds are blamable." Moreover, "If, after an exchange of shots, neither party be hit, it is the duty of the second of the challengee to approach the second of the challenger and say 'Our friends have exchanged shots; are you satisfied, or is there any cause why the contest should be continued?' If the meeting is of no serious cause of complaint, where the party complaining had in no way been deeply injured or grossly insulted, the second of the party challenging should reply: 'The point of honor being settled, there can, I conceive, be no objection to a reconciliation and I propose that our friends meet on middle ground, shake hands, and be friends.' "

Unless this course is followed and accepted, "It will be the duty of the second of the challenger to say in reply to the second of the challengee: 'We have been deeply wronged, and if you are not disposed to repair the injury, the contest must continue.' And if the challengee offers nothing by way of reparation, the fight must continue until one or the other of the principals is hit. . . . When the duel is ended by a party being hit, it is the duty of the second to the party so hit to announce the fact to the second of the party hitting, who will forthwith tender any assistance he can command to the disabled principal. If the party challenging hit the challengee, it is his duty to say he is satisfied and will leave the ground. If the challenger be hit, upon the challengee being informed of it, he should ask through his second, whether he is at liberty to leave the ground, which should be assented to."

Special stipulations govern who may be permitted on the ground other than principals and seconds: "One surgeon and one assistant surgeon are allowable, though the latter may be dispensed with," and usually was, perhaps to save doctor's bills. The seconds had the liberty to allow as large an attendance of outsiders as they cared to, barring relatives of the parties involved. Persons so attending, it was ruled, "are to carefully abstain by word or behavior from any act that might be the least exceptionable; nor should they stand near the principals or seconds, or hold conference with them."

The pistol, it is specified, should, in being presented, never be placed in the "pistol hand," of a principal, but in the other, whence the individual could transfer it. As a rule the pistol was to be held "muzzle down," though in cases where the duellist found it more convenient to lower it when taking aim, it might be held aloft unless objected to.

As to what might be considered insulting conduct; "Intoxication is not a full excuse, but it will greatly palliate. If it were a full excuse, it might be well counterfeited to wound feelings or destroy character," and "insults given at a wine table . . . must be answered for."

"Blows," the Governor states, "may be compromised in many cases."

The Governor supplemented his code with one

adopted in Ireland, during the summer of 1777, at the Clonmel assizes by a convention of gentlemen delegates from Tipperary, Galway, Sligo, and Roscommon, designed for use throughout the Green Island. He found it in an extended notice of Sir Jonah Barrington's "Personal Sketches of His Own Times," published in the *American Quarterly Review* for September, 1827. The *Review* was a Philadelphia publication, extremely well made, and the reviewer of Barrington's book got in some digs at the practice of duelling south of Mason and Dixon's uneasy line, which roused Wilson's ire.

"The grave reviewer," observes the Governor, "has spoken of certain states in terms so unlike a gentleman that I would advise him to look at home and say whether he does not think that the manners of his own countrymen do not require great amendment. I am very sure that the citizens of the states so disrespectfully spoken of would feel a deep humiliation to be compelled to exchange their urbanity for the uncouth civility of the people of Massachusetts. Look at their public journals, and you will find them very generally teeming with abuse of private character, which would not be countenanced here (South Carolina). The idea is about as fanciful as Bolingbroke's idea of a patriot king. I like their *fortiter in re,* but utterly eschew their *suaviter in modo.*"

The Irish code follows:

Rule 1. The first offense requires the first apology, although the retort may have been more offensive than the insult; example: A tells B he is impertinent, &c. B retorts that he lies; yet A must make the first apology, because he gave the first offense, and then (after one fire) B may explain away the retort by subsequent apology.

Rule 2. But if the parties would rather fight on, then, after two shots each (but in no case before), B may explain first and A apologize afterwards.

Rule 3. If a doubt exists who gave the first offense, the decision rests with the seconds; if they won't decide or can't agree, the matter must proceed to two shots or a hit, if the challenger requires it.

Rule 4. When the lie direct is the first offense, the aggressor must either beg pardon in express terms; exchange two shots previous to apology, or three shots followed up by explanation; or fire on till a severe hit be received by one party or the other.

Rule 5. As a blow is strictly prohibited under any circumstances, among gentlemen, no verbal apology can be received for such an insult; the alternatives therefore are the offender handing a cane to the injured party to be used on his own back, at the same time begging pardon; firing on until one or both is disabled; or exchanging three shots, and then asking pardon without the proffer of the cane. If swords are used, the parties engage till one is well blooded, disabled, or disarmed; or until after receiving a wound, and blood being drawn, the aggressor begs pardon.

N.B. A disarm is the same as a disable; the disarmee may (strictly) break his adversary's sword; but if it be the challenger who is disarmed, it is considered ungenerous to do so. In case the challenged be disabled and refuses to ask pardon or atone, he must not be killed as formerly; but the challenger may lay his own sword on the aggressor's shoulder, then break the aggressor's sword and say, "I spare your life." The challenged can never revive the quarrel, the challenger may.

Rule 6. If A gives B the lie, and B retorts by a blow (being the two greatest offenses), no reconciliation can take place till after two discharges each, or a severe hit, after which B may beg A's pardon for the blow and then A may explain simply for the lie—because a blow is never allowable, and the offense of the lie merges in it. (See preceding rule.)

N.B. Challenges for undivulged causes may be reconciled on the ground after one shot. An explanation or the slightest hit should be sufficient in such cases, because no personal cause transpired.

Rule 7. But no apology can be received in any case, after the parties have actually taken their ground, without exchange of fire.

Rule 8. In the above case, no challenger is obliged to reveal the cause of his challenge (if private) unless required by the challenged to do so before their meeting.

Rule 9. All imputations of cheating at play, races, etc., to be conceded equivalent to a blow; but may be reconciled after one shot, on admitting their falsehood, and begging pardon publicly.

Rule 10. An insult to a lady under a gentleman's care or protection, to be considered as, by one degree, a greater offense than if given to the gentleman personally, and to be regulated accordingly.

Rule 11. Offenses originating or accruing from the support of ladies' reputation, to be considered as less unjustifiable than any other of the same class, and as admitting of lighter apologies by the aggressor; this is to be determined by the circumstances of the case, but always favorable to the lady.

Rule 12. In simple, unpremeditated *rencontres* with the small sword or *couteau-de-chasse,* the rule is, first draw, first sheath; unless blood be drawn; then both sheath and proceed to investigation.

Rule 13. No dumb-shooting; or firing in the air admissible in any case. The challenger ought to have challenged without giving offense and the challenged ought, if he gave offense, to have made an apology before he came on the ground; therefore, children's play must be dishonorable on one side or the other, and is accordingly prohibited.

Rule 14. Seconds, to be of equal rank in society with the principals they attend, in so much as a second may choose or chance to become a principal and equality is indispensable.

Rule 15. Challenge is never to be delivered at night, unless the party to be challenged intend leaving the place of offense before morning; for it is desirable to control all hot-headed proceedings.

Rule 16. The challenged has the right to choose his own weapon, unless the challenger gives his honor that he is no swordsman; after which, however, he cannot decline any second species of weapon proposed by the challenged.

Rule 17. The challenged shall choose his ground; the challenger chooses his distance; the seconds fix the time and terms of firing.

Rule 18. The seconds load in presence of each other, unless they give their mutual honors that they have charged smooth and single, which should be held sufficient.

Rule 19. Firing may be regulated, but by signal; secondly, by word of command; or thirdly, at the latter case the parties may fire at their reasonable leisure, but second presents and rests are strictly prohibited.

Rule 20. In all cases miss-fire is equivalent to a shot, and a snap or a non-cock is to be considered as a miss-fire.

Rule 21. Seconds are bound to attempt a reconciliation before the meeting takes place, or after sufficient firing or hits, as specified.

Rule 22. Any wound sufficient to agitate the nerves and necessarily make the hands shake, must end the business for that day.

Rule 23. If the cause of meeting be of such nature that no apology or explanation can or will be received, the challenged takes his ground, and calls on the challenger to proceed as he chooses; in such cases firing at pleasure is the usual practice, but may be varied by agreement.

Rule 24. In slight cases the second hands his principal but one pistol, but in gross cases, two, holding another case ready charged in reserve.

Rule 25. When seconds disagree, and resolve to exchange shots themselves, it must be at the same time and at right angles with their principals. If seconds are used, side by side, at five paces interval.

N.B. All matters and doubts not herein mentioned will be explained and cleared up by application to the committee, who meet alternately at Clonmel and Galway, at the quarter sessions for the purpose.

CROW RYAN
President

JAMES KEOG
AMBY BODKIN } *Secretaries*

To this seemingly sufficient code Galway added two articles:

Article 1. No party can be allowed to bend the knee or cover his side with his left hand; but may present at any level from the hip to the eye.

Article 2. One can neither advance or retreat if the ground be measured. If the ground be unmeasured, either party may advance at pleasure—even to touch muzzle—but neither can advance on his adversary after the fire, unless his adversary step forward on him.

The seconds stand responsible for this last rule being strictly observed; bad cases have occurred from neglecting it.

In closing his curious compilation Wilson discovers from Barrington that Tipperary and Galway vied in combativeness, and there was much rivalry between the gentry of the two counties as to which witnessed the most "call-outs." "By this sort of criticism," the Governor observes amiably, "Tennessee, Kentucky, Georgia, and South Carolina would bear away the palm for gentility among the states of the Union."

The code prevailing in France during the modern duelling days was a very elaborate affair, numbering eighty-four rules, based upon three kinds of causes: "1. A simple offense; 2. An offense of an insulting nature; 3. An offense with personal acts of violence."

Rule one prescribes that the person offended is the injured party. If the injury is followed by a blow this is unquestionably the case. To return one blow by another of a more serious nature, severely wounding— for instance, after a slap in the face—does not shift the insult from the first to the second party, who may properly demand satisfaction in spite of his retaliation. A son may espouse the cause of a father provided that the disparity in age is not too great, but not in a case where the parent is the aggressor. Acts of violence in return for insult are deprecated as liable to lead to mortal combat.

Rule nine prescribes that in cases of violence, or degrading insult, the offended party has the right to name his duel, his arms, and to fix the distance, and may insist upon the aggressor not using his own weapons, as having had practice. In such instances he is also barred from employing familiar weapons. Arms allowable are limited to the sword, the saber, and the pistol. The saber may be objected to by a civilian challenged by an officer. All duels must take place within forty-eight hours after the provocation. Each second is required to have a witness. They also decide whether or not a duel is warranted and may apologize in the name of their principals. Persons with one leg or one arm may decline to employ the sword or saber. In sword or saber combats the breast must be bared. No young man may fight another over sixty years of age unless the cause rests on a blow. Relations are barred as seconds. Only by the consent of a wounded man can the combat be continued. In cases of pistol fighting the wounded man is allowed two minutes to come to the scratch and fire if he so desires.

The distances for pistol duels is fixed at fifteen paces, but the principals start towards each other at the word "march" from points forty or fifty paces apart and fire on reaching their stations. In some cases the "march" is longer and by zig-zag steps. The man who fires first must stand and receive the fire of his opponent. Two pistols are allowed each principal in cases where the affront has been a blow.

There are several varieties of the Gallic pistol duel. One requires that, "at the first signal weapons are to be raised; at the second, aimed; and at the third, fired."

An English Code was published in 1824 by Knight and Lacey. The author's name is not given, but the text reveals that he was a punctilious person. This English compilation is less complex than the others quoted, as becomes the simplicity of the race. It deprecates the use of the sword as unfair and limits the duties of seconds to examining weapons, inspecting the ground, measuring distance, and giving the word.

Three shots were deemed sufficient to satisfy the most exacting sense of honor. As the Code states: "Three fires should be the ultimatum in any case; any further reduces a duel to conflict for blood, or must subject it to the ridicule of incapacity in arms." "Posting" for lack of satisfaction, "horse-whipping," or "pulling of the nose" are deprecated as not in keeping with a lofty sense of honor.

CHAPTER III

HENRY PHILLIPS *vs.* BENJAMIN WOODBRIDGE

THE earliest recorded duel in American history appears to have been an encounter near the Powder House on Boston Common, July 3, 1728, between Henry Phillips and Benjamin Woodbridge. The conflict occurred in the evening, swords being the weapons. Phillips was a kinsman of Peter Faneuil, builder of the hall that became the "True Cradle of Liberty." His mother, Mrs. Marie Phillips, was a sister of Faneuil, and his brother Gillam was associated with the latter in business. Phillips was little more than a boy. Woodbridge was the elder, one of the first graduates of Harvard College, a partner of Jonathan Sewall, a prominent merchant of the day and forbear of many eminent persons of that name. What the quarrel was about never became known. The Reverend Lucius Menlius Sargent gives great space to the affair in his *Dealings with the Dead,* Vol. II. Kneeland's *New Weekly Journal* of July 8, 1728, had this to say of the encounter:

"On Thursday last, July 4th, the current, about three in the morning, after some hours search, was found dead near the Powder House the body of Mr. Benjamin Woodbridge, a young gentleman merchant of this place. He had a small stab under the right arm; but what proved fatal to him was a thrust

he received under his right breast, which came out
at the small of his back. The forefinger of his left
hand was almost cut off at the uppermost joint, supposed to be done by grasping a naked sword. The
coroner's inquest at once sat upon the body and, after
the best information and evidence they could obtain,
upon their oaths say that the said Benjamin Woodbridge was killed with a sword run through his body
at the hands of Henry Phillips, of Boston, merchant,
in the Common of said Boston, on the third instant
as appears to us."

Boston had never before been so excited in its hundred years of existence. Law and order were at stake,
the sober citizens thought, and under the public pressure
Governor William Dummer issued a proclamation on
July 4, 1728, reading:

"Whereas a barbarous murder was last night committed on the body of Benjamin Woodbridge, a young
gentleman resident in the town of Boston; and Henry
Phillips of said town, is suspected to be the author of
said murder, and is now fled from Justice; I have
thought proper therefore, to issue this proclamation,
hereby commanding all justices, sheriffs and constables,
and all other officers within this province, and requiring
all others in his Majesty's name, to use their utmost
endeavors, that the said Henry Phillips may be apprehended and brought to justice; and all persons who-
soever are commanded, at their utmost peril, not to
harbor nor conceal him. The said Henry Phillips is a
fair young man, about the age of twenty-two years,
well set, well dressed; and has a wound in one of his
hands. Given at Boston, the 4th of July, 1728, in the

second year of the reign of our Sovereign Lord and King, George II."

The proclamation was not swift enough to catch Phillips. His brother Gillam, Peter Faneuil, and other friends saw to that. A heavy fog prevailed the night of the duel, and the young man was taken from Gibb's Wharf by rowboat to the pink-sterned schooner *Molly,* owned by Faneuil. Her skillful captain steered her through the mist to a point between Castle and Spectacle Islands, where lay the British warship *Sheerness.* Phillips was transferred to the frigate and welcomed there by Captain Conrad and a friend, Lieutenant Pritchard.

Indignant Boston, on the morning of July 4, was pretty sure that Phillips was on board the *Sheerness,* but no one was in a position to ask questions of a man-of-war. Besides, the mist was too thick to make it safe to seek her out. When the fog lifted, it was found that the *Sheerness* had put to sea.

A coroner's jury sat upon the case and took much testimony—mostly hearsay—though it examined Thomas Baker, who admitted that he had attended Phillips as a friend, and Robert Handy, who had performed like service for Woodbridge, rather informally it would appear.

The young man's body was taken to Jonathan Sewall's house and thence interred "handsomely and decently," as the current account states, in the Granary burying ground. The tombstone is still visible from Tremont Street.

Phillips was promptly indicted, but was well out of reach upon the sea. Some sympathy developed for him, however. The Faneuils and thirty other friends entered a petition favoring his case, in which he was described as a "youth of a very affable, courteous, and peaceable behavior and disposition," not addicted to quarreling and "soberly brought up," as behooved a Boston boy of that day. They "verily" believed him to be "slow to anger, and with difficulty moved to resentment."

Adverse to this the Reverend Timothy Cutler preached a sermon on the sin of duelling, and the town talked for days about the event and the nerve of His Majesty's Captain Conrad carrying off a murderer to safety across the mighty deep—it was most mighty then. Young Phillips made his way to France, where he was consigned by Peter Faneuil to the care of his brother Jean, who looked out for Boston business at that end of the line. He was kindly received, but he went into a decline and died about May 20, 1729.

CHAPTER IV

WILLIAM WHATELY vs. JOHN TEMPLE

TO speak after the manner of Sir Boyle Roche, this famous American duel was not American at all. It was fought in England between Englishmen, but the provocation was American, and the provocateur no less a personage than Benjamin Franklin. At the time (1773), this wise and great man had long been the Agent of the Colonies in Great Britain. Relations between these and the parent country had become tense, growing out of governmental attempts to treat the Colonists as sources of gain, to stifle commercial enterprise in the interest of British merchants and British ship owners, besides enforcing taxation without representation.

The wit and prudence of Franklin had gained him much support, yet conditions grew intolerable. The bureaucrats were resentful and oppressive; Parliament was inactive; and intriguers were busy. The Commissioners of the Tax Office found that their expenses in America had amounted to twelve thousand pounds for the year, while the return was barely fifteen hundred, coming for the most part from the West Indies and the more docile Canada.

Luxuries like tea and liquors were smuggled in through ports on the long coast by Dutch ships. England was powerless against the tacit conspiracy in the

SIR JOHN TEMPLE

colonies to send no revenues overseas so long as no representatives in Parliament accompanied them. Thomas Hutchinson, Governor of Massachusetts Bay, and Andrew Oliver, his Lieutenant, were living helpless amid a hostile people and did not know what to do. Both relieved their feelings by writing very frank letters to James Whately, Secretary of the Treasury. Peter Oliver, the Chief Justice, was paid his salary for the year 1772 out of the Royal Treasury, not as before by Massachusetts, whose people chose to interpret this as a form of bribing his honor to induce decisions favorable to the Crown. For taking the money from the King, the Assembly impeached Oliver. In turn it was dissolved by Hutchinson, who soon found himself in great difficulty. This his letters voiced. His woes were echoed by Andrew Oliver and Charles Paxton, the Royal Revenue Collector, at Boston.

James Whately died. The letters fell into the hands of William Whately, his brother and administrator. They were confidential missives, but William Whately handed them about. Members of Parliament friendly to Benjamin Franklin, saw them. He was advised to procure the letters, and with his customary resource and cunning did so. How he obtained them he had sworn never to reveal, and he kept his pledge. Thinking it his duty to make Massachusetts aware of the feeling manifested by her officials, he sent the letters to Boston. The signatures had been effaced and the envelopes were missing. He knew the handwriting would reveal the writers to his Boston correspondent, Thomas Cushing, Speaker of the General Court, to whom he wrote: "All good men wish harmony to subsist between the Colonies and the Mother Country. My resentment against this country for its arbitrary measures in governing us has been exceedingly abated since my conviction by these papers that the measures were projected, and vised and called for by men of character among ourselves." These he saw "bartering away the liberties of their native country for posts, negotiating for salaries and pensions extorted from the people," besides "exciting jealousies in the Crown and provoking it to wrath against so great a part of its faithful subjects." Though he had asked that the letters be handed about among the Liberal group and not made public, the Massachusetts malcontents seized eagerly upon the communications and published them. They caused intense excitement, which reacted in London through a petition from the Massachusetts Assembly, in which, on the strength of the letters, it begged leave "particularly to complain of the conduct of his Excellency Thomas Hutchinson, Esq., Governor, and Andrew Oliver, Esq., Lieutenant-Governor, of this Your Majesty's provinces," and asked that they be removed. The Privy Council, to which this was referred, did not hurry about dealing with the question. Franklin forwarded it by the friendly Earl of Dartmouth, on August 21, 1773, but it did not come up for action until the New Year.

Meanwhile, William Whately, who had prospered as a banker for the Treasury, through his brother,— among other things collecting Dr. Samuel Johnson's pension for him—was deeply disturbed and feared that he might suffer blame for the consequences. This disturbance was increased by two letters published in the

Public Advertiser, signed "Antenor," which more than intimated that breach of confidence lay at the door of John Temple, a prominent member of Parliament, and a warm friend of Doctor Franklin. One of these, printed on December 8, 1773, made a special stir, laying stress, as it did, on Temple's alleged share in the scandal. To this he responded under date of December 8, 1773, in a note to the editor of the *Public Advertiser.* This read:

SIR,—

Having read in your paper of this day an imputation on my character, under the signature of Antenor, I called on Mr. Whately, the banker, whose name is mentioned, to know whether he had authorized that charge, or avowed any proof of the pretended facts upon which it is founded. Mr. Whately totally disclaimed them, and denied that he had authorized any person to use his name, or knew the writer. I then read to him the state of facts relative to me in the said paper; all of which he acknowledged were false, except that about a year ago he gave me some letters of my own, written to his late brother when Secretary of the Treasury; and that we had together read some other letters from gentlemen in America, but none of these lately published of Messrs. Hutchinson, Oliver, Paxton, &c., which Mr. Whately assured me he had never seen until they appeared in print.

Anonymous attacks are not to be regarded; but if no note were taken of them when names are mentioned, concealed villains might in some measure answer their infamous purposes.

J. TEMPLE

Great George Street
Dec. 8, 1773.

Just what there was in this to take exception to is hard to perceive, but Whately responded in a laborious letter to the *Public Advertiser,* which appeared on the following day, December 9. He observed in his reply that he had no knowledge of the authorship of the Antenor letters, and seemed on the face of it to withdraw himself from the complication. He recited that Temple having asked to select certain letters from Thomas Whately's correspondence, "I made no scruple to lay before him, and occasionally during his visit to leave with him, several parcels of letters from my late brother's correspondents in America, in the exact state into which they had come into my possession; some regularly sorted and some promiscuously tied together; and some of them from Mr. Temple himself, and his brother, and from Governor Hutchinson, Mr. Oliver, and others; and, during the intervals that I was in the room with Mr. Temple, we did cast our eyes on one or two letters of Governor Hutchinson, and, I believe, of one or two other correspondents of my late brother. In July last I received information from Mr. Oliver, of Boston, that several letters to my late brother had been laid before the Assembly of the Province; upon which I waited upon Mr. Temple and told him I thought myself entitled to call upon him to join his name with mine in asserting the integrity and honor of both of us; that he, and he only, had ever had access to any of the letters of my brother's correspondents in America, and that I was called to account for the letters in question. Mr. Temple assured me, in terms the most precise (that except some letters from himself and his brother which he received from me by my permission), he had not taken a single letter, or an extract of any I had communicated to him. I

saw him twice afterwards on the subject and the same
assurances were invariably returned by him, and confirmed by him in the most solemn manner."

"A Member of Parliament," in a letter to the *Public
Advertiser,* caustically pointed out that this was not an
exoneration, and Temple himself came again into print
to observe concerning Whately's letter: "He omitted
to state what was solely essential, that he did not know
the letters in question were among those he put in my
hands, and that none of those he had intrusted to me
appeared to be missing; but related in such a manner as
strongly to corroborate the anonymous charge; and
gave me, to my understanding, the lie direct."

In further proceedings: "Mr. Whately's answer not
being deemed satisfactory by Mr. Temple, his friend
Mr. Izard waited upon Mr. Whately with a letter
desiring Mr. Whately to wait upon him that evening,
the consequences of which the public need not be informed, was, Mr. Whately received many wounds."

"Friend Izard" was no less a person than young
Mr. Ralph Izard, of North Carolina, then residing
in London. Whately accepted the challenge as noted,
but declined seconds.

A London evening paper issued on the next day decorously added this detail:

"The gentlemen who lately fought a duel in Hyde
Park met about four in the afternoon under the wall,
near the spot where soldiers are usually shot. They
had no seconds, nor was any person within sight of
them but a boy who was exercising a horse. This boy,
we are told, rode up to the combatants and threatened
to ride over them if they did not desist, but he was

ordered to keep off at his peril. As the boy tells the
story, the lusty gentlemen fell in making a lunge at
his antagonist and received a wound after he fell;
on which the boy exclaimed against the unfairness of
such conduct, which put a stop to further injury, and
so the duel ended. A man who heard the report of
the pistols had the curiosity to clamber over the wall,
but, it is said, not time enough to be a witness to the
transaction."

Franklin was absent from London when the duel
occurred, but on returning he made haste to write to
the printer of the *Public Advertiser*:

Sir,—

Finding that two gentlemen have been unfortunately engaged in a duel, about a transaction and its circumstances; I
think it incumbent upon me to declare (for the prevention of
further mischief, and as far as such a declaration may contribute
to prevent it) that I alone am the person who transmitted to
Boston the letters in question. Mr. W. could not communicate
them, because they were never in his possession; and for the same
reason they could not be taken from him by Mr. T. They were
not of the nature of private letters between friends. They
were written by public officers to persons in public stations on
public affairs and intended to procure public measures; they
were therefore handed to other public persons who might be
influenced by them to produce these measures. Their tendency
was to influence the mother country against her colonies, and
by the steps recommended, to widen the breach; which they
effected. The chief caution expressed with regard to privacy,
was, to keep their contents from the colony agents, who, the
writers apprehended might return them, or copies of them, to
America. This apprehension, was, it seems, well-founded, for

the first agent who laid his hands on them thought it his duty
to transmit them to his constituents.

B. FRANKLIN

Agent for the House of Representatives
  of Massachusetts Bay, Craven Street
    December 25, 1773.

A Merry Christmas, indeed, did the good doctor
usher in! Naturally, all this roused a prodigious stir
and more correspondence in the press. A letter attack-
ing Temple, published in the *Public Advertiser,* on
December 28, 1773, called from him a full account of
the duel, which was published December 30, in which
he said:

"Mr. Whately declined having any second, and
therefore I brought none. He appeared at the place
armed with a sword only. I gave him one of my
pistols. We discharged them mutually, mine being, at
his request, the first, without effect. If his was not
directed at me, it escaped my observation. I then drew
my sword and approached him, who also unsheathed
his, with a persuasion grounded on his coming with a
sword only, when the choice of weapons was in him,
that I was to encounter an adversary much superior to
myself in skill. I soon found my mistake; and, as far
as I could reason in such a situation, determined, by
wounding him in the sword arm, to end the business
without a fatal shot. But my skill was not equal to my
intention; it soon became a struggle, exposed parts,
which in regular encounter could never have been
touched. When he turned to seize the blade of my

sword with his left hand, I supposed he received the wounds in his left side; and in some violent effort, his shoulder must have been exposed. The extreme smallness of the wound in that part, being, as I am well informed, a mere puncture, proves it to have been accidental. Had my purpose been unfair, I should have taken the life that was in my power; had it been mortal, every wound would not have been sufficient, and one only, dangerous, not from its depth, but the direction. I understand it has been said he was down. In such circumstances it is as impossible to account for everything that happens, as to remember everything that passes. But of this I am very sure, that though he slipt once, he never fell."

Temple reiterated his denial that he had "any concern, directly or indirectly, in procuring or transmitting the letters which were sent to Boston."

The gossip continuing, Temple appealed to Whately to state through the *Public Advertiser,* whether he "did or did not, in every respect, behave like a gentleman and man of honor." Whately responded with a long statement that intimated nothing to Temple's discredit. He revealed that his wounds were five in number and soon healed. Temple got off with a scratch on the hand. He was in the closest sort of intimacy with the Americans in London, who included, besides Franklin and Izard, Arthur Lee. Izard and Lee were handy to Hyde Park when the fight occurred. They had a carriage, and after hearing the pistol shots, strolled toward the spot from whence they came. The two met the wounded Whately, who was placed in the carriage and escorted home by Izard, while Lee walked with

Temple to Izard's house, where no doubt there was
some exciting conversation. Temple, by the way, was
quite deaf, a fact that may have made him more than
ordinarily sensitive and suspicious.

The full story, together with the correspondence,
is told in detail in a very rare pamphlet, issued in
London at the time and entitled: "A Faithful Account
of the Whole of the Transactions relating to the late
Affair of Honour between J. Temple and W. Whately,
Esqs. Containing a particular History of that unhappy
Quarrel. Likewise, the whole of the Letters that passed
on that Occasion, with those signed Antenor. An
Enemy of Villains of every Denomination, &c., &c.
London, 1774."

One wonders if Franklin had a hand in its produc-
tion. He was pretty good at pamphleteering. The outcome was to be severe against him and the direct consequence was the American Revolution.

The Privy Council, stirred by events, including the
duel, took up the Cushing petition on January 11, 1774.
Franklin, coming before it, found that Hutchinson's
agent, Israel Maduit, had asked, quite properly, to be
heard by counsel on behalf of his principal. So when
Franklin apeared on the scene, he found Alexander
Wedderburn, afterwards Baron Loughborough, and
first Earl of Rosslyn, on the ground to defend the
governor and his lieutenant, while upon him fell the
duty of representing the petitioners. He therefore
asked for three week's time in which to select counsel
and prepare his case, remarking that he "had thought it
a matter of politics, not of law."

The Council very reasonably gave him until January

26 to secure counsel and prepare. Dr. James Priestly, the eminent scientist, who became an American, wrote later, in discussing the event:

"On the morning of the day on which the cause was to be heard, I met Mr. Burke (Edmund) on Parliament Street, accompanied by Doctor Douglas, afterwards Bishop of Carlisle; and after introducing us to each other as men of letters, he asked me whither I was going? I said I could tell him where I wished to go. He then asked me where it was. I said to the Privy Council, but I was afraid I could not get admission. He then desired me to go along with him. Accordingly, I did; but when we got to the ante-room, we found it quite filled with persons as desirous of getting admission as ourselves. Seeing this, I said we should never get through the crowd. He said, 'Give me your arm!' and locking it fast to his, he soon made his way to the door of the Privy Council. I then said, 'Mr. Burke, you are an excellent leader.' He replied, 'I wish other persons thought so too.'

"After waiting a short time, the door of the Privy Council opened, and we entered the first, when Mr. Burke took his stand behind the first chair next to the President, and I behind that next to him. When the business was opened, it was sufficiently evident, from the speech of Mr. Wedderburn, who was counsel for the Governor (Hutchinson) that the real object of the Court was to insult Dr. Franklin. All this time he stood in the corner of the room, not far from me, without the least apparent emotion.

"Mr. Dunning, who was the leading counsel on the

part of the colony, was so hoarse that he could hardly make himself heard; and Mr. Lee, who was the second, spoke but feebly in reply; so that Mr. Wedderburn had a complete triumph. At the sallies of his sarcastic wit all the members of the Council, the president himself —Lord Gower—not excepted, laughed outright. No person belonging to the Council behaved with decent gravity except Lord North, who, coming late, took his stand behind the chair opposite me.

"When the business was over, Dr. Franklin, in going out, took me by the hand in a manner that indicated some feeling. I soon followed him, and going through the ante-room, I saw Mr. Wedderburn there surrounded with a circle of friends and admirers. Being known to him, he stepped forward as if to speak to me; but I turned aside, and made what haste I could out of the place.

"The next morning I breakfasted with the Doctor, when he said that he had never before been so sensible of the power of a good conscience; for that if he had not considered the thing for which he had been insulted, as one of the best actions in his life, and what he should certainly do again in the same circumstances, he could not have supported it. He was accused of clandestinely procuring certain letters containing complaints of the governor and sending them to America with a view to excite their animosity against him (Hutchinson), and thus embroil the two countries. But he assured me that he did not even know such letters existed until they were brought to him as agent for the colony, in order to be sent to his constituents; and the cover of the letters on which the direction had been written, being lost, he only guessed at the person to whom they were addressed by the contents."

It may be certain that Franklin guessed correctly. Nor could his shrewd mind have failed to tell him that the letters were loaded. It is true, as Priestly states, that John Dunning, afterwards Lord Ashburton, and John Lee, though both able attorneys, did badly. Wedderburn had things all his own way, handling the case, not on the evidence, but upon the way it had been procured. His "insults" follow in part:

"The letters could not have come to Dr. Franklin by fair means. The writers did not give them to him, nor yet the deceased correspondents, who, from our intimacy, would otherwise have told me of it. Nothing, then, will acquit Dr. Franklin of the charge of obtaining them by fraudulent or corrupt means, for the most malignant of purposes, unless he stole them from the person who stole them. This argument is irrefragable.

"I hope, my Lords, you will mark and brand the man, for the honor of this country, of Europe, and of mankind. Private correspondence has hitherto been held sacred in times of the greatest party rage, not only in politics, but religion.

"He has forfeited all the respect of societies and of men. Into what companies will he hereafter go with an unembarrassed face, or the honest intrepidity of virtue? Men will watch him with a jealous eye; they will hide their papers from him, and lock up their escritoires. He will henceforth esteem it a libel to be called a man of letters, *homo trium literarum*.

"But he not only took away the letters from one

brother, but kept himself concealed till he nearly occasioned the murder of the other. It is impossible to read his account, expressive of the coolest and most deliberate malice, without horror. (Here he read Franklin's letter to the *Public Advertiser.*) Amidst these tranquil events, of one person nearly murdered; of another answerable for the issue; of a worthy governor hurt in his dearest interests; the fate of America is in suspense; here is a man, who, with the utmost insensibility of remorse, stands up and avows himself the author of all. I can compare it only to Zanga, in Dr. Young's *Revenge*:

> Know then, t'was—I,
> I forged the letter—I disposed the picture—
> I hated—I despised, and I destroy.

"I ask, my Lords, whether the temper, attributed by poetic fiction only to the bloody African, is not surpassed by the coolness and apathy of the wily American?"

The Lords of the Privy Council agreed with him. Wedderburn's speech led him to become the chief defender of Lord North's administration and made him Lord Loughborough. Hutchinson and Oliver were absolved. Franklin was dismissed from his position as assistant postmaster general of the colonies, where he had made the service pay while much improving it. He stood convicted as a marplot, which was far from what he had intended to be if his word is to be taken.

But in one thing Wedderburn was wrong. The Doctor not only continued to keep the best of company, but joined that of the immortals. He was right in another, however. The fate of America was in suspense, and he himself broke the slender skein that held it when he affronted the greatest American we have yet produced.

Dr. Edward Bancroft, who was present in the "Cockpit," as the Privy Council Chamber was popularly known, during this arraignment of Franklin, records that:

"The Doctor was dressed in a full dress suit of spotted Manchester velvet, and stood conspicuously erect, without the smallest movement of any part of his body. The muscles of his face had been previously composed so as to afford a placid, tranquil expression of countenance, and he did not suffer the slightest alteration of it to appear during the continuance of the speech in which he was so harshly and improperly treated. In short, to quote the words which he employed concerning himself on another occasion, he kept his countenance as immovable as if his features had been made of wood."

This outer stoicism belied what was boiling inside. Up to that time, to use his own words, he had "represented the people of America as proud of Britain, concerned for its interests and glory, and without the least desire for a separation from it." He therefore viewed with concern the sending of troops to Boston at the call of Hutchinson, while their "behavior to the people there gave me infinite uneasiness, as I apprehended from that measure the worst of consequences—a break between the two countries." Having often discussed the situation in this light, he was "to my great surprise, assured by a gentleman of character and distinction. . . . that not only the measure I particularly censured so warmly, but all the other grievances we complained of took their rise, not from the government here (England), but were projected, proposed to administration, solicited, and obtained by some of the most respectable among the Americans themselves, as necessary measures for the welfare of that country. As I could not readily assent to the probability of this, he undertook to convince me, and he hoped through me—as their agent here—my countrymen. Accordingly, he called upon me some days after, and produced to me these very letters from Governor Hutchinson, Lieutenant-Governor Oliver, and others, which have since been the object of so much discussion.

"Though astonished, I could not but confess myself convinced, and I was ready, as he desired to convince my countrymen; for I saw, I felt indeed, by its effect upon myself, the tendency it must have towards a reconciliation, which for the common good I earnestly wished."

Thinking mere copies would not have the full effect desired, he acquired the originals, on the express conditions that they should not be printed, that no copies should be taken of them; that they should be shown only to a few leading people of the government, and that they should be carefully returned. Unfortunately, or perhaps more accurately, fortunately, the person to whom Franklin sent the letters, passed them on to others, who, regardless of his injunction, made them public, with all the consequences previously narrated.

Whately followed up his complaint to the Privy Council with a bill in chancery which required that Franklin give the source from which he obtained the letters. To this the Doctor demurred. His demurrer was overruled, and he was ordered to make the revelation. To avoid doing this, "feeling that it would be a violation of his engagement" and "probably injurious to the person to whom they had been sent," he "thought it incumbent upon him to return to America." So he resigned his agency and returned home after a long absence, to become the most important figure in the Revolution. Nor did he ever reveal the name of the person from whom he received the letters. He did let it become known at the time that the man in Boston to whom he sent them was Thomas Cushing.

Franklin had no mind for war at the outset, having always held that "there was never a good war, nor a bad peace" and that "as between friends every affront is not worth a duel, and between nations every injury is not worth a war." Nor was "every mistake in government, every encroachment upon rights . . . worth a rebellion."

But he carried the insults of Wedderburn in his heart, and on the day in Paris when he signed the Treaty that brought men and money to the aid of the almost cornered colonies and insured their liberty, he wore the "spotted suit of Manchester velvet" in which he had stood silent under abuse.

According to George Bancroft:

"That Temple was privy to the plan of getting the letters, he knew from Hutchinson and under his own hand. That he kept aloof, and at the time concealed his agency in the matter, appears from his own statement and from that of Franklin. Franklin gave his word not to name his informer. English writers have not noticed that the English Ministry and Hutchinson seem to have had the means of discovering the secret, that the Ministry discouraged inquiry, and that Temple was subsequently forgiven and appointed to a good place." The "good place" was that of Consul General to the United States after the peace. He was next adorned with the order of Knighthood. Also, it might be noted that Franklin's grandson and biographer was named William Temple Franklin, the "William" for his father, the governor of New Jersey, and "Temple" in honor of his grandfather's friend.

CHAPTER V

PHILIP HAMILTON vs. GEORGE I. EACKER

GENERAL ALEXANDER HAMILTON had eight children, the eldest of whom, Philip, was named for his grandfather, General Philip Schuyler. Philip was a lively youth of twenty, in 1801, having just graduated from Columbia College, and he was beginning the study of law. He had taken on the color of his father's Federalism, and though not yet of age, was active among the youngsters in a political way, as well as being a brisk blade about town. As such he was much in evidence in social affairs and at the theater sharing in temperament the vivacity of his father rather more than the sedate character of Elizabeth Schuyler, his mother.

New York, at the period, possessed but one place of amusement, the Park Theater. Philip Hamilton and his friend, Price, attended the play at this house on the evening of Friday, November 1, 1801. In a box adjacent to them sat George I. Eacker, a young lawyer, who was already of some reputation in the city, with a party of friends. Eacker was a member of the Republican Party headed in the city and state by Aaron Burr. The Republicans, under Jefferson and Burr, had ousted the Federalists—Jefferson being President of the United States and Burr Vice-President. Eacker was twenty-seven years of age, and at the Fourth of July celebration held by Tammany Hall, in 1801, had been the orator of the day. In his address he had paid his respects to the fallen foe in emphatic terms, mentioning by name their Federalist leader, Alexander Hamilton. He had not, however, transgressed the bounds of propriety, and had no reason to expect any affront on account of his utterances. Indeed, he seems to have been greatly respected and to have been a "rising" young man in both law and politics.

The enjoyment of the play by Mr. Eacker and his friends was interrupted by loud talking and derisive laughter in the adjoining box. Looking about for its source, Eacker recognized Hamilton and Price, who seemed delighted to have attracted his attention and increased their offensiveness. Price, the son of a well-to-do merchant, was of good social position, but he had made a reputation for himself as a rake. Eacker, aware of their purpose, paid no further attention to them. But in the interlude preceding the presentation of the afterpiece—always a feature of the evening's performance in that day—the two lively youngsters crowded into the Eacker box and began making ironic comments on Mr. Eacker's Fourth of July eloquence. The intrusion and impudence of the pair roused Eacker to remonstrate. He did not speak to them while in the box, but stepped toward the lobby, observing as he went, "It is too abominable to be publicly insulted by a pair of damned rascals."

The pair had followed him, bent, obviously, upon picking a quarrel. On hearing his remark, Hamilton and Price echoed in chorus: "Whom do you call 'damned rascals'?"

Eacker, not desiring a public altercation, said, "I live at 50 Wall Street, where I am always to be found."

"Your place of residence," remarked Hamilton, angrily, "has nothing to do with it."

With this, Hamilton and Price made a hostile move toward Eacker. Before they could clinch, friends intervened to prevent fisticuffs and succeeded in persuading all three to adjourn to a near-by tavern to continue the discussion. They walked to the inn, arguing as they went under increasing excitement. On reaching the hostelry, both demanded that Eacker name his specific "damned rascals."

In retort Eacker asked, "Did you come into the box on purpose to insult me?"

"That is nothing to the purpose," was the response from one of the young gentlemen. "We insist on your particularizing the person you meant to distinguish by the appellation of 'rascal'."

Eacker's reply was a query. "Did you mean to insult me?"

"We insist upon an answer," responded the young men in chorus.

"Well, then," said Eacker, firmly and with indignation at the obvious purpose of the pair, "you are both rascals."

The two, who had been drinking, raised a great uproar and made for the street. Their denunciations and bad behavior moved Eacker to observe: "Gentlemen, you had better make less noise. I shall expect to hear from you."

"That you shall!" both responded in one breath. Eacker went back to the theater and rejoined his party.

Soon a messenger came with a note from Price challenging him to a duel. This was followed after a short interval by one from Philip Hamilton.

"Tell him," said Eacker, "that I am already engaged to Mr. Price. After that obligation is fulfilled, I will be prepared to deal with Mr. Hamilton."

The meeting took place at Weehawken, on the following Sunday afternoon, between noon and one o'clock. Three shots were exchanged without damage. This seemed sufficient to the seconds to appease any reasonable sense of honor, and they advised a reconciliation. To this neither would assent, and a fourth exchange followed. This, too, was ineffective.

Price, who had a sense of humor and who was a reckless soul, was now ready to desist. "Eacker," he remarked jocosely, "is such a lath of a fellow that I might shoot all day without purpose."

This provoked a laugh all around. The fighters shook hands and departed for the city with much good will and a great rejoicing that all had turned out so happily. On reaching town Eacker at once advised Hamilton's friend that he was now ready for that gentleman. He named his own representative. The two seconds came together and did their best to bring about an understanding that would prevent a meeting, the reasons for which were altogether ridiculous. Hamilton—like his father, later—was quite aware that he had been the original offender, but he could not bring himself to own up and apologize. Duelling was the fashion, and he feared for his social future more than he did Eacker's aim, which the encounter with Price did not demonstrate as especially accurate. He stood stiffly on the ground of "requiring an explanation" from Mr. Eacker "for the expression he had made use of in the theater on Friday night."

In bearing this bit of impertinence Hamilton's friend politely offered to give Mr. Eacker time to consult his friends. Eacker took fifteen minutes to consider. Then, after a failure to frame a verbal response, he extracted a piece of paper from his waistcoat pocket and wrote upon it the following:

"The expressions I made use of toward Mr. Hamilton at the theater on Friday night were produced by his conduct on that occasion. I thought them applicable then, and I think so still."

This he read to the messenger of fate. The immediate result was a meeting arranged for Monday. The two young men met on the Weehawken ground. Hamilton, knowing himself to be in the wrong, had determined not to fire. Eacker's aim this time was sure. He fired at the word, hitting his antagonist, who, under the impact of the shot, touched the hair trigger of his weapon, which went off harmlessly in the air. The wound Hamilton received was evidently mortal. Friends rowed the handsome, foolish lad across the Hudson and bore him to a house near the shore. His father and mother were sent for, as well as surgeons. The latter found the ball had entered his right side above the hip, and passing through the body, had lodged in his left arm.

The New York *Historical Magazine* published in season an account of the result of the duel, written by one of the boy's friends;

"All the physicians in town were called for, and the

news spread like a conflagration. At the theatre I was informed of it about nine o'clock Monday evening. I immediately ran to the house near the State's prison, from which I was told they dare not remove him. Picture to yourself the emotions which must have assailed me on my arrival at his room, to which I was admitted as his old college classmate! On a bed without curtains lay poor Phil, pale and languid, his rolling, distorted eyeballs darting forth flashes of delirium. On one side of him, on the same bed, lay his agonized father; on the other, his distracted mother; around him were numerous relatives and friends, weeping and fixed in sorrow. Blanched with astonishment and affright was the countenance which, a few minutes before, was illumined by the smile of merriment. I could continue in the room but a very short time. Returning home, I quickened my pace almost unconsciously, hoping to escape the image as well as the reality of what I had witnessed."

The unfortunate young man suffered great agony through the night and died about five o'clock on Tuesday morning, November 25. So great was the grief of his father that he had to be supported at the graveside by two friends. Like his father, Philip was gay and attractive in face and maner. With the high lineage of the Schuylers, a liberal allowance and a taste for pleasure, he was the central light among the fast young people of the town. He led in all the routs and by later standards would have been accounted dissolute. To his father his death was as a shadow cast before.

The pistol used by the youth in this encounter was not his own. It was one of a pair owned by his uncle,

John B. Church, husband of his mother's sister, Angelica Schuyler. One of the pair had been used not so long before in a duel between Church and Aaron Burr that came off harmless at Hoboken. That was also rather ridiculous and caused more laughter than criticism. The pistols were to be used again, but tragically, with Burr once more facing one of them. They are now in the New York State museum at Albany. For years they were the property of the late Colonel Walter S. Church of Albany, whom the author knew well. He has often handled them. They are thick-barreled, of small bore, with hair triggers and a bull-dog look.

Despite the power of Hamilton, no untoward consequences followed Eacker.

The Burr-Hamilton feud was now growing more intense. But before it came to a head, another bloody but not fatal affair occurred. This took place in 1802, when John Swartwout, a stout supporter of Burr, fought DeWitt Clinton, later Governor of New York and father of the Erie Canal. Swartwout and Clinton exchanged five shots, the last of which wounded Swartwout in the leg. He was so intent on getting his man that while the surgeon was picking out the ball, he demanded another shot. The seconds declined to permit this. George Clinton, Governor of the state of New York at the time of the duel—was young Clinton's uncle. Governor Clinton was later to succeed Burr as Vice-President of the United States. Another tragic outgrowth was the Killing in a duel, of Collector of Customs Thompson, by William Coleman, editor of the Evening Post.

CHAPTER VI

Aaron Burr vs. Alexander Hamilton

FROM the day when little more than lads, they passed each other as aides to General George Washington, Commander-in-Chief of the Continental Army, Aaron Burr and Alexander Hamilton competed with each other for a place in the public eye.

Burr was a bit the older, having been born at Newark, New Jersey, February 6, 1756, while Hamilton came into the world, on the West Indian Island of Nevis, January 11, 1757.

Each possessed an amazing intellectuality. Burr inherited his from the blood of the English family of Downings, via Jonathan Edwards, the distinguished orthodox divine, and from that of the Reverend Aaron Burr, President of Princeton College, descendant of an eminent line of clergymen. Hamilton's ancestry was clouded. Like Junot, he was his own ancestor. Burr had already enjoyed a vivid military experience before joining Washington at his New York headquarters in a mansion called Richmond Hill, near the so-called Greenwich Village section. The youth had gained a reputation for courage and address with Benedict Arnold and James Montgomery in the essay against Quebec, but found life at Richmond Hill dull. In six weeks he resigned. Hamilton liked it little better but held on. Burr was soon a Lieutenant-colonel, with a command of his own. Hamilton saw the end of the Revolution at Yorktown, leading a column in the final assault. Burr had held the post of honor at Valley Forge and distinguished himself on the lines in Westchester.

Both Burr and Hamilton became lawyers. Both located in New York. Both went into politics, Burr following the faith of Thomas Jefferson, and Hamilton founding a creed of his own, which became known as Federalism. Though he was compelled by a scandal to resign as President Washington's Secretary of the Treasury, Hamilton remained no less active and potent in politics. His followers formed a Federalist party. John Adams was their only president, though he hated Hamilton, but the presidency came to him as one of the Fathers of the Republic.

Now came Jefferson to dispute the Hamiltonian theory of government that had so far prevailed under the Constitution which Hamilton had done much to form. Burr had become a United States Senator, beating Hamilton's father-in-law, General Philip Schuyler. At the next turn of the wheel Hamilton elected Schuyler, defeating Burr in New York. The latter appeared out of luck, but rallied and became a formidable candidate for President against Jefferson. Adams had muddled things so that the Federalists were third in the Electoral College, but Jefferson and Burr were tied. This threw the choice in the House, where the Federalists held the balance of power. Hamilton turned the vote to Jefferson, his opposite in politics, rather than give the Presidency to Burr.

Under the rule then prevailing, Burr was made Vice-

President. This office had not then become a nonentity. The Vice-President appointed the committees of the Senate and exercised much power that no longer exists. Burr's outlook seemed bright but for an obstacle that was always in his path—Alexander Hamilton. At the beginning of their careers Hamilton had invited Burr to become his partner in law, but Burr had declined. In an adverse moment, after losing the Senate seat, Burr had sought a brigadier's commission in the army. This appointment was prevented, Burr believed, by Hamilton sowing mistrust in Washington's mind.

As presiding officer of the Senate, Burr was a complete success; but politically his progress was barred by continuous calumny emanating from a source that could not be mistaken—and that was marvelously effective in its purpose. He was conscious long before the end of his term that he had no prospect of continuing as Vice-President, or of being promoted to the higher office. The venom of the Federalists spent itself against him, the animus for which originated with their leader. Burr's hope of succeeding either himself or Jefferson was killed off by an amazing piece of misrepresentation. It was charged that in 1801 he had plotted with the Federalists to secure enough of their votes to make him President. The fact that Hamilton threw all his influence to elect Jefferson instead of Burr was completely ignored, and Burr stood marked as a potential traitor. With Burr held in Washington, Hamilton, busy in New York, undermined him at home. Burr found himself so circumstanced that he appealed to Jefferson, whose own succession was assured, to send him as Ambassador to France, an office commensurate to his talents and of a dignity worthy of the position from which he was to retire. The calumniators had done their work so thoroughly that Jefferson declined to accede to the request, a decision greatly to his discredit, because he must have known that the charge of conniving with the Federalists was false. "My enemies," said Burr, in making the appeal, "are using your name to destroy me; and something is necessary from you to prevent it, and deprive them of that weapon—some mark of favor from you which will declare to the world that I retire with your confidence."

Jefferson evaded what should have been his duty, the absolving of Burr from the charge of treachery. The Vice-President had been too close to his heels to be comfortable. He did nothing either by word or act to clear him of the stain, loftily taking the ground that he had not interfered in the event of 1801, which may have been true. Hamilton had attended to all that.

George Clinton of New York was selected for Vice-President. Burr, aware that he was out, but not considering himself down, then took the fatal step of calling Hamilton to account for his share in his discomfiture. The Senate not being in session, Burr spent his time in the spring of 1804 in New York, where he speedily discovered that, not content with what he had already done, Hamilton was still busy injuring his repute. Determined to end it once for all at whatever hazard, Burr called his foe to account by sending this icy letter:

New York, June 18, 1804

Sir,—

I send for your perusal a letter signed Charles D. Cooper,

which, though apparently published some time ago, has but very recently come to my knowledge. Mr. Van Ness, who does me the favour to deliver this, will point out to you that clause of the letter to which I particularly request your attention.

You must perceive, Sir, the necessity of a prompt and unqualified acknowledgement or denial of the use of any expression which would warrant the assertions of Cooper.

I have the honour to be,
Your obedient serv't,
A. Burr

General Hamilton

Hamilton took two days to formulate his reply. It came at length on June 20, saying:

Sir,—

I have maturely reflected on the subject of your letter of the 18th inst., and the more I have reflected the more I have become convinced, that I could not, without manifest impropriety, make the avowal or disavowal which you seem to think necessary. The clause pointed out by Mr. Van Ness is in these terms: "I could detail to you a *still more despicable* opinion which General Hamilton *has expressed* of Mr. Burr." To endeavour to discover the meaning of this declaration, I was obliged to seek in the antecedent part of this letter for the opinion to which it referred, as having been already disclosed. I found it in these words: "General Hamilton and Judge Kent have declared in *substance,* that they looked upon Mr. Burr to be a *dangerous man,* and one *who ought not to be trusted with the reins of government."*

The language of Cooper plainly implies that he considered this opinion of you, which he attributes to me, as a *despicable* one; but he affirms that I have expressed some other, *more despicable,* without, however, mentioning to whom, when, or where. 'Tis evident that the phrase, "still more despicable," admits of infinite shades, from very light to very dark. How am I to judge of the degree intended? Or how shall I annex any precise idea to language so indefinite?

Between gentlemen, despicable and more despicable are not worth the pains of distinction; when, therefore, you do not interrogate me as to the opinion which is specifically ascribed to me, I must conclude, that you view it as within the limits to which the animadversions of political opponents upon each other may justifiably extend, and consequently as not warranting the idea of it which Doctor Cooper appears to entertain. If so, what precise inference could you draw, as a guide for your conduct, were I to acknowledge that I had expressed an opinion of you still more despicable than the one which is particularized? How could you be sure that even this opinion had exceeded the bounds which you would yourself deem admissible between political opponents?

But I forbear further comment on the embarrassment, to which the requisition you have made naturally leads. The occasion forbids a more ample illustration, though nothing could be more easy than to pursue it.

Repeating that I cannot reconcile it with propriety to make the acknowledgement or denial you desire, I will add that I deem it inadmissible on principle, to consent to be interrogated as to the justness of the inferences which may be drawn by others from whatever I may have said of a political opponent, in the course of fifteen years competition. If there were no other objection to it this is sufficient that it would tend to expose my sincerity and delicacy to injurious imputations from every person who may at any time have conceived the import of my expressions, differently from what I may then have intended or may afterwards recollect. I stand ready to avow or disavow promptly and explicitly any precise or definite opinion which I may be charged with having declared of any Gentleman. More than this cannot fitly be expected from me; and especially it cannot be reasonably expected that I shall enter into an explanation upon a basis so vague as that which you have adopted. I trust on more reflection you will see the matter in the same light with me. If not, I can only regret the circumstance and must abide the consequences.

The publication of Doctor Cooper was never seen by me till after the receipt of your letter.

I have the honour to be, &c.

A. HAMILTON

Colonel Burr

The unmoved and unappeased Burr could not accept this ingenious sophistry. He continued to press his point, replying to the following effect:

New York, 21st June, 1804

SIR,—

Your letter of the 20th instant has been this day received. Having considered it attentively, I regret to find in it nothing of that sincerity and delicacy which you profess to value.

Political opposition can never absolve gentlemen from the necessity of a rigid adherence to the laws of honour, and the rules of decorum. I neither claim such privilege nor indulge it in others.

The common sense of mankind affixes to the epithet adopted by Cooper, the idea of dishonour. It has been publicly applied to me under the sanction of your name. The question is not, whether he has understood the meaning of the word, or has used it according to syntax, and with grammatical accuracy; but, whether you have authorized this application, either directly or by uttering expressions or opinions derogatory to my honour. The time "when" is in your own knowledge, but no way material to me, as the calumny has now first been disclosed, so as to become the subject of my notice, and as the effect is present and palpable.

Your letter has furnished me with new reasons for requiring a definite reply.

> I have the honour to be,
> Sir, your obedient,
> A. BURR

General Hamilton

This note caused Hamilton to call his friend Nathaniel Pendleton into consultation on Saturday, June 22, 1804. William P. Van Ness had been the bearer of Burr's letters. Hamilton informed Pendleton that he had told Van Ness he considered Burr's last letter rude and offensive; he could not see his way to return any other answer than that, leaving to Mr. Burr such further steps as he saw fit. Van Ness had advised that he take time to deliberate. When the latter came for the decision, Hamilton had, he said, again advised him that he could make no other reply unless Burr would recall his last letter and send one that would admit of a different response. This Burr had not done. Accordingly, Hamilton handed Pendleton a note for Burr, expressing his view. It read:

> *New York, June 22, 1804*

SIR,—

Your first letter, in a style too peremptory, made a demand, in my opinion, unprecedented and unwarrantable. My answer, pointing out the embarrassment, gave you an opportunity to take a less exceptionable course. You have not chosen to do it; but by your last letter received this day, containing expressions *indecorous* and improper, you have increased the difficulties to explanation intrinsically incident to the nature of your application.

If by a "definite reply," you mean the direct avowal or disavowal required in your first letter, I have no other answer to give, than that which has already been given. If you mean anything different, admitting of greater latitude, it is requisite you should explain.

I have the honour to be,
Sir, your obedient servant,
ALEX HAMILTON

Aaron Burr, Esq.

Pendleton did not present this letter at the moment, awaiting some word from Van Ness as to the result of his report to his principal of the interview with Hamilton. Burr was absent from the city and Van Ness did not see him until June 23. Then Van Ness wrote Hamilton asking most politely when it would be convenient for him to accord an interview. Hamilton replied that if the matter were pressing, he could see him that same day at his country home, on Washington Heights, if convenient. If not, he would be at his city home in Cedar Street at nine o'clock on the morning of June 24. Meanwhile, parleyings had gone on between Van Ness and Pendleton, the latter urging that Burr write a letter to Hamilton requesting to know in substance, whether, in the conversation to which Doctor Cooper referred, any particular instance of dishonest conduct was imputed to Colonel Burr, or whether there was any impeachment of his private character, in which case General Hamilton "would declare to the best of his recollection" what passed at that conversation. In making this request, Mr. Pendleton read from a written sheet the substance of what he understood Hamilton would state in that event, viz:

"General Hamilton says he cannot imagine to what Dr. Cooper may have alluded, unless it were to a conversation at Mr. Taylor's in Albany, last winter (at which he and Gen. Hamilton were present). Gen. Hamilton cannot recollect distinctly the particulars of that conversation so as to undertake to repeat them, without running the risk of varying, or omitting what might be deemed important circumstances. The expressions are entirely forgotten, and the specific ideas imperfectly remembered; but to the best of his recollection it consisted of comments on the political principles and views of Col. Burr and the results that might be expected from them in the event of his election as Governor, without reference to any particular instance of past conduct, or to private character."

Pendleton also delivered the Hamilton letter of June 22. Van Ness, at a further interview, asked Pendleton to put in writing what he proposed on the part of General Hamilton. This Pendleton did, as follows:

"In answer to a letter properly adapted to obtain from General Hamilton a declaration whether he had charged Col. Burr with any particular instance of dishonourable conduct, or had impeached his private character, either in the conversation alluded to by Dr. Cooper, or in any other particular instance to be specified; he would be able to answer consistently with his honour, and the truth, in substance, that the conversation to which Dr. Cooper alluded, turned wholly on political topics, and did not attribute to Col. Burr any instance of dishonourable conduct, nor relate to his private character; and in relation to any other language or conversation of General Hamilton which

Col. Burr will specify, a prompt and frank avowal or denial will be given."

This brought the following response from Van Ness:

SIR,—

The letter which you yesterday delivered me, and your subsequent communication, in Colonel Burr's opinion, evince no disposition on the part of General Hamilton to come to a satisfactory accommodation. The injury complained of and the reparation expected, are so definitely expressed in Colonel Burr's letter of the 21st instant, that there is not perceived a necessity for further explanation on his part. The difficulty that would result from confining the inquiry to any particular times and occasions must be manifest. The denial of a specified conversation only, would leave strong implications that on other occasions improper language had been used. When and where injurious opinions and expressions have been uttered by General Hamilton must be best known to him, and of him only will Colonel Burr inquire. No denial or declaration will be satisfactory, unless it be general, so as wholly to exclude the idea that rumours derogatory to Colonel Burr's honour have originated with General Hamilton, or have been fairly inferred from any thing he has said. A definite reply to a requisition of this nature was demanded by Colonel Burr's letter of the 21st instant. This being refused, invites the alternative alluded to in General Hamilton's letter of the 20th.

It was required by the position in which the controversy was placed by General Hamilton on Friday last, and I was immediately furnished with a communication demanding a personal interview. The necessity of this measure has not, in the opinion of Colonel Burr, been diminished by the General's last letter, or any communication which has since been received. I am consequently again instructed to deliver you a message, as soon as it may be convenient for you to receive it. I beg there-

fore you will be so good as to inform me at what hour I can
have the pleasure of seeing you.

Your most obedient, and
Very humble servant,
W. P. Van Ness

Nathaniel Pendleton, Esq. June 26th

Pendleton responded thus:

26th June, 1804

Sir,—

I have communicated the letter which you did me the honour
to write to me of this date, to General Hamilton. The expectations now disclosed on the part of Colonel Burr appear to him
to have greatly extended the original ground of inquiry, and
instead of presenting a particular and definite case for explanation, seem to aim at nothing less than an inquisition into his most
confidential conversations, as well as others through the whole
period of his acquaintance with Colonel Burr.

While he was prepared to meet the particular case fairly
and fully, he thinks it inadmissible that he should be expected
to answer at large as to every thing that he may possibly have
said, in relation to the character of Colonel Burr, at any time
or upon any occasion. Though he is not conscious that any
charges which are in circulation to the prejudice of Colonel
Burr have originated with him, except one which may have
been so considered, and which has long since been fully explained between Colonel Burr and himself,—yet he cannot consent to be questioned generally as to any rumours which may
be afloat derogatory to the character of Colonel Burr, without
specification of the several rumours, many of them probably unknown to him. He does not, however, mean to authorize any
conclusion as to the real nature of his conduct in relation to
Colonel Burr, by his declining so loose and vague a basis of
explanation, and he disavows an unwillingness to come to a

satisfactory, provided it be an honourable, accommodation. His objection is the very indefinite ground which Colonel Burr has assumed, in which he is sorry to be able to discern nothing short of predetermined hostility. Presuming, therefore, that it will be adhered to, he has instructed me to receive the message which you have it in charge to deliver. For this purpose I shall be at home and at your command tomorrow morning from eight to ten o'clock.

I have the honour to be, respectfully,

Your obedient servant,

NATHANIEL PENDLETON

William P. Van Ness, Esq.

Van Ness's reply follows:

SIR,—

The letter which I had the honour to receive from you, under date of yesterday, states, among other things, that in General Hamilton's opinion, Colonel Burr has taken a very indefinite ground, in which he evinces nothing short of predetermined hostility, and that General Hamilton thinks it inadmissible that the inquiry should extend to his confidential as well as other conversations. In this Colonel Burr can only reply, that secret whispers traducing his fame, and impeaching his honour, are, at least, equally injurious with slanders publicly uttered; that General Hamilton had, at no time, and in no place, a right to use any such injurious expressions; and that the partial negative he is disposed to give, with the reservations he wishes to make, are proofs that he has done the injury specified.

Colonel Burr's request was, in the first instance, proposed in a form the most simple, in order that General Hamilton might give to the affair that course to which he might be induced by his temper and his knowledge of facts. Colonel Burr trusted with confidence, that from the frankness of a soldier and the candour of a gentleman, he might expect an ingenuous declaration. That if, as he had reason to believe, General Hamilton had used expressions derogatory to his honour, he would have had the magnanimity to retract them; and that if, from his language, injurious inferences had been improperly drawn, he would have perceived the propriety of correcting errors, which might thus have been widely diffused. With these impressions Colonel Burr was greatly surprised at receiving a letter which he considered as evasive, and which in manner he deemed not altogether decorous. In one expectation, however, he was not wholly deceived, for the close of General Hamilton's letter contained an intimation that if Colonel Burr should dislike his refusal to acknowledge or deny, he was ready to meet the consequences. This Colonel Burr deemed a sort of defiance, and would have felt justified in making it the basis of an immediate message. But as the communication contained something concerning the indefiniteness of the request; as he believed it rather the offspring of false pride than of reflection, and as he felt the utmost reluctance to proceed to extremities, while any other hope remained, his request was repeated in terms more explicit. The replies and propositions on the part of General Hamilton have, in Colonel Burr's opinion, been constantly in substance the same.

Colonel Burr disavows all motives of predetermined hostility, a charge by which he thinks insult added to injury. He feels as a gentleman should feel when his honour is impeached or assailed; and without sensations of hostility or wishes of revenge, he is determined to vindicate that honour at such hazard as the nature of the case demands.

The length to which this correspondence has extended, only tending to prove that the satisfactory redress, earnestly desired, cannot be obtained, he deems it useless to offer any proposition except the simple message which I shall now have the honour to deliver.

I have the honour to be with great respect,
Your obedient and very humble servant,
W. P. VAN NESS

Wednesday Morning, June 27th, 1804

This message was, of course, a formal challenge. Pendleton notified Van Ness that he would meet him the next day, pending which he gave the letter to Hamilton, who asked him to confer further on the following morning. Hamilton was plainly confused by the pitiless process of forcing him to act. Assuming that Van Ness's dictum might not necessarily be final, he gave Pendleton a paper to present to Van Ness. This the latter declined to receive. It read:

"Remarks on the letter of June 27, 1804*"*

"Whether the observations on this letter are designed merely to justify the result which is indicated in the close of the letter, or may be intended to give an opening for rendering any thing explicit which may have been deemed vague heretofore, can only be judged of by the sequel. At any rate it appears to me necessary not to be misunderstood. Mr. Pendleton is therefore authorized to say, that in the course of the present discussion, written or verbal, there has been no intention to evade, defy, or insult, but a sincere disposition to avoid extremities if it could be done with propriety. With this view, General Hamilton has been ready to enter into a frank and free explanation on any and every object of a specific nature; but not to answer a general and abstract inquiry, embracing a period too long for an accurate recollection, and exposing him to unpleasant criticisms from, or unpleasant discussions with, any and every person, who may have understood him in an unfavorable sense. This (admitting that he could answer in a manner the most satisfactory to Col. Burr) he should deem inadmissible, in principle and precedent, and humiliating in practice. To this therefore he can never submit. Frequent allusion has been made to slanders said to be in circulation. Whether they are openly or in whispers, they have a form and shape, and might be specified.

"If the alternative alluded to in the close of the letter is definitively tendered, it must be accepted; the time, place, and manner, to be afterwards regulated. I should not think it right in the midst of a Circuit Court to withdraw my services from those who may have confided important interests to me, and expose them to the embarrassment of seeking other counsel, who may not have time to be sufficiently instructed in their causes. I shall also want a little time to make some arrangements respecting my own affairs."

Van Ness for Burr would not recede. Accordingly, on Friday, July 6, 1804, Pendleton informed him that General Hamilton would be at Colonel Burr's service at any time after Sunday following. The seconds met on Monday and arranged for a meeting at Weehawken, where it was that Philip Hamilton had fallen before George Eacker's pistol, on the Wednesday morning following, at seven o'clock. Hamilton and Burr met accordingly. The details of all that occurred were afterwards set down by the seconds as follows:

"Colonel Burr arrived first on the ground, as had been previously agreed; when General Hamilton ar-

AARON BURR
From a painting by J. Sharples, the Elder

rived, the parties exchanged salutations, and the seconds proceeded to make their arrangements. They measured the distance, ten full paces, and cast lots for the choice of position, as also to determine by whom the word should be given, both of which fell to the second of General Hamilton. They then proceeded to load the pistols in each other's presence, after which the parties took their stations. The gentleman who was to give the word, then explained to the parties the rules which were to govern them in firing, which were as follows: 'The parties being placed at their stations . . the second who gives the word shall ask them whether they are ready; being answered in the affirmative, he shall say, Present! After this the parties shall present and fire when they please . . . If one fires before the other, the opposite second shall say one, two, three, fire . . . and he shall then fire or lose his fire.' He then asked if they were prepared; being answered in the affirmative, he gave the word 'Present!' as had been agreed on, and both parties presented and fired in succession . . . the intervening time is not expressed, as the seconds do not precisely agree on that point. The fire of Colonel Burr took effect, and General Hamilton almost instantly fell. Colonel Burr then advanced toward General Hamilton, with a manner and gesture that appeared to General Hamilton's friend to be expressive of regret, but without speaking, turned about and withdrew, being urged from the field by his friend as has been subsequently stated, with a view to prevent his being recognized by the surgeon and bargemen, who were then approaching. No further communication took place between the principals, and the barge that carried Colonel Burr immediately returned to the city. We conceive it proper to add that the conduct of the parties in this interview was perfectly proper as suited the occasion."

This is the bare account. To elaborate further it may be said that General Hamilton, Pendleton, and Doctor David Hosack, a distinguished surgeon, who had also some considerable literary attainments, arrived together after Burr and Van Ness, whom they found, with their coats off, removing brush and clearing the ground. There was little delay in placing the parties. Burr raised his arm slowly, aimed deliberately, and fired when Pendleton gave the word. The ball struck Hamilton on the right side, causing him to raise himself involuntarily on his toes, turn his body to the left, and fall upon his face. He had neither aimed or fired, but as he swayed the pistol went off and the ball cut the leaves over his head. Pendleton called Hosack, who ran to his fallen friend, while Van Ness covered Burr's face with an umbrella as he passed so Hosack could swear that he had not seen him on the field. For the rest, let us quote Hosack:

August 17th, 1804

DEAR SIR,—

To comply with your request is a painful task; but I will repress my feelings while I endeavour to furnish you with an enumeration of such particulars relative to the melancholy end of our beloved friend Hamilton, as dwell most forcibly on my recollection.

When called to him, upon his receiving the fatal wound, I found him half sitting on the ground, supported in the arms of

Mr. Pendleton. His countenance of death I shall never forget. He had at that instant just strength to say, "This is a mortal wound, Doctor"; when he sank away, and became to all appearances lifeless. I immediately stripped up his clothes, and soon, alas! ascertained that the direction of the ball must have been through some vital part. His pulses were not to be felt; his respiration was entirely suspended; and upon laying my hand on his heart, and perceiving no motion there, I considered him as irrecoverably gone. I, however, observed to Mr. Pendleton, that the only chance for his reviving was immediately to get him upon the water. We therefore lifted him up, and carried him out of the wood, to the margin of the bank, where the bargemen aided us in conveying him into the boat, which immediately put off. During all this time I could not discover the least symptom of returning life. I now rubbed his face, lips, and temples, with spirits of hartshorne, applied to his neck and breast, and to the wrists and palms of his hands, and endeavoured to pour some into his mouth. When we had got, as I should judge, about fifty yards from the shore, some imperfect efforts to breathe were for the first time manifest; in a few minutes he sighed, and became sensible to the impression of the hartshorne, or the fresh air of the water. He breathed; his eyes, hardly opened, wandered, without fixing upon any objects; to our great joy he at length spoke. "My vision is distinct," were his first words. His pulse became more perceptible; his respiration more regular; his sight returned. I then examined the wound to know if there was any dangerous discharge of blood; upon slightly pressing his side it gave him pain; on which I desisted. Soon after recovering his sight, he happened to cast his eye upon the case of pistols, and observing the one that he had had in his hand lying on the outside, he said, "Take care of that pistol; it is undischarged, and still cocked; it may go off and do harm. Pendleton knows (attempting to turn his head towards him) that I did not intend to fire at him." "Yes," said Mr. Pendleton, understanding his wish, "I have already made Dr. Hosack acquainted with your determination as to that."

He then closed his eyes and remained calm, without any disposition to speak; nor did he say much afterwards, excepting in reply to my questions as to his feelings. He asked me once or twice how I found his pulse; and he informed me that his lower extremities had lost all feeling; manifesting to me that he entertained no hopes that he should long survive. I changed the posture of his limbs, but to no purpose; they had totally lost their sensibility. Perceiving that we approached the shore, he said, "Let Mrs. Hamilton be immediately sent for—let the event be gradually broken to her; but give her hopes." Looking up, we saw his friend Mr. Bayard standing on the wharf in great agitation. He had been told by his servant that General Hamilton, Mr. Pendleton, and myself, had crossed the river in a boat together, and too well he conjectured the fatal errand, and foreboded the dreadful result. Perceiving, as we came nearer, that Mr. Pendleton and myself only sat up in the stern sheets, he clasped his hands together in the most violent apprehension; but when I called to him to have a cot prepared, and he at the same moment saw his poor friend lying in the bottom of the boat, he threw up his eyes and burst into a flood of tears and lamentation. Hamilton alone appeared tranquil and composed. We then conveyed him as tenderly as possible up to the house. The distresses of this amiable family were such that till the first shock was abated, they were scarcely able to summon fortitude enough to yield sufficient assistance to their dying friend.

Upon our reaching the house, he became more languid, occasioned probably by the agitation of his removal from the boat. I gave him a little weak wine and water. When he recovered his feelings, he complained of pain in his back; we immediately undressed him, laid him in bed, and darkened the room. I then gave him a large anodyne, which I frequently repeated. During the first day he took upwards of an ounce of laudanum; and tepid anodyne fomentations were also applied to those parts nearest the seat of his pain. Yet were his sufferings, during the whole of the day, almost intolerable. I had not the shadow of a hope of his recovery, and Dr. Post, whom I requested might be sent for immediately on our reaching Mr. Bayard's house, united with me in this opinion. General Rey, the French Consul, also had the goodness to invite the surgeons of the French frigates in our harbour, as they had had much experience in gun-shot wounds, to render their assistance. They immediately came; but to prevent his being disturbed I stated to them his situation, described the nature of his wound and the direction of the ball, with all the symptoms that could enable them to form an opinion as to the event. One of the gentlemen then accompanied me to the bedside. The result was a confirmation of the opinion that had already been expressed by Dr. Post and myself.

During the night, he had some imperfect sleep; but the succeeding morning his symptoms were aggravated, attended however, with a diminution of pain. His mind retained all its usual strength and composure. The great source of his anxiety seemed to be in his sympathy with his half distracted wife and children. He spoke to me frequently of them. "My beloved wife and children," were always his expressions. But his fortitude triumphed over his situation, dreadful as it was; once, indeed, at the sight of his children brought to the bedside together, seven in number, his utterance forsook him; he opened his eyes, gave them one look, and closed them again, till they were taken away. As a proof of his extraordinary composure of mind, let me add, that he alone could calm the frantic grief of their mother. "Remember, my Eliza, you are a Christian," were the expressions with which he frequently, with a firm voice, but in a pathetic and impressive manner, addressed her. His words, and the tone in which they were uttered, will never be effaced from my memory. At about two o'clock, as the public well knows, he expired.

"Incorrupta fides—nudaque veritas
Quando ullum invenient parem?
Multis ille quidem flebilis occifit."

I am, Sir,
Your friend and humble serv't,
DAVID HOSACK

Wm. Coleman, Esq.

They found in Hamilton's desk a letter to Pendleton thanking him for his pains. They also found his will and a statement setting forth his reasons for so foolishly taking the risk that was to prove fatal. It read:

On my expected interview with Burr, I think it proper to make some remarks explanatory of my conduct, motives, and views.

I was certainly desirous of avoiding this interview for the most cogent reasons.

1. My religious and moral principles are strongly opposed to the practice of duelling, and it would ever give me pain to be obliged to shed the blood of a fellow creature in a private combat forbidden by the laws.

2. My wife and children are extremely dear to me, and my life is of the utmost importance to them, in various views.

3. I feel a sense of obligation towards my creditors; who in case of accident to me, by the forced sale of my property, may be in some degree sufferers. I did not think myself at liberty as a man of probity, lightly to expose them to this hazard.

4. I am conscious of no ill will to Colonel Burr, distinct from political opposition, which, as I trust, has proceeded from pure and upright motives.

Lastly, I shall hazard much, and can possibly gain nothing by the issue of the interview.

But it was, as I conceive, impossible for me to avoid it. There were intrinsic difficulties in the thing, and artificial embarrassments, from the manner of proceeding on the part of Colonel Burr.

Intrinsic, because it is not to be denied, that my animadversions on the political principles, character, and views of Colonel Burr, have been extremely severe; and on different occasions I, in common with many others, have made very unfavorable criticisms on particular instances of the private conduct of this gentleman.

In proportion as these impressions were entertained with sincerity, and uttered with motives and for purposes which might appear to me commendable, would be the difficulty (until they could be removed by evidence of their being erroneous) of explanation or apology. The disavowal required of me by Colonel Burr, in a general and indefinite form, was out of my power, if it had really been proper for me to submit to be so questioned; but I was sincerely of opinion that this could not be, and in this opinion, I was confirmed by that of a very moderate and judicious friend whom I consulted. Besides that, Colonel Burr appeared to me to assume, in the first instance, a tone unnecessarily peremptory and menacing, and in the second, positively offensive. Yet I wished, as far as might be practicable, to leave a door open to accommodation. This, I think will be inferred from the written communications made by me and by my direction, and would be confirmed by the conversations between Mr. Van Ness and myself, which arose out of the subject.

I am not sure whether, under all the circumstances, I did not go further in the attempt to accommodate, than a punctilious delicacy will justify. If so, I hope the motives I have stated will excuse me.

It is not my design, by what I have said, to affix any odium on the conduct of Colonel Burr, in this case. He doubtless has heard of animadversions of mine which bore very hard upon him; and it is probable that as usual they were accompanied with some falsehoods. He may have supposed himself under a necessity of acting as he has done. I hope the grounds of his proceeding have been such as ought to satisfy his own conscience.

I trust, at the same time, that the world will do me the justice to believe, that I have not censured him on light grounds, nor from unworthy inducements. I certainly have had strong reasons for what I may have said, though it is possible that in some particulars, I may have been influenced by misconstruction or misinformation. It is also my ardent wish that I may have been more mistaken than I think I have been, and that he, by his future conduct, may show himself worthy of all confidence and esteem, and prove an ornament and blessing to the country.

As well because it is possible that I may have injured Colonel Burr, however convinced myself that my opinions and declarations have been well founded, as from my general principles and temper in relation to similar affairs, I have resolved, if our interview is conducted in the usual manner, and it pleases God to give me the opportunity, to reserve and throw away my first fire, and I have thoughts even of reserving my second fire— and thus giving a double opportunity to Colonel Burr to pause and to reflect.

It is not, however, my intention to enter into any explanations on the ground. Apology from principle, I hope, rather than pride, is out of the question.

To those who, with me, abhorring the practice of duelling, may think that I ought on no account to have added to the number of bad examples, I answer, that my relative situation, as well in public as private, enforcing all the considerations which constitute what men of the world denominate honour, imposed on me (as I thought) a peculiar necessity not to decline the call. The ability to be in future useful, whether in resisting mischief or effecting good, in those crises of our public affairs which seem likely to happen, would probably be inseparable from a conformity with public prejudice in this particular.

A. H.

It will be noted in the chronology that this miserable affair went on for a month, during all of which time both men attended to business as usual; they even met at a banquet of the Cincinnati, but never a word leaked out. Had the least hint of the controversy become known, public sentiment would not have permitted the meeting. The news gave the city the greatest shock in its history. It was plunged in grief. All classes shared in mourning. The funeral, held on the Saturday following the duel, was attended with high ceremony. The military, commanded by Lieutenant-Colonel Morton, were drawn up before John B. Church's house in Robinson Street, where the body lay. It was borne to the hearse to "melancholy music by a large and elegant band," as William Coleman's chronicle puts it. The procession moved at noon through Beekman, Pearl, and Whitehall streets, up Broadway to Trinity churchyard. There a grave had been opened on the side adjacent to Rector Street, and there the remains rest to this day, in the center of the great financial district, of which Hamilton was the founder. Matthew Clarkson, Oliver Wolcott, Richard Harrison, Abijah Hammond, Josiah Ogden Hoffman, Richard Varick, William Bayard, and Judge Lawrence, were the pallbearers.

Hamilton's gray horse, draped in mourning and led by two black servants who were dressed in white, their turbans trimmed with black, followed the coffin. Across its saddle were his boots and spurs, reversed. His hat and sword lay on the coffin. Gouverneur Morris gave the funeral oration, with Hamilton's four sons, the oldest then sixteen and the youngest six, gathered about him.

In the harbor lay his British Majesty's ships *Boston* and *Lord Charles Spencer,* commanded respectively by Captain Douglas and Captain Cotesworth. Both peaked their yards in mourning and fired minute guns during the services. So did two of Napoleon's frigates, the *Cybelle* and *Didon,* which also slanted their yards and reversed their flags.

"Our Troy has lost its Hector," said the Albany *Sentinel,* voicing the universal grief. The press and pulpit in general joined in manifestations of respect and regret. To the cold and callous Burr, all this was most surprising. He had thought Hamilton hated equally with himself; he had certainly earned a greater portion by his political activities. But such was not the case. Alarmed at consequences, he left the state, going first to Cranbury in South Jersey, then to West Chester, Pennsylvania, where he lodged with Commodore Thomas Truxton, and then he departed South. New Jersey sought to find and punish him for murder by hanging. New York disfranchised him, though he was still Vice-President of the United States. Verily the brand of Cain was upon him, and there it rested to the end of his long life. His story has been too often told to be repeated here. Yet, if ever there was justification for a duel to the death, Burr should be granted it. He had been hounded and thwarted to an unbearable degree.

That Burr's conscience was clear is seen in this letter written by him to his friend Charles Biddle, of Philadelphia, under date of July 18, 1804:

MY DEAR SIR,—

Your letter of the 13th was particularly acceptable. It is too well known that Gen'l H. had long indulged himself in illiberal freedom with my character. He had a peculiar talent for saying things improper and offensive in such a manner as could not be well taken hold of. On two different occasions, however, having reason to apprehend that he had gone so far as to afford me reason for calling on him, he anticipated me by coming forward voluntarily and making apologies and concessions. From delicacy to him and from a sincere desire for peace, I have never mentioned these circumstances, always hoping that the generosity of my conduct would have some influence on him. In this I have been constantly deceived, and it became impossible that I could consistently with self-respect again forbear. With regard to the immediate cause of the late events, I refer you to the *Morning Chronicle* of the 17th inst. Though in this many circumstances not favorable to H. are suppressed, the following incidents will show what reliance may be placed in these declarations of H. which assert that he did not intend to injure me, &c. &. (contemptible disclosures, if true). When the parties had taken their places, having their pistols in their hands, cocked, Mr. P. [Pendleton], who was to give the word, asked the gentlemen if they were ready. "Stop," said General H., "in certain light one requires glasses." He then levelled his pistol in several directions to try the light. After this he put on his spectacles and repeated the same experiment several times. He kept on his spectacles and said he was ready. When the word "present" was given, he took aim at his adversary and fired very promptly. The other fired two or three seconds after him and the Gen'l instantly fell, exclaiming, "I am a dead man." Both he and Mr. P., while on the ground, appeared a good deal agitated and not to be in a state of mind suitable for observing accurately what passed. H. looked as if possessed by the horrors of conscious guilt. It is the opinion of all considerate men here that my only fault has been in bearing so much and so long.

You will remark that all of our intemperate and unprincipled Jacobins who have for years been reviling H. as a disgrace to the country and a pest to society are now the most vehement in his praise, and you will readily perceive that their motive is not respect for him but malice to me.

The last hours of Gen'l H. (I might include the day preceding the interview) appear to have been devoted to malevolence and hypocrisy. All men of honor must perceive with disgust the persecutions which are practiced against me. Among other unusual steps, a coroner's jury has been called and will meet for the fourth time this evening. The object is to procure an inquest of murder, which will probably be effected, though the transactions took place in another state. Upon such an inquest a warrant may issue to apprehend me, and I should be taken, bail would probably be refused. The friends of Gen'l H. and even his enemies, who are still more my enemies, are but too faithful executors of his malice.

William P. Van Ness, Burr's second, also writing to Biddle, had the following to say about the affair:

DEAR SIR,—

I shall answer without hesitation the interrogations you put to me, as I conceive it my duty to communicate with freedom the circumstances which attended the interview between Colonel Burr and General Hamilton. After the necessary preparations had been made, which you will find detailed in the printed statements of the seconds, the parties took their places; General Hamilton raised his pistol as if to try it, and again lowering it said, "I beg your pardon for delaying you, but the direction of the light sometimes renders glasses necessary. "He then drew forth his spectacles and put them on. The gentleman whose duty it was to give the word, then asked the parties if they were prepared, which being answered in the affirmative, the word "present" was then given, on which both parties presented. The pistol of General Hamilton was first discharged, and Colonel Burr fired immediately after. On this point I have the misfortune to disagree with the friend of General Hamilton, and without doubting the sincerity of his opinion, I can safely declare that I was never more firmly convinced of any fact that came under my observation. On the discharge of General Hamilton's pistol I observed a slight motion in the person of Colonel Burr, which gave me the idea that he was struck. On this point I conversed with Colonel Burr, when he returned, who ascribed the motion of his body to a small stone under his foot, and added the smoke of General Hamilton's pistol for a moment obscured his sight.

When General Hamilton fell, Colonel Burr advanced toward him, but I immediately urged the importance of returning to the barge. He complied with my request, and in a few minutes I followed him. He said to me, "I must go and speak to him." I replied it would be obviously improper, as General Hamilton was surrounded by the surgeons and the bargemen, by whom he ought not to be seen, but that if he would remain, I would go and see the General, which I did, and on my return to the boat, ordered the bargemen to proceed immediately to the city, which was so done.

Thus, Sir, I have related to you such circumstances respecting the late unfortunate interview between Colonel Burr and General Hamilton, as has not hitherto been published. It is but just to add that Colonel Burr, so far from exhibiting any degree of levity on the occasion to which I have alluded, or expressing any satisfaction at the result of the meeting, his whole conduct while I was with him was expressive of regret and concern.

Popular feeling against duelling expressed itself loudly after Hamilton's death. The pulpits rang with sermons, and the press joined in protest against this method of settling disputes between gentlemen.

"Duelling is no criterion of bravery," wrote Charles Cotesworth Pinckney in commenting on the affair. "I have seen," he continued, "cowards fight duels, and I am convinced real courage may be better shown in the refusal than in the acceptance of a challenge." He urged the Society of the Cincinnati to set its influence against the practice in an attempt "to annul this odious custom." The society took action accordingly, the South Carolina branch memorializing the legislature to forbid the practice by law.

CHAPTER VII

WILLIAM H. CRAWFORD vs. GENERAL JOHN CLARK

WILLIAM HARRIS CRAWFORD is a faded figure in American history, where he once filled a considerable place. He was born in Virginia, February 24, 1774, his family removing to Georgia when he was young. Being unprosperous, they forced the likely lad to look out for himself. He became a student under Dr. Hugh Waddell, a famous instructor in his day, worked his way along as usher and tutor, acquired a rudiment of law, and set himself up to practice that profession. He was to rise to the high positions of United States Senator, Minister to France in the last days of Napoleon, and to be Secretary of the Treasury under Madison and Monroe. More than this, he was slated by the political powers to succeed the latter in the office of President of the United States.

Oglethorpe County, where young Crawford settled into the practice of the law, was a fertile and prosperous section of Georgia, watered by the Broad River. It was the seat of many wealthy planters, among whom were included numerous Virginians, who were clannish and worked together against the "crackers," as the natives were known. Not that there was a lack of native aristocracy, for it was there in plenty. For example, there was Thomas W. Cobb, a devoted friend of Crawford, Governor George Matthews, Colonel Benjamin Taliaferro—a name that drifted across the mountains and became Tolliver in Kentucky and Tennessee; Hugh McGehee, John Lumpkin—whose name lives in that of a county; Frank Meriwether, Stephen Upson, and John Thomas. All these men were active in the fervid politics of the day.

Oglethorpe County lay in what was called the Western Circuit, of which Thomas Peter Carnes, who had married a sister of the great William Wirt, was judge. There was much litigation. Statutes were few in the early days, and the law was mainly judge-made—*obiter dicta* uttered from the bench on the causes as presented. This usually served for lack of something better and made practice picturesque and results problematical. Thus Aaron Burr's famous dictum, "That is law which is boldly asserted and most plausibly maintained," became almost a fact on the Circuit.

Old lawyers, long in practice, had well-loaded memories that gave them great advantage over newcomers, and Crawford found plenty of antagonism, especially when he took a hand in politics as well as law. He founded a partnership with Peter Early, a Virginian, like himself, and was soon in a commanding, as well as an offensive, position. Early went to Congress in 1802 and turned the business of the firm over to Crawford, who was soon at the head of the bar in the Circuit. Naturally, where law was absent and opinions ruled, it became hard to satisfy litigants, and the lawyers frequently had to settle their differences under the *Code Duello*. This was a ruling force at the time. J. E. D. Shepp, who wrote an all too brief life of Crawford, published in 1909, observed critically on this point:

"In the early history of the State of Georgia the crime of duelling was prevalent among the better class of her citizens; perhaps more so than in any other state. The fatal practice became general when the virtuous and best citizens—Governors, Congressmen and Legislators—on the most trivial excuses and slightest provocations, were shedding each other's blood. The horror of shedding human blood was not regarded."

In proof of this the historian cites numbers of examples. General James Jackson, Governor of Georgia, in 1780 killed Lieutenant-Governor Wells, stating in explanation that he could not longer endure "the overbearing disposition of the lieutenant-governor." He himself was badly wounded.

Judge Taliaferro, in 1796, while on the bench, fought with Colonel Wells. He wounded his antagonist so severely at the first fire that the latter declined the courtesy of a second shot. The Judge had served in the Revolution under Light Horse Harry Lee, and the weapon he employed on this occasion was a horse pistol carrying a bullet almost as big as a walnut. Wells, struck in the breast, needed no more to satisfy his injured honor. He had been the challenger.

In this connection Mr. Shepp observes:

"Duelling was looked upon by society as the honorable way of settling differences between gentlemen. A coward was contemptible, and no man could remain long in the public eye without distinguishing himself for bravery. True, common law declared that homicide in a duel was murder. Yet Georgia was too 'high toned' to enforce this law, which had in practice become obsolete. The trial in the courts of all the Southern states turned entirely on the fairness with which the duel was conducted, and, if fair, a verdict of acquittal was invariably rendered."

It was in this atmosphere that Crawford had to hold his place at the bar and in politics. Tall, handsome, and courtly, he was indeed a fine figure of a man, and by his prominence he soon became a target for slings and arrows.

With the driving out of the Indians, there had been developed what became a great speculation, if not a swindle, in the sale of rich bottom lands along the Yazoo River. One year's cotton crop paid for the land, a second for the slaves, and a third for a palatial mansion. The fever ran wild. Great fortunes were made by the insiders, who included numbers of prominent Georgians and South Carolinians; notable among the latter was the first General Wade Hampton. They operated under a Georgia incorporation of a corrupt character, involving as it did the sale by the state of 2,500,000 acres of land to the company for one and a half cents an acre! This land lay between the Chattanooga and the Yazoo rivers.

Many members of the Legislature who held stock voted for the bill when it was passed; others were bribed to do so. The promoter, Henry Wilson, of Pennsylvania, and his associates were regarded as honorable men engaged in a laudable enterprise. They proved to be quite otherwise. Governor George Matthews signed the bill over a popular protest led by Crawford. To the latter's support came Senator James

Jackson, who resigned his seat in Washington to return to Georgia and lead the fight for the repeal of the act by the next Legislature. The backers of the bill were called "Yazooists," and at the end of a fierce campaign they were beaten. The enraged people hunted down those who had profited by the measure. Some were killed in duels; others were lynched, horsewhipped, and compelled to flee the state. The act was repealed, the money paid the state was returned, and the land was retrieved as far as possible. To crown its virtue the Legislature directed that the obnoxious act should be publicly burned, with all records appertaining thereto. This was consummated in the square before the Capitol —which was then at Louisville, Georgia—Governor Jared Irwin calling fire from Heaven by means of a sun glass to start the flame.

Thus vindicated, the state might, it would be thought, have succeeded in getting along without more shooting. But it did not. Indeed, Jackson, who became governor, fought three "bloody duels," as the chronicle relates, with Robert Watkins, who had made a compilation of Georgia laws which included the act plus the repeal. The Governor would not permit the work to be paid for so long as the hated words were in it, contending that as the act had been repealed, it no longer existed.

In spite of the duels, the book never became validated, though Watkins was paid a little money for his work. In the last of the three duels "Jackson and Watkins conversed with great eloquence and entire politeness" before taking their stations. On the third fire the Governor was shot through the right thigh. He could stand after being lifted to his feet and wanted to try again, but the surgeon would not permit it. To the Governor's credit, he is said to have affably apologized to Watkins, as he was borne from the field with, "Damn it, Watkins, I thought I could give you another shot."

The question of a digest was then settled by appointing Crawford, George Watkins, and Horatio Marbury, Secretary of State, a commission to have the work done. It was completed, and after 1801 the state had printed statutes for the first time.

The *Code Duello,* however, continued to supersede the law, and Crawford was now to come under its terms. General John Clark, famous as a fighter in the Revolution and the Indian Wars, was prominent in politics and in a large measure dominated the state. Crawford speedily became an obstacle in his path. Clark had an itch also for grabbing rich Indian lands, and the process of pushing the redskins toward the setting sun went on apace. This was done under the guise of legality, by the speculators retaining all the able lawyers and owning the judges on the bench. Crawford's part in the Yazoo matter made it desirable that he should be annexed. He declined the proffer and continued his opposition to the crooked proceedings, until, as Shepp records, "Finding his talents and integrity very much in the way of their success, a conspiracy was entered into to kill or drive him away." Peter Lawrence Van Alen, "an impudent fellow from New York, was chosen to play the bully."

It is a curious psychological fact that men transported to new climates take on the more violent characteristics of their surroundings. For example, Sargent S.

Prentiss, of Mississippi, born in Portland, Maine, became the most pronounced fire-eater of the South. His contemporary, from the same town, the Rev. J. H. Ingraham, preacher and novelist, always carried a pistol into his pulpit at Holly Springs, and, indeed, died by what was called its accidental discharge in his robing-room in the Episcopal church. So it was that Van Alen, scion of a Knickerbocker family, became a sensitive soul in Georgia. He had progressed in politics and was then state solicitor for the Western District. He was a kinsman of Martin Van Buren, who had sought and found fortune in the new South. The West was then undreamed of, and the slave states held out the best inducements as the Indians were forced to move on. John Clark, provoked by Crawford's stand, had no difficulty in turning Van Alen into a tool. The young lawyer, by his ability and personality, was making great headway, and it was highly desirable to put a stop to it.

"Never," according to Shepp, "was a plot more ingeniously planned or boldly attempted. Crawford must either fight or be driven from the country." The conspirators, knowing Crawford had been a school-master reckoned that he would not have the spirit to fight, being without skill as a marksman, and refusal was counted upon. This "would result in his political ruin," as "a refusal would render him without power to be useful in repelling mischief or achieving good thereafter, as public prejudice was too strong to be resisted."

Van Alen was a Federalist, while Crawford was a firm Jeffersonian. This political divergence was made a basis for picking a quarrel. Van Alen's home was in Elbert County, where he had a considerable following.

He began operations by picking on Judge Charles Tait, through the medium of a lawsuit brought against one George Cook, who had been in Tait's confidence, before whom the suit was heard. Van Alen was employed to defend Cook and he managed to put in the record some foolish letters written by the judge to Cook which aroused his Honor to challenge the solicitor.

Van Alen declined on the ground that Tait was not a gentleman, and that he was also deficient in respectability. Crawford, representing Tait, was expected to take umbrage at this and carry on the affair, but he did not do so. Tait posted Van Alen as a coward, after the custom under the code. Upon this Van Alen set aside his scruples and challenged Tait, one Tankerly, of Washington, Georgia, acting as the intermediary "friend." Tait failed to reply in writing, but after some delay sent a verbal acceptance by Crawford. Tankerly informed Crawford that Van Alen could go no further by reason of Tait's lack of formality in failing to come promptly to the scratch. Pausing on his way home, after delivering his message at the hotel in Washington, Crawford was met by Van Alen, who, after becoming grossly insulting, challenged him to combat. Here again Van Alen counted on the fact that Crawford had failed to take up Tait's cause, believing that he would now keep out of the difficulty and so expose himself to the consequences of popular contempt.

Convinced that he was in the clutch of a conspiracy to either kill him or drive him out of public life, Crawford accepted the challenge. It was arranged that the meeting should take place at Fort Charlotte, in South Carolina, twelve miles below Petersburg.

WILLIAM H. CRAWFORD

This was a common ground for duellists. It is related that Crawford went to the appointed spot without any preparation whatsoever, having furbished up an old pair of pistols, which he did not take the trouble to examine until the morning of the appointed day. Then when he snapped them, both missed fire. Indeed, he owned no weapons, having borrowed these from a Mr. Pain.

Van Alen, contemptuous of the schoolmaster, and quite resolved to kill him, made a hideous grimace as they faced the word. This, Crawford afterwards related, much disconcerted him, so that he fired wildly. Evidently, twisting his visage disturbed Van Alen's aim as well as that of his antagonist. Both missed. On the second fire Crawford shut out the distorted face of Van Alen by pulling down his hat brim. The fates were with him. Van Alen's ball went wide; Crawford's true. The solicitor fell, mortally hurt.

Victory brought Crawford public approval of his conduct, and he rose higher than ever in popular esteem. He did not, however, escape further trial at the pistol point. John Clark continued his purpose to get him out of his way. Judge Carnes retiring, Charles Tait and John Griffin became rivals for the office, which rested with the Legislature. Crawford supported Tait, while Clark backed Griffin, who was his brother-in-law. Tait won, but trouble grew out of the contest, Clark calling Crawford to account for some remark about his misuse of influence on behalf of a relative. A copious correspondence resulted that grew in heat as it progressed, until, on December 6, 1804, Crawford wrote the General:

SIR,—

In your last publication you assure me that you are not restricted in the mode of warfare hitherto pursued. My friend, Colonel Flournoy, is therefore authorized on my part to make necessary arrangements.

WM. H. CRAWFORD

General Clark

Clark responded at once:

6th December, 1804

SIR,—

Your challenge of this morning by Colonel Flournoy is received and accepted. My friend Captain Cobb will adjust and settle with him the necessary preliminaries.

JOHN CLARK

Wm. H. Crawford, Esq.

Clark was an expert with arms, and Crawford took a great chance in sending his "defi." The basis of it all was, of course, who should be master of politics in Georgia, but it is reasonable to assume that Crawford's luck in killing Van Alen had made him confident, and as the leader of a faction, he determined to force the fighting. So it was that Crawford once more made his way to Fort Charlotte. Colonel Thomas Flournoy went along as his second. Captain Howell Cobb was in like attendance upon Clark. The two did not, however, meet upon the ground where Van Alen died two years before, but eleven miles away. It fell out, before shots could be exchanged, that Governor John Milledge, of Georgia, having got wind of the matter, appeared on the scene and urged both sides to desist, with such purpose that both agreed to accept the decision of a

Court of Honor composed of Jared Irwin, Abraham Jackson, James Seagrove, D. B. Mitchell, and J. Ben Maxwell. These eminent gentlemen found that "Upon the whole we are fully and clearly of the opinion that General Clark and Mr. Crawford have been led into a dispute, the foundation of which has not sufficient weight, and ought not to have produced the subsequent heat and animosity, which might have led to consequences truly serious and calamitous to themselves and families, their friends, and their country. We have no hesitancy in declaring it to be our opinion that both gentlemen are brave and intrepid and do decree and arrange that they acquit each other of any imputations to the contrary." The pair were asked to shake hands "as friends and fellow citizens." They did so, but gingerly. Clark went away with a poor opinion of courts of honor, feeling that they had acted too much in Crawford's interest.

Not long after Judge John M. Dooly, a Clark follower, was challenged by Judge Charles Tait, Crawford bearing the message. Dooly was an Irishman and a wit. He selected Clark as his second. When Crawford and Tait went to the appointed spot, they found Dooly sitting on a stump alone in the forest.

"Where is General Clark?" asked Crawford.

"He is in the woods, sir."

"And will soon be present, I presume?"

"Yes, as soon as he can find a gum."

"May I inquire, Colonel Dooly, what use you have for a gum in the matter under settlement?"

It may be explained here that one of Judge Tait's

legs was wooden, and that gum trees were very likely to be hollow.

"I want to put my leg in it, sir," replied the complacent Dooly. "Do you suppose I can risk my leg of flesh and blood against Tait's wooden one? If I hit his leg, he will have another tomorrow and be pegging about as well as usual; if he hits mine, I may lose my life by it, but almost certainly my leg, and be compelled, like Tait, to stump about the balance of my life. I could not risk this and must have a gum to put my leg in; then I am as much wood as he is, and on equal terms with him."

"I understand you, Mr. Dooly. You do not want to fight."

"Well, really, Mr. Crawford, I thought everybody knew that."

"Well, sir," said the angry second, "you shall fill a column in the newspapers in no enviable light."

"Mr. Crawford," replied the judge coolly, "I assure you I would rather fill two newspapers than one coffin."

With that all parties went home. The humor of it all saved Dooly from any obloquy, while Tait's own standing was not high enough to make his status any better. So laughter took the place of blood all around.

The rivalry with Clark, however, continued, and refused to down. Clark tried to secure Tait's impeachment, and the old sore reopened wide. Finally, after an angry controversy, Clark now challenged Crawford, on December 2, 1806, in these terms:

The various injuries I have received from you make it necessary for me to call on you for the satisfaction usually offered in similar cases. My friend, Mr. Forsyth, is authorized to make the necessary arrangements on my part.

With due respect, I am, Sir,

Your humble servant,

JOHN CLARK

In reply Crawford wrote:

Your challenge of this date is accepted, and my friend, Captain Moore, will, on my part, make the necessary arrangements.

John Forsyth, being busy on court cases, declined to serve Clark as second, and Major Gilbert Henry took his place. The terms agreed upon were put in writing and are worth reproduction. They read:

Article 1. The pistols are to be smooth-bore and to be loaded with a single ball by the seconds of the two parties, in the presence of each other and their principals.

Article 2. The distance shall be ten yards, the parties facing.

Article 3. The seconds of each party shall place the pistols in the right hand of his friend, cocked, with the barrel as nearly perpendicular as possible, pointing up or down, and neither of the principals shall alter the position of the pistol until the word of command is given.

Article 4. The signal for a discharge shall be: "Make ready; fire." At the word "fire" each party shall discharge his pistol as nearly as possible after receiving the word; and should either party withhold his fire it shall be lost.

Article 5. A snap or a flash shall be considered the same as a shot.

Article 6. Whenever the challenger shall express himself as satisfied, or shall have received a wound judged by the surgeon as *mortes,* or whenever the challenged shall have received a wound and express himself satisfied, then the contest shall cease.

Article 7. No conversation between the parties, but through their friends.

Article 8. To prevent the possibilities of suspicion of wearing improper covering, each party will submit to an examination by the seconds of his opponent immediately preceding their being placed at their stations.

Article 9. Choice of ground and the word to be decided by lot.

Article 10. The seconds shall be properly armed, to prevent a transgression of these rules, and the interposition of any other person.

Article 11. If either of the principals deviate from the foregoing rules, or attempt to take any undue advantage, either or both of the seconds are at liberty to fire at him.

Article 12. If either party falls, no person except the surgeon shall be admitted until the opposite party leaves the ground.

GEO. MOORE
G. HAY

Dec. 16th, 1806, at the High Shoals on the Appalachee in the Indian Territory

The meeting had been arranged for twelve o'clock on the above date. Clark found some fault with the arrangements and an hour's recess was taken for adjustment. This angered Crawford, who became reckless. Confident in the success that had attended his offhand encounter with Van Alen, he "swaggered to the peg with the same degree of carelessness that he was wont to use to address a country jury." Not so Clark. He was an old hand and took no chances of missing or being hit. Crawford posed unskillfully, failing to protect his left arm with his body, and became an easy mark. Both fired at the word. Clark was unhurt. His bullet, however, struck the wrist of Crawford's unguarded left arm and shattered it severely. He was a long time recovering from the wound. Clark demanded another round, but Captain Moore held that the agreement had been carried out and he would not permit it. At this Clark was much disgruntled, and on July 22, 1807, he again challenged Crawford:

Sir,—

From the understanding at our interview in December last you have no doubt (since the restoration of your health) anticipated this call. It is high time that the differences between us should be brought to a final issue, and from the situation in which the affair was left, I presume nothing more is necessary than for you to appoint the time and place. My friend, Mr. Sherrod, will hand you this and receive your answer.

Crawford replied the next day:

Since the receipt of your note yesterday by the hands of Mr. Sherrod, I have obtained the perusal of the communications which passed between Captain Moore and Major Hay, on the 16th of December, last, from which it appears to be that the contest was brought to a final issue and the difference adjudicated as far as an interview of that kind is intended or calculated for adjustment. Captain Moore, pursuant to the latter part of the sixth article agreed upon, determined that the contest was at an end. I therefore shall decline the appointment of time and place.

Failing to coax Crawford to his doom, Clark continued the controversy in the press and went so far as to horsewhip Judge Tait. For this he was indicted, found guilty, fined two thousand dollars, and sentenced to give a bond covering good behavior for five years. He put out a pamphlet, entitled "Consideration of the Purity of the Principles of W. H. Crawford," in self-justification, and Governor Jared Irwin pardoned him. Clark averred that he had been persecuted by Crawford and his following. He had been a comrade with Irwin in the revolution and the Indian Wars. So the matter ended—but not the opposition. This was to go on for years. Happily, however, circumstances removed Crawford from local surroundings to a safer situation in Washington. Abraham Baldwin, one of the state's senators, resigned in 1807, and Crawford was appointed to his place. Crawford continued to fill this appointment with great distinction, despite Clark's opposition, until he was made Minister to France. On his return, he was appointed Secretary of the Treasury by Madison. Figuring large for the Presidency in 1816, he was persuaded to give way to Monroe, under a promise to be given the succession in 1824. This was defeated by the moves of Andrew Jackson and Henry Clay, for the most part, but also by a stroke of paralysis that really made him unfit to serve, had he been elected. Crawford returned to Georgia, where, at the death of Judge Dooly, the humorous duellist, he was given that gentleman's place on the bench, retaining it until his own death in 1832. In the meantime he precipitated the break between Andrew Jackson and John C. Calhoun.

CHAPTER VIII

ANDREW JACKSON vs. CHARLES DICKINSON

IN 1828 when Andrew Jackson announced his purpose to become President of these United States, a fellow-citizen of Nashville, Tennessee, bearing him no good will, published what is now a rare pamphlet, covering "The Indiscretions of Andrew Jackson." This delicate title covered the details of some fourteen conflicts engaged in by the General between the ages of twenty-three and sixty. The compiler had a record of one hundred and three duels, fights, and altercations, in which the "Hero of New Orleans" had been involved in his lifetime, beginning, perhaps, with the occasion when he "sassed" one of Banastre Tarleton's British troopers, raiding in the Carolinas, and was rebuked with a saber slash across his skull. This, at sixty, would be giving him forty-seven fighting years, with an average of but little better than two rows a year, not a very large item when reckoned by percentages.

Certainly, it must be said, that if ever a man hunted trouble it was Jackson. He was, indeed, a man of spirit. He was licensed to practice law in North Carolina as early as 1787, and from that time on was destined to be heard from. The new country of Tennessee was alluring, and the young Jackson—he was twenty at the time—migrated to a settlement on the Cumberland, that was later to become Nashville. Here he boarded with the widow of Colonel John Donelson, a name to be well known in history. The widow possessed a daughter, Rachel, who was married to Lewis Robards, a Virginian. Robards was jealous in temperament, and not liking the star boarder, departed from the Donelson doors, never to return. To cement his purpose, he applied to the legislature of Virginia for a bill permitting him to secure a divorce—this being the current method of sex-severance—to which he was entitled as a native of that state. He procured the bill, but did not follow it with the court action. Jackson and the lady, assuming that all was well, took a trip to Natchez and were there married—by a Catholic priest, it would appear.

Perhaps had Jackson been a nobody, this would have caused no more than passing comment. Being a somebody, however, it was destined to make him a deal of trouble. The charming Rachel was not welcomed in Nashville society and all too frequently her husband had to resent the charge of living with another man's wife. One of the men who made this accusation was the redoubtable John Sevier, victor at King's Mountain, and founder of Tennessee. Sevier was governor of the state and also major-general of the militia. Jackson wanted the last-named honor and demanded that Sevier resign in his favor, which the Governor refused to do. This led to words and ill-feeling that cropped out whenever the two met. Jackson challenged Sevier to a duel, which the latter declined on the ground that he was too poor to fight and risk leaving a large family penniless.

Jackson would not let the question rest. Meeting Sevier at Knoxville, he reopened his claim on the ground of his services to the state. "Services!" retorted Sevier. "I know of no great services you have rendered the country except taking a trip to Natchez with another man's wife."

The response was a pistol shot. They fired informally, without damage. Later, with friends and relatives, they met on the highway, when Jackson flashed a pistol and warned Sevier to defend himself. The Governor swung from the saddle, but as he did so his horse bolted along with his arsenal, carried in holsters at the saddleside. Sevier's seventeen-year-old son was armed and stood beside his father. Before anything further eventuated, the crowd forced the fighters apart, and so ended the episode. Sevier's sun soon set and that of Jackson rose.

Of the one hundred and three "difficulties" only one resulted in a fatality. This is our story. Jackson's activities were enormous and in all ways successful. He was busy as a lawyer, became the owner of fifty thousand acres of land, a Judge of the Supreme Court, and a member of Congress, all before 1806, when the tragedy occurred. Besides all these activities, he ran a big farm, kept a store, raised fighting cocks, and bred race horses. Storekeeping has always been considered an occupation of the spiritless. Not so with Jackson. He bet on his fighting cocks at the side of the pit, and backed his racers heavily. One of these, called Truxton, after the doughty commodore, was a star performer on the track. There was little cash in the country and wagers were usually met with notes payable on demand. Truxton was frequently challenged. Among those who ventured to question his speed was Captain Joseph Erwin, who owned a very fast steed called Ploughboy. A match was arranged, with stakes of two thousand dollars and an eight-hundred-dollar forfeit. Associated with Erwin in the contest was Charles Dickinson, his son-in-law. This was in the fall of 1805. In the tryouts Ploughboy did not show up to advantage, so Erwin and Dickinson decided to call the race off, paying the forfeit by note. Thus far all was regular and there was no ill-feeling. But there had come to town from Virginia a young man named Thomas Swann, who chose the dangerous method of gaining distinction by getting in Jackson's way. On the occasion of the forfeit, Swann, for no purpose that is discernible, circulated a statement that the notes given by Erwin and Dickinson were not of the sort that Jackson had expected to receive—that is, they were time and not on demand, quoting Jackson as his authority. Dickinson was a lawyer, land speculator, and sporting man, as was Jackson. Their lines often met. Considering the story a reflection on his honor, Dickinson sought Swann, the source, and received in confirmation the statement as coming from Jackson that "Dickinson's notes were the same; but those of Captain Erwin were different," as above cited.

To this Erwin took exception. Erwin and Dickinson met Jackson on December 28, 1805, and, according to Swann's story, he then admitted that the notes were the same as he had agreed to accept in settlement, adding that Swann was a "d—d liar." This was reported to Swann, who thereupon called Jackson to account in a formal note, remarking, "The harshness of this expression has deeply wounded my feelings; it is language to which I am a stranger, which no man acquainted with my character would venture to apply to me, and which, should the information of Mr. Dickinson be correct, I shall be under the necessity of taking proper notice of."

Jackson replied at some length, rather begging the question, but bringing in Dickinson invidiously, thus: "When the conversation dropt between Mr. Dickinson and myself I thought it was at an end. As he wishes to blow the coal, I am ready to light it to a blaze, that it may be consumed at once and finally extinguished. Mr. Dickinson has given you the information, the subject of your letter. In return, and in justice to him, I request you to show him this. I set out this morning for South-West Point. I will return at a short day, and, at all times, be assured I hold myself answerable for any of my conduct, and should anything herein contained give Mr. Dickinson the spleen, I will furnish him an anodine as soon as I return."

Jackson came back in due season and was called upon by Swann for further satisfaction, which he did not get. Threatening a challenge, Jackson told him if he sent it, he, Jackson, would "cane him." Defying this, Swann sent a friend, to whom Jackson would give no answer until he could be sure that "Swann was a gentleman." He was also conciliatory, averring, according to Swann, that he had not meant him in his talk with Dickinson and was not to blame "if I thought proper to trim or pare my head to fit the cap."

The next day Jackson met Swann in a tavern when,

Swann narrates, "he (Jackson), surrounded by his friends, with a large bludgeon and a brace of pistols, assailed me without giving me a moment's warning to defend myself."

Unable to avenge himself on the field of honor, or anywhere else, Swann now accepted Jackson's suggestion and showed his "spleen" letter to Charles Dickinson. The latter was about to depart via flatboat for New Orleans, but left behind this missive for Jackson:

January 10, 1806

GENERAL ANDREW JACKSON, SIR,—

Last evening was shown me by Mr. Thomas Swann a letter from you in answer to a letter he had written you respecting a conversation that took place between you and myself at Mr. Winn's tavern, etc., etc.

I there informed you of a report that Patten Anderson had given publicity to; that a different list was produced when we were about paying the forfeit, from the one we were to make our stake out of, and that he had it from you, which you denied ever sanctioning. I then informed you I had another author who said he did hear you say that a different list was brought by Captain Erwin, which, as soon as I mentioned, and before I could give my author, you declared the author had told a damned lie; that so far from saying so, you had never intimated such a thing to any one, and immediately asked, "Who was the author?" to which I answered, "Thomas Swann." You wished Mr. Swann to be called forward, which I declined, lest Mr. Swann might think I wished to throw the burden off my shoulders on his; and the business being then entirely between Mr. Swann and yourself—Mr. Swann asserting that you had told him that a different list was produced by Captain Erwin, and you as positively denying it.

After the report was circulated by Patten Anderson, Mr.

Swann (as he informed me) was anxious to know if Patten Anderson was your herald; and further, as he had been introduced to Captain Erwin as a gentleman, he was desirous of knowing if any improper conduct had been attempted, and after he had mentioned the business to you, you answered concerning the stake and forfeit as stated above.

Your letter is so replete with equivocations that it is impossible for me to understand you. But in one part of your letter you say, had you "not known that the statement of Mr. Dickinson was not correct." which is denying that you contradicted what Mr. Swann had asserted. Should that be your meaning, I can prove it, not only by the assertions, but oaths of Mr. Samuel Jackson and Captain Erwin, whom I shall have sworn, that the world may know who can prove himself the gentleman and man of truth. Why should you have wished to have Mr. Swann called had you not denied what he had asserted? And do you pretend to call a man a talebearer for telling that which is truth and can be proved? Mr. Swann, after he understood an interview was to take place between you and myself, gave me liberty to make use of his name; and on our meeting, which was a few days after, he asked me if I had made use of his name and what you had said, an impartial statement of which I detailed to him. As to the word "coward," I think it as applicable to yourself as any one I know, and I shall be very glad when an opportunity serves to know in what manner you give your anodines, and hope you will take in payment one of my most moderate cathartics.

Yours at command,
CHARLES DICKINSON

James Parton, most minute of Jackson's biographers, believes, but does not prove, that Dickinson had several times made slighting allusions to Mrs. Jackson, a subject upon which her husband was decidedly sensitive. He also reports a "tradition in Tennessee" that on the slow trip down the big river, Dickinson "spent every leisure moment in practicing with the pistol, expecting on his return to be called out by General Jackson."

Swann, meanwhile, made public his correspondence in *The Impartial Review and Cumberland Repository,* a Nashville newspaper—a rather rash thing to do under the circumstances. The busybody, it would appear, had to try hard to justify the trouble he was causing. Jackson replied at length to Thomas Easton, the editor, who had also taken a chance in publishing Swann's rhetoric. It reads:

"MR. EASTON: The respect I owe to the world makes it necessary that a publication under the signature of 'Thomas Swann,' in your *Impartial Review* of the 1st instant, should be noticed.

"To impose upon the public attention, through the medium of your useful paper, is not my wish; but as Mr. Swann has endeavored to exhibit to the public eye a statement of his case and character, an impartial public will indulge such supplementary remarks as may be necessary to complete the caricature. In justice to Mr. Swann, and lest the figure when finished may appear the work of different artists, the groundwork, and even the various materials of which his drawing is composed, shall be carefully attended to.

"Not, however, in the new-invented style of support adopted by his friends, Mr. N. A. McNairy and Samuel Jackson—one the accredited agent of Mr. Swann, and the other invoked in his support. To a perfect understanding of the case of the complainant, let it briefly be premised, that a course race was made between Captain Erwin and myself, for 2,000 dollars in cash notes, payable at the day of the race. It was suggested that all Captain Erwin's notes were not payable precisely at the day. An accommodation was proposed, and a schedule of the notes, and Charles S. Carson's verbal assumpsit (being present) was offered for 440 dollars, or thereabouts, which was accepted. Mr. Erwin was previously informed that I had not any power over one half of the bet, as Major Verrell and Captain Pryor, who were interested in the other half, were about to leave the country; that one half must be payable at the day of the race, the other, which respected myself and Major W. P. Anderson, was not material.

"Mr. Charles Dickinson is the son-in-law to Captain Erwin, and was interested in the race, as it is understood. This race was afterward drawn on account of the indisposition of Captain Erwin's horse, upon an agreement to pay eight hundred dollars as a forfeit. The payment of this forfeit is the circumstance which gave rise to the conduct of Mr. Swann—his publication, the following certificates, and the subjoined remarks. The fact to be decided by the public is, whether Mr. Swann, in his solicitude to 'know the true statement,' though unconcerned, has omitted, in his assertion to Mr. Dickinson and the public, some material fact, or, in other words, whether I asserted that which was untrue?

"Mr. Hutchings has truly stated the assertion to which I have uniformly adhered, upon which Mr. Swann and myself were at issue; that issue has been decided—whether in a moral manner, casuists must determine, upon the following certificates and analysis:

Affidavit of John Hutchings

"Being called on by General Andrew Jackson to state a conversation that took place, on a certain Saturday, in his store, when Thomas Swann was present, with myself and a number of other gentlemen, relative to the payment of the forfeit by Captain Erwin in the race between Ploughboy and Truxton, do certify that the subject was introduced by Captain P. Anderson, who was stating that, on that occasion, Captain Erwin had produced a different memorandum or schedule of notes than that which was produced at the time the accommodation of the race took place in Nashville. General Jackson replied:

" 'In that you are incorrect. Instead of producing a different schedule, he produced none at all.'

"Some person in the room, perhaps Mr. Swann, stepped toward the General, and said he had heard something on this subject, and wished to know the true statement. To which General Jackson observed that when Captain Erwin asked him up to Captain Hoggatt's to receive the forfeit, he, Captain Erwin, produced to, and offered him notes, none of which were due and payable at the time; that he, the General, refused to-receive them because one half were not due and payable; his reason being that one half were the property of Major Verrel and Captain Pryor, who were about to leave the country immediately. Captain Erwin said they were part of the same notes exhibited in the schedule at Nashville. The General then asked Captain

Erwin for that schedule. He put his hands in his pockets, and, after some search, said it was lost or mislaid, but that Mr. Dickinson had his notes and memorandum or schedule (that he might be called in), out of which the forfeit could be paid. Mr. Dickinson was then called in, produced his notes and memorandum, out of which, with an order on King, Carson & King, the forfeit was paid. When the General had finished his statement, Mr. Anderson said, 'Then I have taken up a wrong idea, and am mistaken,' or words to that import, and the subject ended.

"JOHN HUTCHINGS

"February 5th, 1806"

John Coffee's Affidavit

"I do hereby certify that on or about the 12th day of January last I was in company with General Andrew Jackson, at Nashville, in Mr. Winn's tavern, when the General mentioned to me that some communications had come from Mr. Thomas Swann to him some days previous to that, in consequence of which perhaps Mr. Swann, from the pompous airs he put on, might wish to say something on the subject. He requested me to say to Mr. Swann, who was then in the house, that if he had any business with him (General Jackson), to make it known immediately, as he was about to leave Nashville. I complied with his request. Mr. Swann replied he was just waiting to speak with the General, and immediately stepped up to him. They walked out of the house together. After some minutes General Jackson came into the room (Mr. Swann passed by the door), and observed to him, as he passed on, and to the gentlemen in the house, that if Mr. Swann did attempt to support a statement made in a letter addressed from Mr. Swann to General Jackson (which letter the General showed the company), that he would cane him, inasmuch that the statement was false, that the author could not be a gentleman, and that such would be the treatment he deserved. He observed he would probably be in town the next day, or in a few days, as his business would permit, and if Mr. Swann put on any airs with him he would cane him. He then left town.

"The General's business prevented him from returning to Nashville for some days, in which time Mr. Swann addressed another letter, by his friend, Mr. Nathaniel A. McNairy, to the General, observing that the statements made were substantially correct, etc. The General then was under a promise to cane him on sight. The day after the receipt of the last letter mentioned, General Jackson and myself went into Nashville together, he, under a determination to make good his promise. We stopped at Mr. Winn's tavern; had not been in the house but a few minutes when Mr. Swann came walking into the room. As soon as the General saw him he rose from his chair, observing, he was glad to meet with him, drew up his cane and gave him a very severe blow, which appeared to stagger Mr. Swann forward. The General gave back, as I supposed, to repeat his blows, came in contact with some chairs that stood behind him, and fell backwards over them to the fire or hearth; but before he was down, the gentlemen present caught him and prevented further blows.

"Mr. Swann stepped back, put his hand behind him

under his coat, as I supposed, to draw a pistol. Some person forbade his drawing. The General replied to the company, 'Let him draw and defend himself.' The General put his hand behind him and drew a pistol. The company all immediately gave back, and I supposed that a fire would immediately take place. But when Mr. Swann saw the General draw a pistol, he withdrew his hand, observing that he had no such intention. The General observed to him, that such was the treatment he deserved, and such he would always give young men conducting themselves as he had done; that had he acted in a proper manner to him he would have treated him otherwise. Mr. Swann observed, that he had just learned that he (the General) was come into the house, and that he had come downstairs to speak with him to pave the way for accommodation, or words to that purpose. Mr. Swann then withdrew from the room.

"Some short time after, in the same day, I was called on to hear a conversation between General Jackson and Mr. Nathaniel A. McNairy, the friend of Mr. Swann, as he expressed himself. The General observed to Mr. McNairy, that he knew not Mr. Swann as a gentleman; that he would not degrade himself by accepting his challenge; that he was a stranger to him; that his conduct towards him had been ungentlemanly. Consequently, he would not have any correspondence with him; but if Mr. Swann was dissatisfied with him from the treatment he had received, that he would accommodate him thus far; that he would ride with him anywhere, on any ground he would name; he would meet him in any sequestered grove he would point out; or he would see him in any way he would suggest, through him, Mr. McNairy. He further observed, that if Mr. Swann had any friend, that was known to be a gentleman, who would step forward, in his behalf, that he there pledged himself to meet him on any gentlemanly ground. Mr. McNairy observed that his own knowledge of Mr. Swann would not justify his supporting him as a gentleman, but urged that a court of honor should be called; that he would produce such certificates as he thought would support his friend. General Jackson referred him to me for further proceedings on the occasion, and withdrew.

"My reply to Mr. McNairy was, that I thought that gentleman's honor and feelings were too delicate to arbitrate; that, under the existing circumstances, I thought the General's proposals were as far as he ought to go, and that further satisfaction he might not expect. He, Mr. McNairy, declined accepting the proposition. In the meantime he observed, his only wish was to do justice; that if Mr. Swann's papers did not hold him out to be the gentleman, he would withdraw himself from the business. He said it was unfortunate the General had been so rash, as he was fully convinced that had a conversation taken place between the parties before the General had struck Mr. Swann, the thing would have been easily settled; inasmuch as he, Mr. McNairy, and Mr. Swann, on mature reflection, had discovered they had misconstrued the statements that were the original cause of dispute; that Mr. Swann, in seeing General Jackson ride into town, came to see him to have an explanation. Had this been done, he said, a reconciliation would, in all probability, have taken place, but the General's caning him was now the only cause of complaint.

"Some hours after, in the same day, I called on Mr. McNairy, to know if they would accede to the proposition made him by General Jackson, assuring him it was the only one he would get. He declined, saying he supposed the thing would end with a publication in Mr. Swann's defense.

"Some two or three days after, when in Nashville in Mr. Winn's tavern, I was called on by General Jackson to hear a conversation between himself and Mr. McNairy, when General Jackson observed to Mr. McNairy that he had learned since he had just come to town, that McNairy had reported, and caused to be circulated, that when General Jackson refused to treat Mr. Swann as a gentleman, that he, Mr. McNairy, had observed that if Mr. Swann was not known as a gentleman, that he was one, and would meet him in behalf of his friend. Mr. McNairy replied he had never said it, nor wished such an idea to go out; that he had said if General Jackson had a wish to fight him, he would see him; but denied ever offering or wishing to meet him. General Jackson said Major Robert Purdy was his author, and he would call on him. He accordingly called Major Purdy, who asserted firmly that Mr. McNairy had made such a statement to him. Mr. McNairy observed that Major Purdy must have misconstrued his meaning. The Major replied, there could be no misconstruction; that the words were plain and construed themselves. Mr. McNairy observed he never intended to have said such a thing, neither did he wish such an idea to go forth. General Jackson observed to

Mr. McNairy that 'too much had been said on the subject, and for the future, let there be no misunderstanding. I now pledge you my word and my honor, if any gentleman on a standing with myself will come forward as the friend of Mr. Swann, I will at all times meet him on any gentlemanly ground.' Thus the thing rested, so far as the same came to my knowledge.

"JOHN COFFEE"

Statement of Robert Hays Tending To Show That Mr. Swann Was Not A Gentleman

"I certify that, some time in the month of January last, Mr. Samuel Jackson stated to me that Mr. Thomas Swann had (without being asked) proffered him the loan of some cash, and that he would furnish him with as much as 200 dollars or more, if he wished it. Mr. S. Jackson replied (after thanking him), that he would perhaps call on him in a few days for a loan, which he did in a day or two following, and observed that 100 dollars would answer him. Mr. Thomas Swann observed that he might have it at any time. The said S. Jackson called on him the day following for it, and the said Swann answered he had loaned it out, and he could not furnish him with any. The said S. Jackson further observed to me, that he had found out Mr. Thomas Swann, and that he had not acted the gentleman with him; to which I observed, if he acted in that manner, he treated you like a rascal, and said S. Jackson made answer, he did.

"ROBERT HAYS

"*Haysborough, February 3, 1806*"

Letter of Robert Butler, Showing that Samuel Jackson Thought that Mr. Swann was not a Gentleman

"*Haysborough, February 3, 1806*

"GENERAL ANDREW JACKSON:—SIR, agreeable to your request, the following certificate is a correct statement of a conversation that passed from Mr. Samuel Jackson, in the street of Haysborough, in my presence:

"I certify that, on or about the 24th day of January, 1806, when standing in the street of Haysborough, with two or three gentlemen, Samuel Jackson, Esq., and Mr. —— Lee rode up to the place where we were standing, and the conversation taking a turn to the subject of General Andrew Jackson's and Mr. Thomas Swann's quarrel, Samuel Jackson, Esq., did state in my presence, that Mr. T. Swann treated him very rascally, and commenced the statement of the circumstances; but was interrupted through some cause unknown to me. The day or two following the said S. Jackson having returned to Haysborough, and renewing the conversation, stated to me, that Mr. Thomas Swann had proffered him the loan of some money, without being questioned by said S. Jackson on the subject; his (Mr. Samuel Jackson's) answer was (after thanking him), if he really stood in need of it, he would call on him for 100 dollars. Said S. Jackson, finding necessity for making application, did so (on the day following), and was answered by Mr. Swann that he had loaned his money out.

"ROBERT BUTLER"

Robert Purdy's Statement

"Some time since Mr. Thomas Swann and myself had a conversation respecting Mr. Samuel Jackson. Mr. Swann asked me if I did not suppose that Mr. Jackson was one of the damnedest rascals on earth, and observed he, Jackson, was a damned rascal. Some further conversation took place, which I can not recollect.

"Robert Purdy

"*February 8, 1806*"

General Jackson Resumes

"Mr. Swann, in his letter and publication in your paper of the 1st instant, states 'that the notes offered by Captain Joseph Erwin at the time of paying the forfeit, etc., were different from those General Jackson agreed to receive.' What does Dickinson, his informant, state? That Swann said a different list was produced. Mr. Swann should have recollected that the list of notes and the notes offered were different. The first was produced when an accommodation was proposed respecting the commutation of notes not payable for those that were; the second, to the payment of the forfeit a fact which took place some time after the accommodation. By the accommodation, one half was payable; when the notes were offered, no list was produced.

"How does Mr. Swann prove the position he has taken, that different notes from the list were produced?

"1st. By his own assertion. Mr. Hutchings was present; see his affidavit.

"2d. Mr. Charles Dickinson's information is referred to; see Mr. Dickinson's letter. He states no such thing, but refers to a different list. These two corrective informants speak—one of different notes actually offered, the other of a different list of notes. Happy concordance! These two gentlemen possess the key of consistency.

"3d. Mr. Samuel Jackson is next referred to. Mr. Swann has not been so obliging as to give us any certificate, nor even a quotation from Mr. Jackson, of whom he was so polite as to say in the presence of Major Purdy that he was a damned rascal! (an appropriate witness for Mr. Swann). It is to be lamented that he did not, but it is to be hoped that Colonel Hay's and Mr. Robert Butler's certificates may ease Mr. Swann of the labor of vindicating his friend Samuel from any imputation. No doubt of their having well understood each other. Mr. Jackson flatly calls Mr. Swann a rascal. That they have confidence in each other we have no doubt. Mr. Jackson, in his opinion of Mr. Swann, has disclosed the ground on which this good understanding rests. Upon principles of reason and of law, a man cannot discredit his own witness.

"4th. Mr. Nathaniel A. McNairy is quoted by Mr. Swann in support of his assertion of my inconsistency. This young man has industriously acquired such a reputation as to make it an arduous task to add to it. But as the selected supporter of Mr. Swann in the cause of consistency and bravery, it would be doing injustice to omit him. His certificate, which is only marked by a quotation, is introduced with triumph; his *I* without date or signature. This hopeful youth, who forgets today what he has uttered yesterday, thinks himself secure; but read Messrs. Baird and Purdy's certificates and Mr. Coffee's affidavit, and see what credit can or ought to be attached to the statement of such a character.

"Mr. Coffee states in substance that I would cane Mr. Swann if he attempted to support the statement he had made; that he understood Mr. Swann afterwards wrote me that the statement was substantially correct; that, agreeable to promise, I did cane him; that Mr. Swan said, after this chastisement, that he had wished to pave the way for an explanation; that he was present at a conversation immediately afterwards between Mr. N. A. McNairy, the friend of Mr. Swann, and myself, when, among other things, Mr. McNairy proposed a court of honor, saying at the same time that his acquaintance with Mr. Swann would not justify his supporting him as a gentleman; and if Mr. Swann's papers did not support that character, he would withdraw himself. Note that Mr. Baird and Major Purdy state in substance that this young squire of high renown told them, he observed to me that if Swann's character as a gentleman was not known, he would meet me.

"Mr. Coffee further states that this friend of Mr. Swann expressed much concern that this affair had terminated in so rash a manner; that Mr. Swann had wished to see me for the purpose of an explanation; that Mr. Swann and himself had misconstrued the statement made, or, in other words, found out that they were in an error. How shameful is it, then, to persist in it.

"But Mr. McNairy tells Mr. Coffee that the caning was the only cause of complaint. Then why bring the points of veracity and consistency into view in the publication? When Mr. Coffee called on Mr. McNairy to know what he thought of my proposition for redress, observing to him that it was all he might expect, he declined taking any further part in the affair, and observed, that he supposed it would end in a publication in Mr. Swann's defense. The squire had recourse to the same method on a former occasion, and what effect it produced 'the world might judge.' Mr. Coffee further tells us, that he was present when I called on Mr. McNairy to know if he had made use of the language stated in Major Purdy's certificate. Here the valiant squire's memory failed him; he denies that he ever said it, nor did he 'wish such an idea to go forth.' Major Purdy, being convenient, was called on. He told the squire what he had asserted, to which the squire answered, Major Purdy must have misunderstood him. Modest youth! But the Major tells him he could not, for he gave his own words. Misunderstood? How? This young man has either a vicious habit of deviating from the truth, or a natural weakness of memory, either of which is equally pernicious to society, and renders him a fit compeer for his friend.

"It is difficult to find an appropriate epithet for a character who descends to state falsehoods, where the honor of a man is at stake; where truth and justice ought to be the order of the day, with a person chosen to accompany another on the field of honor; and, in many cases, where integrity is the only shield of innocence. However, the squire's conduct is in perfect unison with a recent act on the field of honor; he fired before the word and it was declared to be an accident; and this prevarication, or whatever you may please to call it, I suppose he will declare to be another. Combine these two acts with the whole military feats of this young squire, and his deviations from the path of candor and truth in civil life. He is in my opinion (and I think the world will agree with me) deprived of that privilege in society which the gentleman and man of honor ought, in all cases, in justice to obtain.

"Thus, reader, I have endeavored to finish the picture. The ground-work only appears to be conceived by the author of the publication. The materials existing in the statements of his witnesses may with propriety be said to have been selected by the author. They see, however, the natural result of those chosen by himself; an application of such as were offered have only been made. It is true that the drapery sometimes exhibits black instead of white; but this the reader will excuse when he considers that, consistently with the plan I adopted, no other material could be had. A little more indulgence whilst a few other parts of the publication are noticed.

"Mr. Swann states in substance he was attacked in a defenseless situation, and off his guard; read the certificates of Messrs. Coffee and Claiborne. Judge for yourselves. His own declaration shows that he came into the room, knowing I was there, for the purpose (to make use of his own words) 'to pave the way for an accommodation.' These gentlemen state that Mr. Swann was about drawing a pistol! Why did he not do it? Any man can answer this question. Recollect,

reader, his boast for a certain death in case I attempted
to cane him. He had previously every assurance that I
would not treat him like the gentleman, but that a caning would be given him in return for a challenge.

"Here, then, the hero steps forward with all the
ostensible bravery of a duellist. The faithful promise
was executed. And notwithstanding his gasconading expressions, 'that no power terrestrial should prevent
the settled purpose of his soul,' he shrank at the sight
of a pistol, and dropped his hands for quarter, although one of them was placed on, and in the act of
drawing his own. Is this like the man of courage who
said, 'that instant death should be the consequence'?
Or is it like the coward when his settled purpose fails
him? When true bravery is assailed or attacked in any
way, it will show to the world its genuineness. Yes, as
much bravery is necessary in the act of self-defense in
all cases as in the act of duelling—see Mr. Coffee's
affidavit.

"Mr. Swann, on this occasion, has impertinently and
inconsistently obtruded himself. He has acted the puppet and lying valet for a worthless, drunken, blackguard scoundrel, who is now at war with, and flatly
contradicts, and gives Mr. Swann the lie. Here the
reader can compare Charles Dickinson's letter with
Mr. Swann's publication.

"Mr. Swann states his desire to obtain satisfaction;
'but an ingenious evasion had been discovered.' How
does this agree with the evidence of Mr. Coffee and
Mr. Purdy? He is told he can have satisfaction in any
manner, in any way or situation, but that I will not
degrade myself by the acceptance of a challenge from

a stranger whose acts and conduct had been inconsistent with that of the gentleman—from a man who was capable of acting and writing to me in the manner Mr. Swann had done in his letters of the 3d and 12th of January.

"But Mr. Swann complains I would not acknowledge him a gentleman, and calls for proof of the contrary. If, therefore, I have not shown sufficiently that he has no just claim to the appellation of a gentleman, let him bring forth his letters introductory, or certificates, so much talked of. I was badly advised the day I chastised Mr. Swann, if those vouchers were not given by men in Virginia of known immoral and disreputable character.

"Is it worth while before I take my everlasting farewell of this group, to notice the last falsehood asserted by Mr. Swann in his publication? The fact is, I am only thirty-nine years of age, and if God should permit me to live thirty-nine years more, I will never again be caught before the public in competition with Mr. Swann or any of his auxiliaries.

"ANDREW JACKSON

"*February 10th, 1806*"

This is a curious combination of fact, feeling, and insolence. To describe Dickinson as he finally did, would indicate deep-laid hatred, for which the feminine factor may have been responsible. Certainly, there was small excuse for the language toward one with whom he had been so recently involved in a sporting transaction and whose paper he had taken without protest. Jackson's statement touched off a good deal of "honor."

Young McNairy supplied Editor Easton with a letter for his next issue, taunting Jackson in scurrilous terms. He was considered a boy by the victim and let alone. John Coffee, however, took up the quarrel. The two fought over the line in Kentucky, on March 1, 1806. McNairy fired at the word "two" prematurely and perforated Coffee's thigh. Coffee's second, Major Robert Purdy, was inclined to shoot him for this, but proper apologies all around patched the matter up. Swann kept his pen busy and produced another broadside, devoted to demonstrating his claim to be a gentleman and branding Jackson as a coward. He secured a Virginia certificate of character from no less personage than Edmund Randolph, George Washington's discredited Secretary of State. A dozen others endorsed this. Swann again offered pompously to hold himself "answerable for his conduct."

The general ignored him. But on May 20, 1806, Charles Dickinson reached Nashville on his return from New Orleans. He was speedily appraised of all that had occurred. Dickinson at once took his pen in hand and sent this vitriolic letter to Editor Easton.

"MR. EASTON:—In looking over the tenth number of your *Impartial Review* I discover that a certain Andrew Jackson has endeavored to induce the public to believe that some inconsistency had been attempted by me relative to his dispute with Mr. Thomas Swann. My letter to Andrew Jackson, as published by Mr. Joseph Erwin, is, I consider, a sufficient answer with any impartial person.

"I should have never condescended to have taken

any notice of Andrew Jackson or his scurrilous publication had it not been promised by Mr. Joseph Erwin, when he published my letter at length, which Mr. Jackson, for some cause unknown but to himself, had not the generosity to have published but in part.

"I shall take notice but of those parts of his publication which are intended for myself. The first is in his publication of the 8th of February, which reads thus: 'Mr. Charles Dickinson's information is referred to; see Mr. Dickinson's letter. He states no such thing, but refers to a different list. These two corrective informants speak, one of different notes actually offered, the other of a different list of notes. Happy concordance! These two gentlemen possess the key of consistency.'

"I have no such accommodating disposition as to compare what I intend to offer to the public with that of any witness whatever, and, if it should differ, to correct in such manner as to correspond. What any person offers for publication, if called on, I think it is his duty to swear to. Andrew Jackson has had several disputes, which have appeared in different prints of this State, and, if his mode of publishing his thoughts on his different quarrels is such as to alter his publications to make them answer with those of his witnesses, I can only exclaim, *O tempora! O mores!*

"Another part of his publication of the same date, is as follows: 'He,' alluding to Mr. Thomas Swann, 'has acted the puppet and lying valet for a worthless, drunken, blackguard scoundrel,' etc., etc. Should Andrew Jackson have intended these epithets for me, I declare him, notwithstanding he is a Major General of the militia of Mero district, to be a worthless scoundrel, 'a poltroon and a coward'——a man who, by frivolous and evasive pretexts, avoided giving the satisfaction which was due to a gentleman whom he had injured. This has prevented me from calling on him in the manner I should otherwise have done, for I am well convinced that he is too great a coward to administer any of those anodines he promised me in his letter to Mr. Swann. His excuse I anticipate, that the anodines have been in such demand since I left Tennessee that he is out of the necessary ingredients to mix them. I expect to leave Nashville, the first of next week, for Maryland. Yours, etc.,

"CHARLES DICKINSON

"May 21st, 1806"

With the knowledge aforesaid, General Thomas Overton advised Jackson, on May 22, 1806, that the letter would appear in the next issue of the *Impartial Review and Cumberland Repository*. He urged Jackson to challenge Dickinson forthwith. "This is a matter of life and death," replied Jackson. "I'll see the piece and form my own judgment on it." He rode to the printing office and perused the note, to which he made immediate response in these terms:

CHARLES DICKINSON, SIR,——

Your conduct and expressions relative to me of late have been of such a nature and so insulting that it requires and shall have my notice. Insult may be given by men, and of such a kind that they must be noticed and treated with the respect due a gentleman, although (in the present instance) you do not merit it.

You have, to disturb my quiet, industriously excited Thomas Swann to quarrel with me, which involved the peace and harmony of society for awhile.

You, on the 10th of January, wrote me a very insulting letter, left this country, caused this letter to be delivered after you had been gone some days, and viewing yourself in safety from the contempt I held you, have now in the press a piece more replete with blackguard abuse than any of your other productions. You are pleased to state that you would have noticed me in a different way, but my cowardice would have found a pretext to evade that satisfaction if it had been called for, etc., etc.

I hope, sir, your courage will be an ample security to me that I will obtain speedily that satisfaction due me for the insults offered, and in the way my friend who hands you this will point out. He waits upon you for that purpose, and with your friend will enter into immediate arrangements for this purpose. I am, etc.,

ANDREW JACKSON

In the afternoon Dr. Hanson Catlett brought a reply from Dickinson. It read:

Your note of this morning is received, and your request shall be gratified. My friend who hands you this, will make the necessary arrangements.

Jackson selected General Overton as his representative. He and Catlett drew up the agreement, which was:

"On Friday, the 30th instant, we agree to meet at Harrison's Mills, on Red River, Logan County, State of Kentucky, for the purpose of settling an affair of honor between General Andrew Jackson and Charles Dickinson Esq. Further arrangements to be made. It is understood that the meeting will be at the hour of seven in the morning."

Jackson demurred at the week's delay, one reason for which was Dickinson's lack of weapons. Overton then wrote Catlett:

Sir,—

The affair of honor to be settled between my friend General Jackson and Charles Dickinson, Esq., is wished not to be postponed until the 30th instant (say Friday) agreeable to your time appointed, if it can be done sooner. In order that no inconvenience on your part may occur, if you cannot obtain pistols, we pledge ourselves to give you choice of ours.

Catlett did not reply, so Overton wrote again the next day:

Sir,—

I pressed you in favor of my friend General Jackson for immediate satisfaction for the injury that his feelings had received from a publication of Charles Dickinson. You replied that it might not be in your power to obtain pistols. In my note yesterday, in order to remove any obstacles as it respected pistols, I agreed to give you choice of ours, the other we pledged ourselves to make use of. For God's sake, let this business be fought to an issue immediately, as I cannot see, after the publication, why Mr. Dickinson should wish to put it off until Friday.

Catlett declined to change the date. The seconds then met to arrange the details. These were:

"It is agreed that the distance shall be twenty-four feet; the parties to stand facing each other, with their pistols down perpendicularly. When they are ready, the single word, 'Fire,' to be given; at which they are to fire as soon as they please. Should either fire before the word is given, we pledge ourselves to shoot him down instantly. The person to give the word to be determined by lot, as also the choice of position. We mutually agree that the above regulations shall be observed in the affair of honor depending between General Andrew Jackson and Charles Dickinson, Esq."

Dickinson was credited with having boastfully exhibited to friends the night before the duel a ten-spot card with all the spots cut out at duelling distance.

Both parties, attended by their seconds and a retinue of friends, set out by differing roads for the Red River, on the morning of May 29. No public intelligence had been disseminated of the coming encounter, though it was generally known to inside circles that the combat was impending. Bets were freely placed, with the odds in favor of Dickinson, who was known to be an expert shot. He left his wife without word of his intention, with a promise to be home the next evening. On the road he made fancy shots demonstrating his skill with the pistol, in one instance cutting a string at twenty-four paces, remarking, "If General Jackson comes along this road, show him that." Current tales relate that Dickinson and his party showed great bravado en route, riding recklessly, shouting and shooting along the way.

Jackson and his escort traveled in dignity, discussing the tasks of the next morning. Dickinson was a snap-shooter. That is to say, he took no aim; but when his pistol was raised to the right level, he fired instinctively. Jackson was unused to this and required aim. He and Overton both were certain that Dickinson would have the first shot. They knew also that it was to be a duel to the death. Jackson felt he would not get off unscathed, but was firm in the faith that he would get his man. "I should have hit him if he had shot me through the brain," he said afterwards.

They stopped at David Miller's cross-roads inn on the Red River. Dickinson and his escort arrived later, to be told the house was full. They went on two miles down stream to the hotel kept by William Harrison, where they lodged for the night. Jackson, it is related, was composed during the evening; he ate a hearty supper and smoked his corn-cob pipe before going to bed. In the morning both parties were promptly at the rendezvous. This involved crossing the river. There was no ferryman visible at the hour. Jackson spurred his steed into the stream, and so forded it, leading the others. The chosen spot was a glade in the forest. Jackson was cheery and confident. "I shall wing him, never fear," he said in reply to an inquiring friend. In the lot-drawing Dickinson won the choice of position, Jackson the word. Upon this much depended and Overton had rehearsed for it, should the chance befall him, as it did. Dickinson was a large, florid man; Jackson thin and ascetic. He had dressed for the occasion in large loose garments, within which he shrank his slender shape as much as possible. He was required to face the foe and did so, but twisted his body within his coat so that it was almost sidewise, making a lean target. This saved his life, as the event proved.

The moment of seven having arrived, Overton called out:

"Are you ready?"

"I am ready," answered Dickinson.

"I am ready," echoed Jackson.

"Fi-r-e!" shouted the General. There was but one shot. It came from the pistol of Dickinson. Jackson had deliberately held his fire. He had been hit—that was plain—but stood steadily on his feet, with his left arm drawn tightly across his chest. Slowly he raised his right arm and with it his weapon. Dickinson, startled, slipped back a pace or two and faltered: "Great God! Have I missed him?"

Overton ordered him back to the mark. The doomed man stepped forward. He stood erect, but turned his eyes away from the cold gaze of his antagonist. Jackson pulled his trigger, but there was no response from the charge. It had stopped at half-cock. A merciful man would have tossed it aside and thanked God that he had no need to redden his hands. There was no mercy in Andrew Jackson's soul. He examined the pistol, ascertained the cause of its balkiness, and recocked it. Then he took a new and deliberate aim, and fired. This time there was no misfire. Dickinson swayed backwards, but before he fell, his friends had him in their arms and lowered him gently to the ground. Red stains appeared on his clothing. This was stripped off. The surgeon found a bullet bulging in the skin that had passed through his body below the ribs. The wound bled freely. That it was fatal there could be no doubt.

General Overton went over and took account of Dickinson's condition. "He won't want anything more of you, General," was his report to Jackson. Together with their surgeon the two walked away from the ground. Then the medico noted that Jackson's shoe was dripping blood.

"My God! General Jackson, are you hit?" he inquired excitedly.

"Oh, I believe he has pinked me a little," was the cool reply. "Let's look at it, but say nothing about it."

When the big loose coat and waistcoat were removed, it was found that Jackson's twist of body had saved his life. Dickinson had aimed true for his heart, had it been in the right place. The breastbone was seared and several ribs fractured, despite which he was able to ride back to the tavern. He had gone to the field without breakfasting, and observing a negro servant working a churn, he asked her if the "butter had come." On her answer that it "was coming," he asked for some buttermilk. She took a quart measure full from the churn and he drank it with what appeared to be a single swallow. Then he had his wound dressed and sent one of his party to Dr. Catlett to inquire about Dickinson, offering at the same time the services of his own surgeon. Word came back that Dickinson was past medical aid, whereupon Jackson forwarded a bottle of wine for his antagonist. His own injury was kept carefully concealed for the reason that the savage Jackson did not want Dickinson to depart for the shades with the knowledge that he had hit his mark. That would have been a source of satisfaction to a man who had been sure that he had shot to kill, and "he did not want him to have the gratification even of knowing that he had touched him."

Word had been sent to Dickinson's wife that he was dangerously hurt and she had hurried to reach his side. The poor woman met the wagon bearing his body on the road. He had died at five minutes after nine in the evening, after a day of terrible suffering, from an unceasing flow of blood.

"Why have you put out the lights?" were his last words as the darkness of death seized him. They buried him from the home of his father-in-law, Joseph Erwin. A great crowd attended his obsequies.

The *Impartial Review and Cumberland Repository,* which was responsible for the outcome, observed in its account of the obsequies:

"In the prime of life, and blessed in domestic circumstances with almost every valuable enjoyment, he fell a victim to the barbarous and pernicious habit of duelling. By his untimely fate the community is deprived of an amiable man and a virtuous citizen."

Seventy-three citizens united in requesting Editor Easton to drape his columns in mourning on the next issue, a small enough amend, it would appear. News of this coming to Jackson as he lay nursing his scarred breastbone at the Hermitage, he wrote in protest:

I am informed that at the request of sundry citizens of Nashville and vicinity, you are about to dress your paper in mourning "as a tribute of regret for the memory and for the untimely death of Charles Dickinson." Your paper is the public vehicle, and is always taken as the public will, unless the contrary appears. Presuming that the public is not in mourning for this event, in justice to that public, it is only fair and right to set forth the names of those citizens who have made the request. The thing is so novel that names ought to appear, that the public might judge whether the true motives of the signers were "a tribute of respect for the deceased" or something else that at first sight does not appear.

The editor obliged everybody. He turned his column

rules upside down, gave the names, and published Jackson's letter. There were no further casualties. Erwin questioned Jackson's right to recock his pistol after it had missed fire, upon which criticism there was some merit. Swann, coming in for just complaint as to his share in the miserable business, published a card: "I do avow that neither Mr. Dickinson nor any other person urged me forward to quarrel with Jackson." Yet it had all the aspects of a picked quarrel.

Jackson was confined to the house for a month, and the wound always troubled him. It never properly healed and was believed to have had much to do with his death, which occurred nearly forty years afterward. The duel did him great harm in Tennessee. Aside from his courage, about which there could never be a doubt, there was nothing in his conduct to admire. It required the Battle of New Orleans to wipe out the stain on his name.

CHAPTER IX

ANDREW JACKSON vs. THE TWO BENTONS

ON Saturday, September 4, 1813, when the War of 1812 was well under way, Andrew Jackson was again embroiled in what came near being fatal consequences. This time the duel was not formal partaking rather of the nature of a free fight. It is usually chronicled as a duel, however, though fought with two men, Jesse and Thomas H. Benton.

Jackson had organized a militia force for service in the conflict with Britain and saw fit to show favor to William Carroll, clerk in a hardware store in Pittsburgh, whence he had come to Nashville and attached himself to Jackson, who made him Brigade Inspector. The troops rendezvoused at Natchez. During their movement Carroll had contrived to pick up some forceful enemies. One of these challenged him to a duel. Carroll took the old Jacksonian ground anent Swann, that the challenger was not a gentleman. The second who received this response then challenged the Inspector on the delicate ground that to say his principal was no gentleman was as good as to say that he was not one.

Man after man was picked to bring Carroll into the field until the succession lighted on Jesse Benton. Benton was the younger brother of Thomas H. Benton, who was attorney for Jackson. The elder Benton at this time was in Washington, attending to some very important matters for the General, the failure of which promised to bankrupt him. The two were very close, Benton having acted as Jackson's aid in the Creek War. He was also a frequent and welcome visitor at The Hermitage.

Jesse Benton now challenged Carroll, who, having exhausted excuses, concluded to fight, and sought out General Jackson at The Hermitage to serve as his second.

"Why, Captain Carroll," exclaimed the astonished General. "I am not the man for such an affair! I am too old. The time has been when I would have gone out with pleasure; but at my time of life it would be extremely injudicious. You must get a man nearer your own age."

Carroll continued his urge. This was a conspiracy to "run him out of the country" and secure his coveted commission. The plea had its effect. The General had heard that phrase before—more than once applied to himself. "Well, Carroll," he responded after reflection, "you may make up your mind on one point. They shan't run you out of the country as long as Andrew Jackson lives in it. I'll ride with you to Nashville, and inquire into this business myself."

Inquiry developed the facts as stated by Carroll to be correct. The young bloods were trying to "run him out." Jackson there upon assented to be second. The "duel" that followed was almost as amusing as Mr. Midshipman Easy's three-cornered affair at Malta, both in conduct and outcome.

The men were placed back to back at the customary

twenty-four paces. They were required to wheel about and fire when facing. Benton was not formidable—so little so, indeed, that Jackson remarked, reassuringly, to his principal: "You needn't fear him, Carroll; he'd never hit you if you were as broad as a barn door."

The face-about followed at the word. Benton fired first. His was not a bad shot. It ripped off a bit of Carroll's thumb. In adjusting his position to receive Carroll's shot Benton stooped, pushing out a confidential part of his person so that the well-aimed bullet struck him *a-posteriori,* causing a long gash about a part of his person, that would have gone scatheless probably, had he stood erect. The result was a mighty laugh at both parties, for Carroll would have kept his thumb had he held his hand down to his side, as he ought to have done in observing the proprieties. Of course, the loudest laughter greeted Jesse Benton. Not only was his wound ridiculous, but it kept him laid up for a month, during which time Thomas H. Benton had been successful in disentangling Jackson's troubles at Washington. His letters of triumph were crossed by several from brother Jesse, detailing his discomfiture. Aghast at hearing the part played by Jackson in the silly affair, the elder Benton became vastly indignant. He had great capacity in this respect, and on receiving full accounts of the event, which certainly did his client no credit, took the latter severely to account. Meddling friends added to the tale, and Jackson did not help matters by telling Benton that he should have asked him for the facts before going off half-cocked on the reports of mischievous talebearers. Benton was not mollified by such an attitude. He came back declaring that Jackson was responsible for the duel being carried out in a "savage, unequal, unfair, and base manner."

Coming home by way of Knoxville, Benton illumined the road with denunciations of Jackson, clothed in the pompous style of Gibbon's "Rome," which thundered across East Tennessee and reached the ears of Old Hickory at the Hermitage. The Bentons were North Carolina folk and as neighbors had been more than kind to the Widow Jackson and her brood. The General should have remembered this, but he did not. Though Benton had gone to Washington temporarily on Jackson's behalf, the two men had been together at Natchez where Benton was among the militia officers. The crafty James Wilkinson, Brigadier-General in the Regular Army, had raised a question of outranking Jackson as a Major-General of Volunteers, and Benton had sided with him. This Jackson had forgiven. He was no doubt ashamed of his participation in the duel and at first parleyed with Benton, who would not listen and who finally provoked Jackson into declaring "by the Eternal" that he would horsewhip Tom Benton at the earliest opportunity. The fact was duly proclaimed by the numerous mischief-makers, and from Knoxville to Nashville, Tennessee was all agog for the event.

Ordinarily, Jackson and Benton lodged at the Nashville Inn when in town. Benton arrived on September 3, 1813, and prudently went to the City Hotel, as a precaution against the horsewhip descending upon his shoulders unawares. By coincidence, General Jackson cantered in from The Hermitage, having with him his friend and follower, Colonel John Coffee, who had fought McNairy on his behalf years before. Bystanders, sensing something sensational, quizzed Coffee as to the import of Jackson's sudden coming to town. With a smile, he replied that they were after the mail. It was late in the day, and the pair took rooms at the Inn for the night. Captain Carroll visited the warrior, evidently from a sense of duty that he ought to join in a melée for which he was really responsible. He explained apologetically that he had to leave the city that night to meet an important engagement. "Go, by all means," replied Jackson. "I want no man to fight my battles."

Carroll departed. After breakfast the following morning Jackson and Coffee, on Benton intent, started for the City Hotel via the Nashville post office. Jackson wore a dress-sword and held his riding whip in his right hand. The post office and the City Hotel were adjacent. Looking across the alley that divided them, Jackson saw Thomas H. Benton standing in the doorway of the hostelry.

"Do you see that fellow?" interrogated Coffee.

"Oh, yes," responded Jackson. "I have my eye on him."

They entered the post office, collected some letters, and walked along the sidewalk toward the hotel doorway where Thomas H. Benton was standing, apparently inviting an encounter. In the background stood Jesse Benton. On reaching the doorway, Jackson raised his whip and exclaimed:

"Now, you damned rascal, I am going to punish you. Defend yourself!"

Responding to the suggestion Benton reached to-

ANDREW JACKSON

ward the inside pocket of his frock coat, at which Jackson dropped the whip and flashed a pistol in Benton's face. Benton stepped backward into the hotel, with Jackson following him. In this manner he was pressed across the main floor of the house, toward the rear porch, down which the pair started to walk in this strange fashion, when Jesse Benton came on the scene. His brother was outside, and Jackson had turned to follow him when Jesse fired at him. The pistol was charged with a slug of lead and two bullets. The former struck Jackson's shoulder and broke it into bits. One of the balls perforated his left arm to the bone. The other landed in the wall.

Jackson fell to the floor. He was out of the fighting, and blood gushed from his wounds.

At the report of Jesse Benton's pistol, Coffee came into the conflict. He had been on the watch without. The scene astounded him. His beloved General lay in a pool of blood at Thomas H. Benton's feet, presumably his victim. Jumping to this conclusion, Coffee shot at Benton, but being too excited to aim, the bullet went wide. He raised the heavy weapon to strike Benton with its butt, when the latter, to avoid the blow, stepped backward, inadvertently into a stairway, down which he fell with a resounding crash. This probably saved his life, for Coffee turned his attention to the prostrate Jackson, preceiving that he needed immediate aid. It chanced that Stokley Hays, a nephew of Mrs. Rachel Jackson, was near the scene, and hearing the shooting and tumult, had hurried into the hotel.

Hays spotted Jesse Benton as the man who had

leveled his uncle, and drawing a sword cane, he drove at him with deadly force. The blade was slender and delicate and luck was with the Benton family that day. The point of the needlelike rapier struck a button on Jesse's coat and broke into pieces. Hays, out of all his sober senses with rage, drew a dirk and threw himself upon the younger Benton. The two fell to the floor, with Hays on top. He raised the dirk to stab the young man. Benton succeeded in catching Hays by the sleeve, causing his blow to glance so it pinned an arm, but did not reach the heart, for which it was aimed. Hays was a man of uncommon strength. He broke Benton's grasp and a second thrust would have ensued that meant death. But at this moment he was seized by men whom the rumpus had brought to the scene and held until Benton arose. He tried to resume the attack, but was also restrained by the crowd. This ended the affray with all hands alive.

The wounded General, gasping for breath and bleeding so that his life blood soaked through two mattresses, was taken to the Nashville Inn, where Mrs. Jackson was summoned. The best surgeons in the city came at the call. With one exception, and he the junior of the lot, they advised amputating his arm. "I'll keep my arm," declared the unconquered General, and he did. The ball was allowed to remain, as probing was too risky. It stayed in the flesh for twenty years. Distrusting doctors, Old Hickory had his shoulder poulticed with bark of the slippery elm, and kept refreshed with simples from the pharmacopœia of the Indians. Severe as the injuries were, in three weeks Jackson was up and about again.

The two Bentons remained in possession of the field, uttering loud shouts of triumph and inviting the Jacksonians to mortal combat. They were too busy salvaging the General to accept. In the struggle with Jesse Benton, Jackson had lost his dress-sword. Thomas Benton picked it up and, parading to the public square, broke it with a great blast of defiance, accompanying the act "with words defiant and contemptuous, uttered in the loudest tones of his thundering voice" as one account had it, quite forgetting that he owed his life to having fallen downstairs.

Though the victorious Bentons crowed like chanticleers, they were far from happy. The Jacksonians rallied as soon as the General's life seemed safe and proceeded to make things uncomfortable.

At this time Thomas H. Benton wrote:

I am literally in hell here, having the meanest wretches to contend with—liars, affidavit makers, and shameless cowards. All the puppies of Jackson are at work on me; but they will be astonished at what will happen; for it is not them, but their master whom I will hold accountable. The scalping knife of Tecumseh (*sic*) is mercy compared with the affidavits of these villains. I am in the middle of hell, and see no alternative but to kill or be killed; for I will not crouch to Jackson; and the fact that I and my brother defeated him and his tribe and broke his small sword in the public square, will forever rankle in his bosom, and make him thirst after vengeance. My life is in danger; nothing but a decisive duel can save me, or even give me a chance for my own existence; for it is a settled plan to turn out puppy after puppy to bully me, and when I have got into a scrape, to have me killed somehow in the scuffle, and afterwards the affidavit makers will prove it was honestly done. I shall never be forgiven, having given my opinion in favor of

Wilkinson's authority last winter; and this is the rest of the hell they have turned loose on me.

Benton remained in Nashville for a few days to brave consequences, if there were to be any, and then returned to his home in Franklin, a near-by town. There he published his own version of the encounter. It differs in some details from the preceding account made up from various sources, and follows:

"Franklin, Tennessee September 10, 1813

"A difference which had been brewing for some months between General Jackson and myself, produced on Saturday, the 4th instant, in the Town of Nashville, the most outrageous affray ever witnessed in a civilized country. In communicating the affair to my friends and fellow citizens I limit myself to the statement of a few leading facts, the truth of which I am ready to establish by legal proofs.

"1. That myself and my brother, Jesse Benton, arriving in Nashville on the morning of the affray, and knowing of General Jackson's threats, went and took lodgings in a different house from the one in which he staid, on purpose to avoid him.

"2. That the General and some of his friends came to the house where we had put up, and commenced the attack by levelling a pistol at me, when I had no weapon drawn, and advancing upon me at a quick pace, without giving me time to draw one.

"3. That seeing this, my brother fired upon General Jackson, when he had got within eight or ten feet of me.

"4. That four other pistols were fired in quick succession; one by General Jackson at me; two by me at the General; and one by Colonel Coffee at me. In the course of this firing, General Jackson was brought to the ground, but I received no hurt.

"5. That daggers were then drawn. Colonel Coffee and Mr. Alexander Donaldson made at me, and gave me five slight wounds. Captain Hammond and Mr. Stokley Hays engaged my brother, who, still suffering from a severe wound he had lately received in a duel, was not able to resist two men. They got him down; and while Captain Hammond beat him on the head to make him lie still, Mr. Hays attempted to stab him, and wounded him in both arms as he lay on his back, parrying the thrusts with his naked hands. From this situation a generous hearted citizen of Nashville, Mr. Sumner, relieved him. Before he came to the ground, my brother clapped a pistol to the breast of Mr. Hays, to blow him through, but it missed fire.

"6. My own and my brother's pistols carried two balls each; for it was our intention, if driven to arms, to have no child's play. The pistols fired at me were so near that the blaze of the muzzle of one of them burnt the sleeve of my coat, and the other aimed at my head at a little more than an arm's length from it.

"7. Captain Carroll was to have taken part in the affray, but was absent by the permission of General Jackson, as he had proved by the General's certificate, a certificate which reflects I know not whether less honor upon the General or upon the Captain.

"8. That this attack was made upon me in the house

where the Judge of the District, Mr. Searcy, had his lodgings. Nor has the civil authority yet taken cognizance of this horrible outrage.

"These facts are sufficient to fix the public opinion. For my own part, I think it scandalous that such things should take place at any time; but particularly so at the present moment, when the public service requires the aid of all the citizens. As for the name of courage, God forbid that I should ever attempt to gain it by becoming a bully. Those who know me, know full well that I would give a thousand times more for the reputation of a Croghan in defending his post, than I would for the reputation of all the duellists and gladiators that ever appeared on the face of the earth.

"THOMAS HART BENTON
"Lieut. Col. 39th Infantry"

There was one strange circumstance connected with the affair. Some of the bullets went through the walls and passed over the heads of a young Frenchman and his American wife who, together with an infant son, were lodged in one of the hotel rooms. They were scared but not injured. The boy grew up to be John Charles Fremont, who married Jessie Benton, Thomas H. Benton's brilliant daughter, found pathways to the Pacific, captured California, ran for President of the United States on the first Republican ticket, and made a great noise in the world. Benton soon perceived that Tennessee was no longer tenable. Procuring an appointment as lieutenant colonel in the regular army, he left the state. After the war with Great Britain ended, he resigned and made his home thereafter in St. Louis.

CHAPTER X

Thomas H. Benton vs. Charles Lucas

WHEN Benton settled in St. Louis, his fame as a fighter had preceded him. Soon after his lodgement in Missouri he acted as second to Thomas Hempstead in a duel with Joshua Barton, in which neither principal was hurt. This was in 1816. The next year he was to fight Charles Lucas, another attorney, with a result fatal to the latter. A court quarrel was the cause. In October, 1816, the pair were on opposite sides in the Supreme Court, when Benton, summing up, cited certain points in evidence and asked the judge to instruct the jury to find accordingly, which was in the interest of his client. Upon Lucas's saying that he could recall no such evidence in the record, Benton replied, "I contradict you, sir," in the brow-beating way that was one of his chief characteristics.

Lucas answered, "I contradict you, sir."

Benton then said, "If you deny that, you deny the truth."

To this Lucas answered, "If you assert that you deny that, you assert what is not true."

This resulted in a challenge from Benton, which Lucas declined to accept. Ill-will continued. On election day, August 4, 1817, Lucas inquired if Benton had paid his taxes in time to make his voting legal. Benton, ignoring Lucas, remarked to the judges of the election,

"Gentlemen, if you have any question to ask, I am prepared to answer, but I do not propose to answer
charges made by any puppy who may happen to run
across my path."

This led to a challenge from Lucas in these terms:

St. Louis, August 11, 1817

THOMAS H. BENTON, ESQ.
SIR,—

I am informed you applied to me on the day of the election,
the epithet "Puppy." If so, I shall expect that satisfaction which
is due from one gentleman to another for such an indignity.

I am,

CHARLES LUCAS

Thomas Hempstead, an intimate friend of Benton's,
had just died. Benton had been sitting up all night with
the corpse after the old custom, when the challenge
from Lucas arrived. "I accept," was Benton's response;
"but I must now go and bury a dead friend. That is my
first duty. After that is discharged I will fight tonight
if possible; if not, tomorrow morning at daybreak." He
accordingly secured Colonel Luke E. Lawless for a
second. Joshua Barton acted for Lucas.

The seconds drew up the following rather elaborate
arrangement:

1. The parties shall meet at six o'clock on the morning of
the 12th inst., at the upper end of the Island ("Bloody Island" it was well named, the local resort for duellists) opposite to Madame Roy's.

2. Each party shall choose and provide himself with a smooth-
bore pistol not exceeding eleven inches in length.

3. The pistols shall be loaded on the ground by the friends

Photo by Brown Brothers, New York

THOMAS H. BENTON

of each party in the presence of both friends and parties, if the latter shall require it.

4. The friends of each party shall have the liberty of being armed with two loaded pistols on the ground if they please.

5. The parties respectively shall be examined by the friends of each other on the ground to see that they shall have no personal defense of any kind about them, or anything that can prevent the penetration of a ball.

6. The parties previously to taking their ground shall strip off their coats and waistcoats to their shirts respectively, and shall fire in that situation.

7. Each party to have leave to take a surgeon with them if they please to the grounds.

8. The parties shall stand at the distance of thirty feet, and after being asked if they are ready, and each having answered in the affirmative, they shall receive the word to "Fire," after which the parties may present and fire as they please.

9. The friends of the parties shall cast a lot for choice of stands and the giving of the word.

10. The friends of the parties shall pledge themselves to each other that there are no persons on the island to their knowledge except those seen.

11. If either party shall fire before the word "fire" is given, it shall be the duty of the friend of the opposite party to shoot him who has so fired.

12. The parties by their undersigned friends pledge themselves on their honor for the strict observance of the above articles.

LAWLESS
J. BARTON

St. Louis, 11th August, 1817

The duellists fired at the word. Benton got off with a bruise below the knee. His bullet cut an artery in Lucas's neck, which bled so freely that he could not go on.

It was agreed, however, that the pair should meet again when Lucas had sufficiently recovered. Efforts were made by Lawless to end the difficulty, but during his negotiations, when Benton was ready to drop the matter, "he was assailed with reports of the most offensive nature to his feelings and reputation," which caused him to demand either an explanation or another meeting. Lucas accordingly wrote out a statement in which he declared that he had never said anything about Benton since the first meeting with the view of its becoming public, which Benton accepted after some quibbling. This was thought to have closed the matter, but it did not do so. Benton continued to hear reflections on himself emanating from Lucas, and on September 23, 1817, sent him a challenge. It read:

When I released you from your engagement to return to the island, I yielded to a feeling of generosity in my own bosom, and to a sentiment of deference to the judgment of others. From the reports which now fill the country it would seem that yourself and some of your friends have placed my conduct to very different motives. The object of this is to bring these calumnies to an end, and to give you an opportunity of justifying the great expectations that have been excited. Colonel Lawless will receive your terms and I expect your distance not to exceed nine feet.

Lucas replied, on the 26th, having been absent from town:

Although I am conscious that a respectable man in society cannot be found who will say that he ever heard any of the reports alluded to from me, and though I think it more likely they have been fabricated by your own friends than circulated by any calling themselves mine, yet, even without knowing what the reports are, I shall give you an opportunity of gratifying either your wishes or the wishes of your news-carriers.

This was tart enough and to the point. It was at once arranged that the second meeting should take place at the same spot on Bloody Island, September 26, 1817, at six o'clock in the morning. The retinue was increased. Benton added Major Joshua Pitcher to his company, together with Dr. B. J. Farrar. Barton again represented Lucas, aided by Colonel Clemson, with Dr. Quarles as surgeon.

The distance was shortened to ten paces. Both fired at the word. Benton's bullet went through the left arm of Lucas and lodged near his heart. He lived but an hour. Benton approached the dying man with an expression of condolence. "Colonel Benton, you have persecuted and murdered me; I do not, cannot forgive you." But as his eyes glazed, he murmured, "I can forgive you; I do forgive you," and tendered his hand, which Benton took. So ended this savage and quite unwarranted encounter. Benton felt the outcome deeply. He seldom spoke of it and carefully burned all papers that had any relation to the event.

When, in 1820, Missouri came into the Union she sent Benton to the United States Senate, where he was an important figure for thirty years and was to see much more of Andrew Jackson. The latter came to Washington as Senator from Tennessee in 1823, preparatory to making his first attempt to gain the Presidency of the United States. Defeated in this by the machinations of Henry Clay, he won out in 1828. Benton and Jackson were reconciled, though Clay endeavored to make mischief between them. In 1832, during the course of a debate, Benton having by this time become Jackson's chief supporter in the Senate, Clay charged Benton with having said that if Jackson became President, "We should be obliged to legislate with pistols and dirks by our side."

This Benton vehemently denied as a campaign canard circulated in Missouri, of which no proof had ever been produced. He declared it to be "an atrocious calumny," adding this threat, "And I will pin it to him who repeats it here."

"Then," retorted Clay, "I declare before the Senate that you said to me the very words—"

His further remarks were drowned in loud shouts from Benton, of which "false, false, false!" were the refrain. No fighting followed. Clay had made sneering remarks about the Jackson-Benton fight, implying that Benton was not all that he should be in now defending Jackson, for things he had previously said and done. To this Benton responded: "It is true, sir, that I had an affray with General Jackson, and that I did complain of his conduct. We fought, sir, and I hope we fought like men. When the explosion was over there remained no ill will on either side. No vituperation or system of petty persecution was kept up between us. . . All difficulty between us ended with the conflict; and a few months after it I believe that either party would cheerfully have relieved the other from any peril; and now we shake hands and are friendly when we meet."

During Jackson's stormy eight years in office Benton stood by him and at his death was one of his warmest eulogists. Jesse Benton, however, was unforgiving.

The scar across his buttocks could not be easily effaced. He found much fault with Thomas for his reconciliation with the General, toward whom he maintained his attitude of hostility, but being a person of small account, his ebullitions were passed over. Jackson, with all his faults, had become too great for pinpricks to penetrate. Probably, too, he was ashamed of himself. He had ample reason to be.

Besides sojourning thirty years—five full terms—in the United States Senate, from 1830 to 1850, and earning the sobriquet of "Old Bullion," Thomas H. Benton enjoyed the posthumous felicity of having his biography written by Theodore Roosevelt, as well as of having John C. Fremont for a pretty lively son-in-law.

Some apologists for Benton in the Lucas affair have sought to prove that he was a victim of a local conspiracy to drive him out of town, where his pompous presence excited much ire among members of the bar. Besides, their encounter in court was a good starting point for trouble in those touchy times.

CHAPTER XI

JAMES BARRON *vs.* STEPHEN DECATUR

A N evil fortune seemed to attend the footsteps of
James Barron; but despite it, he eventually became senior commodore of the United States
Navy and its titular head, though he had long been
looked upon as one who had brought dishonor upon its
flag, and whose hands were stained with the blood of its
greatest hero.

The encyclopedias are dark about the date of Barron's birth, fixing it sometime in 1768. He came, however, of a family distinguished in the annals of the
Navy. His father, James Barron, Sr., was commodore
of the navy maintained by Virginia during the Revolution. His uncle, Richard Barron, was one of its
captains. Another uncle, William Barron, was killed
by the bursting of a gun on board the frigate *Boston* in
1778. James Barron's brother, Samuel, was a commodore of distinction in the United States Navy, and a
nephew, Samuel C. Barron, served in the United States
Navy until he joined that of the Confederacy.

James Barron early became a victim of the strange
jealousies that develop so readily in the Army and
Navy. His first clash was with the celebrated John
Rodgers. Both young men were named as lieutenants
on the same day. Later, a like coincidence attended
their promotion to captaincies. Both won equal com-

mendation during the so-called French War from
Secretary of the Navy Benjamin Stoddert, who wrote
to President John Adams: "Lieutenant Rodgers, appointed First Lieutenant of the *Constitution* and now
commanding the *Insurgente,* is a brave man and a good
seaman. Lieutenant Barron . . . is represented by
Barry, and indeed by every officer of the Navy with
whom I have communicated on the subject, as one of
the best officers in the Navy."

When Jefferson essayed his policy of coast defense
by light gunboats, Barron and Rodgers supervised the
building of the first two vessels. Barron began naval
life under his father, as a lad in the Virginia navy. His
promotion into the regular service came when President John Adams discovered that the country needed
warships and a naval department. The Barbary
troubles found him in the Mediterranean in 1802, commanding the 36-gun frigate *New York.* The next year
he was transferred to the *Chesapeake,* with which his
name was to be so tragically associated. He was
ordered home soon to sail back again in command of
the famous *Essex,* and from this ship he began watch-
ing the movements of warships belonging to the
Emperor of Morocco. At this time he served under
Commodore Samuel Barron, his brother, still with the
Essex, in the early operations against Barbary. Here
his trouble with John Rodgers began. Rodgers had
backed the venturesome Connecticut schoolmaster,
William Eaton, in his land war on Tripoli. In this he
was not supported by the elder Barron, who abandoned
Eaton's enterprise. This attempt had ended in the
taking of Derna by a land march from Egypt over the

Libyan Desert, a very extraordinary enterprise for a pedagogue.

Samuel Barron was not well and he wished to give up supreme command. Rodgers stood next in line. According to Rodgers, Commodore Barron was deterred from resigning by his younger brother, who, Rodgers claimed, "used every means which his imagination could invent to induce the Commodore not to give up the command," all the while "assuring me with the gravity of a Judas that he had been endeavoring to prevail upon his brother to resign." However that may have been, Samuel Barron retired in favor of Rodgers on May 22, 1806, leaving his task to be finished by others. May 24, 1806, James Barron sailed in the *Essex* from Malta, bearing Tobias Lear—who had been George Washington's secretary—as a peace commissioner to Tripoli. They arrived at their destination on May 26. Terms were soon concluded. Barron next sat on the court convened to investigate the loss of the *Philadelphia*. This over, he was ordered by Rodgers to sail for home in the *President,* taking his brother Samuel with him. Rodgers liked Samuel Barron, but according to his biographer, C. O. Paullin, he acquired a "strong antipathy for Captain James," which was to have consequences later.

Barron neglected to leave at Gibraltar sundry documents anent the crew of the *President,* which Rodgers made a matter of complaint to the Secretary of the Navy. On reaching America, Barron retaliated and, according to Rodgers, circulated slanders injurious to his reputation. On July 24, 1806, when off Cape Henry, on his way home, Rodgers wrote what amounted to a

JAMES BARRON

challenge. Barron answered curtly that he was ill, but would reply as soon as he was physically able to deal with the consequences. Barron did not recover from his illness during the summer, and through this period the two men kept up an unsatisfactory correspondence. Friends meddled, but no meeting came. By word of mouth and paper the quarrel kept on during the fall and early winter. Finally, enough sense was developed to call the dispute off, Rodgers taking the initiative. He wrote to Commodore Thomas Tingey from Havre de Grace, Maryland, on January 3, 1807, "Impelled by an honorable motive, I have resolved not to push the affair between Captain Barron and myself further."

While this consideration headed off the duel, it did not end the enmity, nor bring peace to Barron, whose career was now to be darkened by a sinister and unfortunate event. The embers of the Revolution were not dead, and the presence of a vigorous American squadron in the Mediterranean, where it had quelled the corsairs, was not welcome in the eyes of our British cousins. There were frequent clashes between sailors ashore, and officers of the rival navies eyed each other malevolently when they met. Lieutenant William Bainbridge had killed the secretary of the British admiral at Gibraltar, as the outcome of a dispute involving the "honor" of the service. Stephen Decatur acted as his second.

John Jay's treaty with England had left several wrinkles unsmoothed, one of which was the right of search at sea, which the British construed to include vessels of war. Under the press-gang system their commanders were always seeking "deserters" or English seamen who preferred the liberty of America to hard lines for life on His Majesty's frigates. This practice kept up a constant friction. The habit of holding up American cruisers and commanding them to send a boat aboard,—a command often made insolently—was a frequent cause of resentment. When Commodore Edward Preble was *en route* for Tripoli in 1803 on board the *Constitution,* not yet celebrated, he was halted near Gibraltar by the presence of a ship of war which loomed up large one evening in the dusk. He silently moved his men to quarters and hailed the stranger with the usual, "What ship is that?"

The answer was a repetition of the same query. This occurred twice. Preble then took the trumpet in hand and roared: "I am now going to hail you for the last time. If a proper reply is not returned, I will fire a shot into you."

"If you fire a shot," came back the stern reply, "I will return a broadside."

Undaunted, Preble repeated his hail. The stranger thought better of it and replied, "This is His Majesty's ship *Donegal,* eighty-four guns, Sir Richard Strachan, an English commodore. Send your boat aboard!"

To this order Preble leaped upon the bulwarks and shouted back: "This is the United States ship *Constitution,* forty-four guns, Edward Preble, an American commodore, who will be damned before he sends a boat on board of any vessel!" Then he turned to the waiting gun captains with, "Blow your matches, boys!"

Soon a rattle of oars indicated the coming of a boat from the *Donegal.* It bore Lieutenant Maidstone with an apology. His ship had equivocated to gain time. They had been equally unaware of the nearby presence of a warship and were not prepared for the always possible trouble. So the incident ended. It is cited to show the touchiness of the times.

The embargo and the English command of the seas during the Napoleonic wars did not soften the temper of our seamen, who chafed under Jefferson's pacific policy, which kept warships rusting at the docks and forbade merchant vessels from adventuring during a profitable period. In this estate the incident of the *Chesapeake* and the *Leopard* came along to darken James Barron's career.

There was more background to this incident than customarily accompanied manifestations of jealousies between the rival navies. In the late spring of 1807, the British Minister at Washington called the attention of the Navy Department to the fact that three deserters from His Majesty's ship *Melampus* were being harbored on the United States frigate *Chesapeake,* then at Norfolk fitting out for sea. His claim was forwarded to Master Commandant Charles Gordon, in charge of the vessel, with the request that he investigate and report. This he did, to the effect that one deserter was found to be a native of the eastern shore of Virginia, the second a Negro, about whose Americanism there could be no dispute, while the third so stoutly defended his citizenship as to be sustained on his word. All three admitted their departure from the British services by desertion, but insisted that they had been impressed therein against their wills, which was no doubt true, as most of the seamen were then procured under the royal mandate. It was a cruel system, made necessary by the peril from France, though long in practice to a lesser degree.

Gordon reported the fact as stated, and His Excellency was informed that our Government would not surrender the three. Apparently, it was not dreamed that Great Britain would resort to any overt act in the matter.

James Barron now hoisted his broad pennant as Captain on the *Chesapeake,* and she went to sea on June 22, 1807. Her departure was hasty, and the ship in disorder. Tackles were out of place, spare spars and stores littered the decks, the crew had not been drilled for action, and on the whole she was a "mess," as sailors say. It was expected that she would be "tidied up" at sea. It was a matter of common knowledge that the British frigate *Leopard,* Captain Humphreys, was at anchor in the near-by harbor of Lynnhaven, but no one seemed to suspect that she was there with a nefarious purpose. The *Chesapeake* was bound for the Mediterranean, there to relieve the *Constitution,* and was proceeding easily out of the bay when the *Leopard* crossed her path. Humphreys hailed to the effect that he had dispatches which he wished to send abroad. As exchange courtesies of this sort were common, Barron lay to and awaited the coming of a boat from the *Leopard.* Instead of dispatches, the lieutenant in charge brought and served upon Captain Barron an order signed by Vice-Admiral George Berkeley, dated June 1, 1807, in which British commanders were instructed to hold up and search the *Chesapeake,* should she come their way. The object, of course, was to seize the three "deserters." In his mandate the Vice-Admiral graciously accorded American war vessels a similar right. The order and its concession were entirely his own. The British government had nothing to do with it, nor had Berkeley in any way advised the Minister at Washington of his intent.

Barron quite properly declined to recognize the demand, or to submit to a search. This he expressed in a formal note to Humphreys. Then he did his best to clear the disordered ship for action. Nothing was in readiness for conflict. Chargers were lacking for the cannon, cartridges unmade, rammers missing, and, in short, the ship was in a disgraceful state. The fault, however, was not Barron's but that of the authorities at the Norfolk navy yard and the Department at Washington.

When the boat of the *Leopard* reached her side and reported, Humphreys hailed Barron, who answered that he could not understand the call. The *Leopard* at once fired a shot across the *Chesapeake's* bow. This was followed by a broadside that wounded Barron, who stood in the gangway, and a number of the crew.

The ships were near each other in a tranquil sea. Barron had not a single gun in order with which to make reply. Broadside followed broadside from the *Leopard* for a quarter of an hour, the solid shot pounding into the *Chesapeake*. The wounded Barron implored his officers to enter some sign of defense by firing a gun. At this Lieutenant William Henry Allen, uncle of the distinguished William Allen Butler, who wrote "Nothing to Wear," took a live coal from the galley stove in his fingers and discharged a single shot that went through the hull of the *Leopard*. Then the *Chesapeake's* flag came down. Three of her men had been killed and eighteen wounded. Her hull had been pierced by twenty-one round shot, her masts were shattered, and her sails were in rags.

Barron demanded his right to surrender his ship, so constituting an act of war. Humphreys declined, but sent an armed force on board and mustered the crew, from whom he took the three men of the *Melampus*—William Ware, John Strachan, and Daniel Martin, the Negro. For full measure they also carried away Jenkin Ratford, enlisted as John Wilson, a deserter from the British sloop *Halifax*. The wreck of the *Chesapeake* was allowed to make its way as best it could back to Hampton Roads.

The unlucky Ratford, it appears, had been recognized on the streets of Norfolk by his former commander, Lord James Townshend, who sought to persuade him to return to his colors. This he rejected in such terms as to win the applause of the crowd that gathered. Taken to the *Halifax*, he was hanged at the yard arm as an example to his fellow tars. The deserters from the *Melampus* were sentenced to endure five hundred lashes—the equivalent to death. This wicked verdict was not carried out.

President Jefferson at once closed our harbors to British men-of-war and ordered them to depart from our coast. His Majesty's Cabinet disavowed Vice-Admiral Berkeley's order and sent two of the three deserters back to the *Chesapeake*, with some money in their pockets and an apology. One died before freedom came.

But for this action, promptly performed, the fury of America would have forced the country into war. As it eventuated, this was but postponed. Barron, however, was put on trial before a naval court-martial, which found him guilty of "neglecting, on the probability of an engagement, to clear his ship for action." The punishment decreed was suspension from rank and pay for five years, dating from February 8, 1808. The ship's gunner was dismissed from the service, and Master Commandant Gordon, who was really the guilty man, if any one person was, escaped with a private reprimand.

Berkeley was recalled from the American Station and given a better post. Despite the disavowal of his order, the searching of American vessels continued with exasperating frequency, but no American was ever caught napping again. His Majesty's ship, *Guerrière,* of which more was to be heard a little later, took a passenger named John Degayo off the brig *Spitfire, en route* from Portland, Maine, to New York. The *President,* Captain John Rodgers, was sent to sea at once in pursuit of the *Guerrière.* He did not find her, but on the night of May 16, he fell athwart a vessel of war that refused to answer a hail. Rodgers ordered a broadside, which brought back so feeble a fire that he desisted, feeling that this was not the ship he sought. When daylight came it was found that the *President* had seriously crippled the British twenty-two gun sloop, *Little Belt,* Captain the Honorable Arthur Butt Bingham. Eleven of her men were dead and twenty-one wounded. The *Little Belt* was still seaworthy and refused all aid. Rodgers declared he had not fired until fired into by a shot that struck his mainmast. Bingham

denied opening the engagement. The country hailed the
episode as avenging the *Chesapeake,* while Rodgers
had exalted himself above his luckless rival.

During the five years of his disgrace, Barron kept
moodily out of sight. His proud spirit had been outraged, and the hostility of his fellow officers grew
greater. He entered the merchant service, sailed to
South America, and spent much time abroad. When
his sentence expired in 1813, he stood next to Rodgers
on the Navy list, but owing to the prejudice against
him he was not called to command in the War of 1812.
During this time he remained in Europe, not returning
to his native land until 1818. He then asked to be restored to active service, and it was out of this that the
tragedy we have to record grew.

Contrasted with the luckless Barron, the career of
Stephen Decatur had been one of shining success. His
victories had placed his name highest in the annals of
the Navy, and his single defeat, the capture of the
United States under his command, by the British frigate *Endymion,* had, if anything, added to his fame.
His toast, "My country, may she ever be right; but
right or wrong, my country!" remains a text of patriotism. Handsome in feature and noble in form, he
was the beau ideal of a naval officer. His grandfather, a
toiler of the sea, had migrated from La Rochelle to
Newport, Rhode Island, in the middle of the eighteenth century. Here he married Miss Priscilla Hill,
who bore him a son, named Stephen, who became a
celebrated privateer captain during the Revolution,
and the father of the second of his name. The elder
Stephen, after the war, sailed merchant ships out of

Philadelphia, where he made his home and where his son came into the world.

He grew up a spirited and gallant youth, with an innate instinct for the sea that attracted the notice of Commodore John Barry. When the lad was eighteen, Captain Barry obtained a midshipman's warrant for him, dated April 30, 1798. He sailed first with Barry on the *United States,* on which ship also served James Barron, as junior lieutenant. The ship's rigging slacked under West Indian heat, and she bid fair to lose her masts, when Barron devised a means of setting up the shrouds, that saved her from wreckage. The unofficial war with France was on, and the *United States,* together with her consort, the *Delaware,* commanded by Decatur's father, captured several French privateers. Decatur now became a junior lieutenant, at the age of twenty.

On the heels of the French clash came the conflict with the Barbary corsairs, who had blackmailed the European powers for centuries and kept thousands of their people captive slaves. To these they had added numbers of Americans, besides exacting a handsome tribute from the far-away Republic. Determined to end this piracy, the American Government sent a stout squadron under Commodore Richard Dale, to bring the pirates of Tripoli to terms. Decatur went along as first lieutenant on the *Essex.* From this time on it is needless to repeat the record of his exploits. They remain immortal among the sagas of the sea.

Following the close of the War of 1812, Decatur became a member of the Board of Naval Commissioners, his colleagues being Commodores John Rodgers and David Porter. He made his residence in Washington and assiduously devoted himself to his duties. He was a popular idol and much besought to appear on public occasions. A toast to his personality at a Baltimore dinner summed up the popular attitude: "Commodore Decatur! The man whom his country delights to honor!" Baltimore emphasized this expression of good opinion with the gift of a splendid silver service. Philadelphia, his native city, not to be outdone, gave him another. A social engagement of a different order was fulfilled on October 10, 1818, when he acted as a second for Commodore Oliver Hazard Perry in a duel with Captain John Heath, of the Marine Corps. Perry faced Heath's fire unscathed and did not return it, after which Decatur announced that his principal had come to the ground determined not to do so. In proof he showed a letter to be used had the outcome been fatal to Perry. Heath expressed himself as satisfied.

At this time the request of Barron for reinstatement came up for consideration. It was opposed by all three of the Navy commissioners and became a burning topic in the Navy. Barron, located at Norfolk, was, of course, in touch with all that was going on. None but Commodore Richard Dale, who had been Paul Jones's lieutenant, and Jesse D. Elliott, who was something of a singed cat himself in naval circles—owing to his dispute with Oliver Hazard Perry as to their several parts in the Battle of Lake Erie—endorsed his claim. The other gentlemen of his rank all opposed it. The ruling reason for rejection seemed to be Barron's stay in Europe during the war. To this Barron replied that he did not have sufficient funds to pay his passage

STEPHEN DECATUR

home. This excuse does not make a strong appeal when made on behalf of a sailor.

While Decatur's opposition to Barron's restoration grew out of what he believed to be a sense of duty to his profession, curiously enough, it was his opinion that Barron was not out of status as an officer that brought on the duel. This reason, so meticulous as to be almost ridiculous, is found in the autobiography of Commodore Charles Morris, who says:

"When I was in Washington, on my way to join the ship for my late cruise, Commodore Decatur detained me at the commissioner's office till the other gentlemen had left it for the day, and showed me a letter which he had received from Commodore Barron, and requested me to act as his friend should it become necessary to meet Commodore Barron. This letter, in substance, called on him to state whether an alleged observation of his at a dinner table, that 'if Commodore Barron chose to challenge him he would accept it,' was intended as an invitation for a challenge or not. Decatur admitted that an expression of the kind had been used by him, but under circumstances which rendered it inoffensive if not rather favorable to Commodore Barron. The conversation had turned on the conduct of Commodore Barron, when the *Chesapeake* was attacked by the *Leopard,* in 1807, and in remaining out of the country during all the subsequent war with Great Britain. Very unfavorable opinions were expressed by some, and, among them, one that he had forfeited all claim to consideration or notice from the officers of the Navy. Decatur dissented from this on the ground that so long as he was recognized as an officer by the Government, he was entitled to consideration as such from others. The question was then put to Decatur, 'If Commodore Barron were to challenge you, would you consent to meet him?' To which he replied that he would, so long as he was considered by the Government worthy to hold his commission in the Navy.

"Although the necessity for an immediate obedience to orders placed it out of my power to comply with Commodore Decatur's request, if any delay was necessary, my opinion was given at once that a simple statement of the facts, given as an answer to Commodore Barron's letter, would effectually prevent any further proceedings. This he declined, because it might have the appearance, to some, of too earnest a wish on his part to avoid meeting Commodore Barron. The unreasonableness of this objection was urged, since his courage was established beyond all question, and his whole course in life placed him above any suspicion of the fear of consequences; that, so far from being injurious to his reputation, such a statement of facts would elevate it still higher, and that the improvement of so favorable an opportunity for setting a good example to the younger officers of the Navy was required from him by the highest consideration. A short answer was drawn up, embracing the facts as he had stated them; but notwithstanding all that could be urged, and his constant assertion that he had no desire to fight Commodore Barron, and that he could gain nothing and might lose his life by it, still all could not induce him to sign a statement which he admitted to be correct and which would probably remove all cause for any further action. He appeared to be governed by an apprehension that his reputation might suffer if he took any means to avoid a meeting with Commodore Barron, if Barron had any disposition to bring about one. Our conversation was continued till dark, and the most I could obtain from him was a promise not to answer the letter for three days, he having refused to wait for the advice of the person whom he might select to act as his friend if a challenge should be sent to him. The whole of the correspondence has been placed before the public and has left a general impression that the challenge was forced from Commodore Barron by the last letter from Commodore Decatur, though few are aware how easily and with what propriety on the part of Commodore Decatur it might have been prevented."

The correspondence in question was considerable. It began with the following note from Barron:

Hampton, Virginia, June 12th, 1819

SIR,—

I have been informed in Norfolk, that you have said that you could insult me with impunity, or words to that effect. If you have said so, you will, no doubt, avow it, and I shall expect to hear from you.

I am, Sir, your obedient servant,

JAMES BARRON

To this Decatur responded:

Washington, June 17th, 1819

SIR,—

I have received your communication of the 12th instant. Before you could have been entitled to the information you have

asked of me, you should have given up the name of your informer. That frankness which ought to characterize our profession required it. I shall not, however, refuse to answer you
on that account, but shall be as candid in my communication to
you, as your letter or the case will warrant.

Whatever I may have thought, or said, in the very frequent
and free conversations I have had respecting you and your conduct, I feel a thorough conviction that I never could have been
guilty of so much egotism as to say, that "I could insult you"
(or any other man) "with impunity."

I am, Sir, your obedient servant,
STEPHEN DECATUR

Barron replied:

Hampton, Virginia, June 25th, 1819

SIR,—

Your communication of the 17th instant, in answer to mine
of the 12th, I have received.

The circumstances that urged me to call on you for the information requested in my letter would, I presume, have instigated you, or any other person, to the same conduct that I
pursued. Several gentlemen in Norfolk, not your enemies, nor
actuated by any malicious motive, told me, that such a report
was in circulation, but could not now be traced to its origin.
I therefore concluded to appeal to you, supposing, under such
circumstances, that I could not outrage any rule of decorum or
candor. This, I trust, will be considered as a just motive for
the course I have pursued. Your declaration, if I understand it correctly, relieves my mind from the apprehension, that
you had so degraded my character, as I had been induced to
allege.

I am, Sir, your obedient servant,
JAMES BARRON

This note Decatur answered curtly:

Washington, June 29th, 1819

SIR,—

I have received your communication of the 25th, in answer to mine of the 17th; and as you have expressed yourself doubtfully, as to your correct understanding of my letter of the aforesaid date, I have now to state, and I request you to understand distinctly, that I meant no more than to disclaim the specific and particular expression, to which your inquiry was directed, to wit, that I had said that I could insult you with impunity. As to the motives of the "several gentlemen in Norfolk," your informants, or the rumors "which cannot be traced to their origin," on which their information was founded, or who they are, it is a matter of perfect indifference to me, as are also your motives in making such an inquiry upon such information.

Your obedient servant,

STEPHEN DECATUR

Barron replied to this in a lengthy statement of his side of his case, reading:

Hampton, October 23d, 1819

SIR,—

I had supposed that the measure of your ambition was nearly completed, and that your good fortune had rendered your reputation for acts of magnanimity too dear to be risked wantonly on occasions, that never can redound to the honor of him that would be great. I had also concluded that your rancor towards me was fully satisfied, by the cruel and unmerited sentence passed upon me by the court, of which you were a member, and, after an exile from my country, family, and friends, of nearly seven years, I had concluded that I should now be allowed, at least, to enjoy that solace with this society, that lacerated feelings like mine required, and that you would have suffered me to remain in quiet possession of those enjoyments. But scarcely had I set my foot on my native soil, ere I learned that the same malignant spirit, which had before influenced you to endeavor to ruin my reputation, was still at work, and that you were ungenerously traducing my character whenever an occasion occurred which suited your views, and, in many instances, not much to your credit as an officer, through the medium of our juniors. Such conduct cannot fail to produce an injurious effect on the discipline and subordination of the navy. A report of that sort, Sir, coming from the respectable and creditable sources it did, could not fail to arrest my attention, and to excite those feelings, which might naturally be expected to arise in the heart of every man, who professes to entertain principles of honor, and intends to act in conformity with them.

With such feelings, I addressed a letter to you, under date of the 12th of June last, which produced a correspondence between us, which, I have since been informed, you have endeavored to use to my further injury, by sending it to Norfolk, by a respectable officer of the navy, to be shown to some of my particular friends, with a view of alienating from me their attachment. I am also informed, that you have tauntingly and boastingly observed, that you would cheerfully meet me in the field, and hoped I would yet act like a man, or that you had used words to that effect.

Such conduct, Sir, on the part of any one, but especially one occupying the influential station under the government which you hold, towards an individual situated as I am, and oppressed as I have been, and that chiefly by your means, is unbecoming you as an officer and a gentleman, and shows a want of magnanimity, which, hostile as I have found you to be towards me, I had hoped, for your own reputation, you possessed. It calls loudly for redress at your hands. I consider you as having given the invitation, which I accept, and will prepare to meet you at such time and place, as our respective friends, hereafter to be named, shall designate. I also, under all the circumstances of the case, consider myself entitled to the choice of weapons, place, and distance; but, should a difference of opinion be entertained by our friends, I flatter myself, from your known personal courage, that you would disdain any unfair advantage, which your superiority in the use of the pistol, and the natural defect in my vision, increased by age, would give you. I will thank you not to put your name on the cover of your answer, as, I presume, you can have no disposition to give unnecessary pain to the females of my family.

I am, Sir, your obedient servant,

JAMES BARRON

To this Decatur replied at length, saying:

Washington, October 31st, 1819

SIR,—

Your letter of the 23d instant has been duly received. Prior to giving it that reply which I intend, its contents suggest the necessity of referring to our June correspondence.

On the 12th of June last, you addressed to me a note, inquiring whether I had said, that "I could insult you with impunity." On the 17th of June, I wrote to you, in reply, as follows: "Whatever I may have thought, or said, in the very frequent and free conversations I have said had respecting you and your conduct, I feel a thorough conviction, that I never could have been guilty of so much egotism, as to say that I could insult you, (or any other man,) with impunity."

On the 25th of June, you again wrote to me, and stated, that the report on which you had grounded your query of the 12th of June "could not now be traced to its origin," and your letter is concluded by the following words: "Your declaration, if I understand it correctly relieves my mind from the apprehension, that you had so degraded my character, as I had been induced to allege." Immediately on receiving your letter of the 25th of June, I wrote to you, on the 29th of June, as follows: "As you have expressed yourself doubtfully, as to your correct understanding of my letter of the 17th of June, I have now to state, I request you to understand distinctly, that I meant no more than to disclaim the specific and particular expressions, to which your inquiry was directed, to wit, that I had said that I could insult you with impunity." Here ended our June correspondence, and with it all kind of communication, till the date of your letter of the 23d instant, which I shall now proceed to notice.

Nearly four months having elapsed since the date of our last correspondence, your letter was unexpected to me, particularly as the terms used by you in the conclusion of your letter to me of the 25th of June, and your silence since receiving my letter of the 29th of June, indicated, as I thought, satisfaction on your part. But it seems that you consider yourself aggrieved by my sending our June correspondence to Norfolk, until three months had expired after your last communication, and not then until I had been informed, by a captain of the navy, that a female of your acquaintance had stated, that such a correspondence had taken place. If that correspondence has, in any degree, "alienated your friends from you," such effect is to be attributed to the correspondence itself. I thought the papers would speak of themselves, and sent them without written comment.

With respect to the court-martial upon you, for the affair of the *Chesapeake,* to which you have been pleased to refer, I shall not treat the officers, who composed that court, with so much disrespect, as to attempt a vindication of their proceedings. The chief magistrate of the country approved them; the nation approved them; and the sentence has been carried into effect. But, Sir, there is a part of my conduct, on that occasion, which it does not appear irrevelant to revive in your recollection. It is this: I was present at the court of inquiry upon you, and heard the evidence then adduced for and against you; thence I drew an opinion altogether unfavorable to you; and when I was called upon, by the Secretary of the Navy, to act as a member of the court-martial ordered for your trial, I begged to be excused the duty, on the ground of my having formed such an opinion. The honorable Secretary was pleased to insist on my serving. Still anxious to be relieved from this service, I did, prior to taking my seat as a member of the court, communicate to your able advocate, General Taylor, the opinion I had formed, and my correspondence with the navy department upon the subject, in order to afford you an opportunity, should you deem it expedient, to protest against my being a member, on the ground of my not only having formed, but expressed, an opinion unfavorable to you. You did not protest against my being a member. Duty constrained me, however unpleasant it was, to take my seat as a member. You, I find, are incapable of estimating the motives which guided my conduct in the transaction.

For my conduct, as a member of that court-martial, I do not consider myself as, in any way, accountable to you. But, Sir, you have thought fit to deduce, from your impressions of my conduct as a member of that court-martial, inferences of personal hostility towards you. Influenced by feelings thence arising, you commenced the June correspondence, a correspondence which I had hoped would have terminated our communications.

Between you and myself there never has been a personal difference; but I have entertained, and do still entertain, the opinion, that your conduct as an officer, since the affair of the *Chesapeake,* has been such as ought to forever bar your readmission into the service.

In my letter to you of the 17th of June, although I disavowed the particular expressions to which you invited my attention, candor required that I should apprize you, that I had not been silent respecting you. I informed you that I had had very frequent and free conversations respecting you and your conduct; and the words were underscored that they might not fail to attract your particular attention. Had you asked what those frequent and free conversations were, I should, with the same frankness, have told you; but, instead of making a demand of this kind, you reply to my letter of the 17th of June, "that my declaration, if correctly understood by you, relieved your mind," &c. That you might correctly understand what I did mean, I addressed you, as before observed, on the 29th of June, and endeavored, by underscoring certain precise terms, to convey to you my precise meaning. To this last letter I never received any reply.

Under these circumstances, I have judged it expedient, at this time, to state, as distinctly as may be in my power, the facts upon which I ground the unfavorable opinion which I entertain, and have expressed, of your conduct as an officer, since the court-martial upon you, while I disclaim all personal enmity towards you.

Some time after you had been suspended from the service, for your conduct in the affair of the *Chesapeake,* you proceeded, in a merchant brig, to Pernambuco; and by a communication from the late Captain Lewis, whose honor and veracity were never yet questioned, it appears, that you stated to Mr. Lyon, the British Consul at Pernambuco, with whom you lived, "that, if the *Chesapeake* had been prepared for action, you would not have resisted the attack of the *Leopard;* assigning as a reason, that you knew (as did also our government) there were deserters on board your ship; that the President of the United States knew there were deserters on board, and of the intention of the British to take them; and that the President caused you to go out in a defenseless state, for the express purpose of having your ship attacked and disgraced, and thus attain his favorite object of involving the United States in a war with Great Britain." For confirmation of this information, Captain Lewis refers to Mr. Thomas Goodwin, of Baltimore, the brother of Captain Ridgely, of the navy, who received it from Mr. Lyon himself. Reference was made to Mr. Goodwin, who, in an official communication, confirmed all that Captain Lewis had said. The veracity and respectability of Mr. Goodwin are also beyond question. You will be enabled to judge of the impression made upon Captain Lewis's mind by the following strong remarks he made on the subject. "I am now convinced that Barron is a traitor; for I can call by no other name a man, who would talk in this way to an Englishman, and an Englishman in office." These communications are now in the archives of the navy department.

If, Sir, the affair of the *Chesapeake* excited the indignant feelings of the nation towards Great Britain, and was, as every one admits, one of the principal causes which produced the late war, did it not behoove you to take an active part in the war, for your own sake, patriotism out of the question?

But, Sir, instead of finding you in the foremost ranks, on an occasion which so emphatically demanded your best exertions, it is said, and is credited, that you were, after the commencement of the war, to be found in command of a vessel sailing under British license! Though urged, by your friends, to avail yourself of some one of the opportunities, which were every day occurring, in privateers, or other fast sailing merchant vessels, sailing from France, and other places, to return to your country during the war, it is not known that you manifested a disposition to do so, excepting in the single instance of the cartel *John Adams,* in which vessel, you must have known, you could not be permitted to return, without violating her character as a cartel.

You say you have been oppressed. You know, Sir, that, by absenting yourself, as you did for years, from the country, without leave from the government, you subjected yourself to be stricken from the rolls. You know, also, that by the tenth article of the act for the better government of the navy, all persons in the navy holding intercourse with an enemy becomes subject to the severest punishment known to our laws. You have not for the offence before stated, to my knowledge, received even a reprimand; and I do know, that your pay, even during your absence, has been continued to you.

As to my having spoken of you injuriously to "junior officers," I have to remark, that such is the state of our service, that we have but few seniors. If I speak with officers at all, the probability is, it will be with a junior.

On your return to this country, your efforts to re-establish yourself in the service were known, and became a subject of conversation with officers, as well as others. In the many and free conversations I have had respecting you and your conduct, I have said, for the causes above enumerated, that, in my opinion, you ought not to be received again into the naval service; that there was not employment for all the officers, who had faithfully discharged their duty to their country in the hour of trial; and that it would be doing an act of injustice to employ you, to the exclusion of any one of them. In speaking thus, and in endeavoring to prevent your readmission, I conceive I was performing a duty I owe to the service, that I was contributing to the preservation of its respectability. Had you made no effort to be reemployed, after the war, it is more than probable I might not have spoken of you. If you continue your efforts, I shall certainly, from the same feelings of public duty, by which I have hitherto been actuated, be constrained to continue the expression of my opinions; and I can assure you, that, in the interchange of opinions I have never met with more than one, who did not entirely concur with me.

The objects of your communication of the 23d, as expressed by you, now claim my notice. You profess to consider me as having given you "an invitation." You say that you have been told, that I have "tauntingly and boastingly observed, that I would cheerfully meet you in the field, and hoped you would yet act like a man."

One would naturally have supposed, that, after having so recently been led into error by "rumors," which could not be traced, you would have received with some caution subsequent rumors; at all events, that you would have endeavored to trace them, before again venturing to act upon them as if they were true. Had you pursued this course, you would have discovered, that the latter rumors were as equally unfounded as the former.

I never invited you to the field; nor have I expressed a hope that you would call me out. I was informed by a gentleman with whom you had conferred upon the subject, that you left Norfolk for this place, some time before our June correspondence, with the intention of calling me out. I then stated to that gentleman, as I have to all others, with whom I have conversed upon the subject, that, if you made the call, I would meet you; but that, on all scores, I should be much better pleased to have nothing to do with you. I do not think that fighting duels, under any circumstances, can raise the reputation of any man, and have long since discovered, that it is not even an unerring criterion of personal courage. I should regret the necessity of fighting with any man; but, in my opinion, the man who makes arms his profession is not at liberty to decline an invitation from any person, who is not so far degraded, as to be beneath his notice. Having incautiously said I would meet you, I will not consider this to be your case, although many think so; and if I had not pledged myself, I might reconsider the case.

As to "weapons, place, and distance," if we are to meet, those points will, as is usual, be committed to the friend I may select on the occasion. As far, however, as it may be left to me, not having my particular prejudice in favor of any particular arm, distance, or mode, (but on the contrary disliking them all) I should not be found fastidious on those points, but should be rather disposed to yield you any little advantage of this kind. As to my skill in the use of the pistol, it exists more in your imagination, than in reality. For the last twenty years I have had but little practice, and the disparity in our ages, to which you have been pleased to refer, is, I believe, not more than five or six years. It would have been out of the common course of nature, if the vision of either of us had been improved by years.

From your manner of proceeding, it appears to me, that you have come to the determination to fight some one, and that you have selected me for that purpose; and I must take leave to observe, that your object would have been better attained, had you made this decision during our late war, when your fighting might have benefited your country, as well as yourself. The style of your communications, and the matter, did not deserve so dispassionate and historical a notice as I have given it; and had I believed it would receive no other inspection than yours, I should have spared myself the trouble. The course I adopted with our former correspondence, I shall pursue with this, if I shall deem it expedient.

I am, Sir, your obedient servant,

STEPHEN DECATUR

The news of the controversy got about and friends began to fear its consequences. The noble Decatur was getting in deeper all the time, while Barron, like Burr, was holding him to the point, which he could have readily evaded had he made clear the position outlined by Charles Morris.

This letter Decatur supplemented on November 5, with a small amende, having "been informed by a gentleman entitled to the fullest credit, that you were not afloat till after the peace; consequently, the report I noticed of your having sailed under the British license must be unfounded." Nothing further was heard from Barron until the 20th, when he pleaded "unavoidable interruption" for his failure to respond and promised a proper reply in a few days. It came in this form:

Hampton, November 30th, 1819

Sir,—

I did not receive until Tuesday, the 9th instant, your very lengthy, elaborate, and historical reply, without date, to my letter to you of the 23d ultimo; which, from its nature and object, did not, I conceive, require that you should have entered so much into detail, in defence of the hostile and unmanly course you have pursued towards me, since the "affair of the *Chesapeake,*" as you term it. A much more laconic answer would have served my purpose, which, for the present, is nothing more than to obtain at your hands honorable redress for the accumulated insults which you, Sir, in particular, above all my enemies have attempted to heap upon me, in every shape in which they could be offered. Your last voluminous letter is alone sufficient proof, if none other existed, of the rancorous disposition you entertain towards me, and the extent to which you have carried it. That letter I should not otherwise notice, than merely to inform you it had reached me, and that I am prepared to meet you in the field, upon anything like fair and equal grounds; but inasmuch as you have intimated that our correspondence is to go before the public, I feel it a duty I owe to myself, and to the world, to reply particularly to the many calumnious charges and aspersions, with which your "dispassionate and historical notice" of my communication so abundantly teems; wishing you, Sir, at the same time, "distinctly to understand," that it is not for you alone, or to justify myself in your estimation, that I take this course.

You have dwelt upon our "June correspondence," as you style it, and have made many quotations from it. I deem it unnecessary, however, to advert to it, further than to remark, that, although "nearly four months" did intervene between that correspondence and my letter of the 23d ultimo, my silence arose not from any misapprehension of the purport of your contumacious "underscored" remarks, nor from the malicious designs they indicated, nor from a tame disposition to yield quietly to

the operation, which either might have against me; but from
a tedious and painful indisposition, which confined me to my bed
the chief part of that period, as is well known to almost every
person here. I anticipated, however, from what I had found
you capable of doing to my injury, the use to which you would
endeavor to pervert that correspondence, and have not at all
been disappointed. So soon as I was well enough, and heard
of your machinations against me, I lost no time in addressing
to you my letter of the 23d ultimo; your reply to which I have
now more particularly to notice. I have not said, nor did I
mean to convey such an idea, nor will my letter bear the in-
terpretation, that your forwarding to Norfolk our "June correspondence" had, in any degree, "alienated my friends from
me," but that it was sent down there with that view.

It is a source of great consolation to me, Sir, to know, that
I have more friends, both in and out of the navy, than you are
aware of and that it is not in your power, great as you may
imagine your official influence to be, to deprive me of their
good opinion and affection. As to the reason which seems to
have promoted you to send that correspondence to Norfolk,
"that a female of my acquaintance had stated, that such a one
had taken place," I will only remark, that she did not derive
her information from me; that it has always been, and ever
will be, with me, a principle, to touch as delicately as possible
upon reports said to come from females, intended to affect injuriously the character of any one; and that, in a correspondence like the present, highly as I estimate the sex, I should
never think of introducing them as authority. Females, Sir,
having nothing, or ought to have nothing, to do in controver-
sies of this kind. In speaking of the court-martial which sat upon
my trial, I have cast no imputation or reflection upon the members, individually, who composed it, (saving yourself,) which
required that you should attempt a vindication of their proceedings, champion as you are, and hostile as some of them may

have been to me; nor does the language of my letter warrant any such inference.

I merely meant to point out to you, Sir, what you appear to have been incapable of perceiving, the indelicacy of your conduct, (to say the least of it,) in hunting me out as an object for malignant persecution, after having acted as one of my judges, and giving your voice in favor of a sentence against me, which, I cannot avoid repeating, was "cruel and unmerited." It is the privilege, Sir, of a man deeply injured as I have been by that decision, and conscious of his not deserving it, as I feel myself, to remonstrate against it; and I have taken the liberty to exercise that privilege.

You say, that "the proceedings of the court have been approved by the chief magistrate of our country, that the nation approved of them, and that the sentence has been carried into effect." It is true, the President of the United States did approve of that sentence, and that it was carried into effect; full and complete effect, which I should have supposed ought to have glutted the envious and vengeful disposition of your heart; but I deny that the nation has approved of that sentence, and, as an appeal appears likely to be made to them, I am willing to submit the question. The part you took on that occasion, it was totally unnecessary, I assure you, "to revive in my recollection"; it is indelibly imprinted on my mind, and can never, while I have life, be erased. You acknowledge you were present at the court of inquiry in my case, "heard the evidence for and against me, and had, therefore, formed and expressed an opinion unfavorable to me"; and yet your conscience was made of such pliable materials, that because the then "honorable Secretary was pleased to insist on your serving as a member of the court-martial, and because I did not protest against it," you conceive that "duty constrained you, however unpleasant, to take your seat as a member," although you were to act under the solemn sanction of an oath, to render me impartial justice, upon the very testimony which had been delivered in your hearing, before the court of inquiry, and from which you "drew an opinion altogether unfavorable to me."

How such conduct can be reconciled with the principles of common honor and justice, is to me inexplicable. Under such circumstances, no consideration, no power or authority on earth, could, or ought to have forced any liberal, high minded man to sit in a case, which he had prejudged; and, to retort upon you your seeing the glaring impropriety of your conduct, for which, although you do not conceive yourself in any way, accountable to me, I hope you will be able to account for it with your God and your conscience.

You say, between you and myself there never has been a personal difference, "and you disclaim all personal enmity towards me." If every step you have taken, every word you have uttered, and every line you have written in relation to me; if your own admission of the very frequent and free conversations you have had respecting me and my conduct, "since the affair of the *Chesapeake*," bear not the plainest stamp of personal hostility, I know not the meaning of such terms. Were you not under the influence of feelings of this sort, why not, in your official capacity, call me, or have me brought before a proper tribunal, to answer the charges you have preferred against me, and thereby give me a chance of defending myself? Why speak injuriously of me to junior officers, "which you do not deny"? Why the "many frequent and free conversations respecting me and my conduct," which you have taken so much pains to underscore? Why use the insulting expression, that you "entertained, and still do entertain, the opinion that my conduct, as an officer, since that affair, has been such, as ought forever to bar my readmission into the service"? and that, in endeavoring to prevent it, "you conceive you were performing a duty you owe to the service, and were contributing to its respectability"? Why the threat, that, if I continued the efforts you say I have been making to be "reëmployed," you "certainly should be constrained to continue the expressions of those opinions"?

Does not all this, together with the whole tenor and tendency of your letter, manifest the most marked personal animosity against me, which an honorable man, acting under a sense of public duty, by which you profess to "have been hitherto actuated," would disdain even to show, much more to feel?

I shall, now, Sir, take up the specific charges you have alleged against me, and shall notice them in the order in which they stand. The first is one of a very heinous character. It is that "I proceeded in a merchant brig to Pernambuco." Could I, Sir, during the period of my suspension, have gone any where in a national vessel? Could I, with what was due to my family, have remained idle? The sentence of the court deprived them of the principal means of subsistence. I was therefore compelled to resort to that description of employment with which I was best acquainted; and on this subject you should have been silent. But you add, that the late Captain Lewis, of the navy, who had it from Mr. Goodwin, who heard it from Mr. Lyon, the British Consul at Pernambuco, with whom you undertake to say I lived, represented me as stating, "that if the *Chesapeake* had been prepared for action, I would not have resisted the attack of the *Leopard;* assigning as a reason, that I knew, as also did our government, that there were deserters on board the *Chesapeake;* and that I said to Mr. Lyon, further, that the President of the United States knew there were deserters on board, and of the intention of the British ship to take them, and that the ship was ordered out, under these circumstances, with a view to bring about a contest, which might embroil the two nations in a war."

The whole of this, Sir, I pronounce to be a falsehood, a ridiculous, malicious, absurd, improbable falsehood, which can never be credited by any man that does not feel a disposition to impress on the opinion of the public that I am an idiot. That I should, two years after the affair of the *Chesapeake,* make such a declaration, when every proof that could be required of a contrary disposition on the part of the chief magistrate had been given, cannot receive credit from any one, but those that are disposed to consider me such a character as you would represent me to be. I did not live with Mr. Lyon, nor did I ever hold a conversation with him so indelicate as the one stated in Captain Lewis's letter would have been. And with what object could I have made such a communication? Mr. Lyon would naturally have felt contempt for a man, that would have suffered himself to have been made a tool of, in so disgraceful an affair. I found Mr. Lyon transacting business in Pernambuco. He produced to me a letter from Mr. Hill, the American Consul in that country, recommending him as entitled to the confidence of his countrymen, every one of whom, in that port, put their business into his hands. I did the same, and thus commenced our acquaintance. He was kind and friendly to me, but never in any respect indelicate, as would have been, in a high degree, such conversation between us.

Of Mr. Goodwin I know nothing. I have never seen him in all my life; nor do I conceive that his hearsay evidence can be of any kind of consequence against me. I was the first that informed the President and the Secretary of the Navy, that such a letter was in the department even before I had seen it. And again, if the mere oral testimony of a British agent was to be considered as evidence sufficient to arraign an American officer, I think the navy would be quickly in such a state, as it might be desirable for their nation to place it in. As to the impressions made upon the mind of Captain Lewis, from this information, and the "strong remarks" he made upon the subject, which you have thought proper to quote, they by no means establish the correctness of that information, but only go to show the effect it produced upon the mind of an individual, who seems to have imbibed a prejudice against me, not otherwise to be accounted for, except your acquaintance with him. He is now in his grave, and I am perfectly disposed there to let him rest. You must, however, have been hard pressed, indeed, to be compelled to resort to such filmsy grounds as those, a degree weaker than even second-handed testimony, to support your charges against me.

These communications, you observe, are now in the archives of the navy department. Of this fact, Sir, I had been long apprized; and had you, when searching the records of that department for documents to injure my character, looked a little further back, you would perhaps have found others calculated to produce a very different effect. Of my desire to return to the United States, during the late war, there are certificates in the navy department of the first respectability, which, if you had been disposed to find and quote, are perhaps lying on the same shelf from whence you took those that you appear so anxious to bring to public view; I mean my letter applying for service, as soon as an opportunity offered, after the term of my suspension expired; and one letter, above all, you should not have passed over unnoticed, that which you received from my hand, of May, 1803, addressed to the Secretary of the Navy, which was one of the principal causes of your obtaining the first command that you were ever honored with; and as you may have forgotten it, I will remind you, on this occasion, that, but little more than one month previous to the date of that letter, I, by my advice and arguments, saved you from resigning the service of your country in a pet, because you were removed from the first lieutenancy of the *New York* to that of second of the *Chesapeake*. But all this, and much more, is now forgotten by you; yet there are others that recollect those circumstances, and the history of your conduct to me will outlive you, let my fate be what it may.

The affair of the *Chesapeake* did certainly "excite," and ought to have excited, the indignant feelings of the nation towards Great Britain; but however it may have justified a declaration of war against that power, it was not, as you assert "every one admits," one of the principal causes of the late war. That did not take place, Sir, until five years after, when that affair had been amicably, and of course honorably, adjusted between the two nations. I mention this fact, not on account of its importance, but because you laid so much stress upon that "affair," as a reason why I ought to have returned home during the late war, and to show, that, although it did happen to be your fortunate lot to have an opportunity of being in the foremost rank on that occasion, of which you seem inclined to vaunt, you are ignorant even of the causes which led to it.

Having, in your letter of the 5th instant, abandoned the charge of my having sailed under "British license," after the commencement of the late war, in consequence of information received by you, from a gentleman entitled to the fullest credit, that I was not afloat until after the peace, consequently the report which you noticed, of my having sailed under British license, must be unfounded; I have only to remark, on this head, that, in advancing a charge against me of so serious a nature, and designed, and so well calculated as it was to affect materially my reputation, not only as an officer of the navy, but as a citizen of the United States, you should first have ascertained that it was founded on fact, and not on rumor, which you so much harp upon; and that, upon a proper investigation, you would have discovered your other accusations to be equally groundless.

For my not returning home during the late war, I do not hold myself, to use your own expressions, "in any way accountable to you," Sir. It would be for the Government, I should suppose, to take notice of my absence, if they deemed it reprehensible; and they, no doubt, would have done so, had not the circumstances of the case, in their estimation, justified it. That they are perfectly satisfied upon this point I have good reason to believe, and trust I shall be able to satisfy my country also. The President's personal conduct to me, and the memorial of the Virginia delegation in Congress to him, prove how I stand with those high characters, your opinion notwithstanding to the contrary. I deny, Sir, that I ever was "urged" by my friends, as you in mockery term them, to return home, during the late war; nor could it have been requisite for me to have been "urged" to do so by any one. Laying patriotism out of the question, as you observe, as well as the reasons why you think "it behooves me" to adopt that course, there were other incentives strong enough, God knows, to excite a desire on my part to return; and I should have returned, Sir, but for circumstances beyond my control, which it is not incumbent on me to explain to you.

Had the many opportunities really presented themselves, which you allege were "every day occurring," of which I might have availed myself to return to my country, in privateers or other fast sailing merchant vessels, from France and other places, but of which you produce no other proof than random assertion, on which most of your other charges rest? There were no such opportunities as you say were "every day occurring"; no, not one within my reach; and some considerable time after the news of the war arrived in Denmark, it was not believed that it would continue six months; but, if I had received the slightest intimation from the department, that I should have been employed on my return, I should have considered no sacrifice too great, no exertion within my power should have been omitted, to obtain so desirable an object, as any mark of my country's confidence would have been to me in such a moment. A gunboat, under my own orders, would not have been refused. But what hope had I, when my letter of application for service was not even honored by an answer? In regard to the *John Adams,* I do not deem it proper, on this occasion, to explain my reasons for making the attempt to return in that ship; but whenever I am called on by any person properly authorized to make the inquiry, I am confident that

I shall convince him, that I had good reason to believe that I should obtain a passage in her, notwithstanding your great knowledge on the occasion.

You say, by absenting myself, for years, from the country, without leave from the government, I "subjected myself to be stricken from the rolls." I knew also by the tenth article of the act for the better government of the navy, that all persons in the navy, holding intercourse with an enemy, became subject to the severest punishment known to the law; and that for these offences, as you are pleased to term them, "I have not received, to your knowledge, even a reprimand"; but I presume, if I have not, it is not your fault. What kind and humane forbearance is this, after what I have already endured! But, Sir, as you seem to be so very intelligent upon other points, pray tell me, where was the necessity of my asking for a furlough until the period of my suspension expired, or even after having reported myself for duty, without being noticed? As to the charge of my holding intercourse with the enemy, I am at a loss to conceive to what you allude, and should degrade myself by giving it any other reply, than to pronounce it, if you mean to insinuate there was any unlawful or improper communication on my part with the government or any individual of Great Britain, as a false and foul aspersion on my character, which no conduct or circumstance of my life, however it might be tortured by your malice or ingenuity, can, in any manner, justify or support.

You say, also, that you do know "that my pay, even during my absence, was continued to me." It is not the fact, Sir. I never, and until very recently since my return, received but half pay. This part of your letter I should not have regarded, were it not to show with what boldness, facility, and *sang froid,* you can make assertions unsustained by the shadow of truth; but if you had made yourself acquainted with the circumstances relative to my half pay, you would have found that not one cent of it was received by me. The Government was so good as to pay the amount to my unfortunate female family, whose kindest entertainment you have frequently enjoyed.

Poor, unfortunate children! whose ancestors, every man of them, did contribute every disposable shilling of their property, many of them their lives, and all of them their best exertions, to establish the independence of their country, should now be told that the small amount of my half pay was considered, by an officer of high rank, too much for them! You have been good enough to inform me, that, on my return to this country, my "efforts," as you have been pleased to call them, "to reinstate myself in the service, were known, and became a subject of conversation with officers, as well as others," and but for those "efforts," it is more than probable you would not have spoken of me.

This would, indeed, have displayed a wonderful degree of lenity and courtesy on your part, of which I could not have failed to be duly sensible. But, Sir, I beg leave to ask how, and where, did you get your information, that such "efforts" were made by me; and even admit they were, why should you alone, disclaiming, as you pretend to do, all "personal enmity" against me, have made yourself so particularly busy on the occasion? Was it because your inflated pride was greater than that of any other officer of the navy, or that you were more tenacious of its honor and "respectability," than the rest of the officers were? You assure me, however, "that, in the interchange of opinion with other officers respecting me, you have never met with more than one, who did not entirely concur with you in the opinion you have expressed of me." Indeed! and what is the reason? It is because, I suppose, you are most commonly attended by a train of dependents, who, to enjoy the sunshine of your favor, act as caterers for your vanity, and, revolving round you like satellites, borrow their chief consequence from the countenance you may condescend to bestow upon them.

You, at length, arrive at the main point; the object of my letter of the 23d ultimo, which you might have reached by a much shorter route, and have saved me the fatigue of being compelled, in self-defence, to travel with you so far as you have gone. The language of defiance, represented to have been used by you, "that you would cheerfully meet me in the field, and hoped I would yet act like a man," is disavowed by you. And you further deny having ever invited me to the field, or expressed a hope I would call you out; but you observe that, "being informed by a gentleman with whom I had conferred upon the subject, that I left Norfolk, for the seat of government, some time before our June correspondence, with the intention of calling you out, you stated to that gentleman, as you have to all others with whom you have conversed upon the subject, that if I made the call, you would meet me; but that, upon all scores, you would be much better pleased to have nothing to do with me."

I certainly do not exactly know who that intermeddling gentleman was, with whom you say I "conferred"; but if I may be allowed a conjecture, I think I can recognize in him the self-same officious gentleman, who, I am creditably informed, originated the report of your having made use of the gasconading expressions you have disowned. In this respect I may be mistaken. Be this, however, as it may, I never gave him, or any other person, to understand that my visit to Washington, last spring, was for the purpose of "calling you out"; nor did I go there with any such view.

How you can reconcile your affected indifference towards me, in the remark "that on all scores you would be much better pleased to have nothing to do with me," with the very active part, it is generally known, and which your own letter clearly evinces, you have taken against me, I am at a loss to conceive. No, Sir, you feel not so much unconcern as you pretend, and wish it to be believed you do, in regard to the course of conduct my honor and my injuries may, in my judgment, require me to pursue. You have a motive, not to be concealed from the world, for all you have done or said, or for any future endeavors you may make, to bar my "readmission" into the service. It is true that you have never given me a direct, formal, and written invitation to meet you in the field, such as one gentleman of honor ought to send to another. But if your own admissions, that you had "incautiously said you would meet me if I wished it," "and that if you had not pledged yourself, you might reconsider the subject," and all this, too, without any provocation on my part, or the most distant intimation from me that I had a desire to meet you, do not amount to a challenge, I cannot comprehend the object or import of such declarations, made, as they were, in the face of the world, and to those, in particular, whom you knew would not only communicate them to me, but give them circulation. Under all the circumstances of the case, I consider you as having thrown down the gauntlet, and I have no hesitation in accepting it. This is, however, a point which it will not be for me or you to decide; nor do I view it as of any other importance, than as respects the privileges allowed to the challenged party in relation to the choice of weapons, distance, &c., about which I feel not more "fastidious," I assure you, Sir, than you do; nor do I claim any advantage whatever, which I have no right to insist upon. Could I stoop so low as to solicit any, I know you too well to believe you would have any inclination to concede them. All I demand is, to be placed upon equal grounds with you; such as two honorable men may decide upon as just and proper.

Upon the subject of duelling I perfectly coincide with the opinions you have expressed. I consider it as a barbarous practice which ought to be exploded from civilized society. But, Sir, there may be causes of such extraordinary and aggravated insult and injury, received by an individual, as to render an appeal to arms, on his part, absolutely necessary. Mine I conceive to be a case of that description; and I feel myself constrained, by every tie that binds me to society, by all that can make life desirable to me, to resort to this mode of obtaining that redress due to me at your hands, as the only alternative which now seems to present itself for the preservation of my honor.

To conclude. You say, "From my manner of proceeding, it appears to you that I have come to the determination to fight some one, and that I have selected you for that purpose." To say nothing of the vanity you display, and the importance you seem to attach to yourself, in thus intimating that, being resolved to fight myself into favor, I could no otherwise do so than by fixing upon you, the very reverse of which you infer is the fact, I never wished to fight in this way; and had you permitted me to remain at rest, I should not have disturbed you; I should have pursued the "even tenor of my way," without regarding you at all. But this would not have suited your ambitious views. You have hunted me out; have persecuted me with all the power and influence of your office, and have declared your determination to drive me from the navy, if I should make any "efforts" to be employed; and for what purpose, or from what other motive than to obtain my rank, I know not. If my life will give it you, you shall have an opportunity of obtaining it. And now, Sir, I have only to add, that if you will make known your determination, and the name of your friend, I will give that of mine, in order to complete the necessary arrangements to a final close of this affair.

I can make no other apology for the apparent tardiness of this communication, than merely to state, that, being on very familiar terms with my family, out of tenderness to their feelings, I have written under great restraint.

I am, Sir, your obedient servant,
James Barron

Decatur did not reply for a month, writing fully, but concluding with what was a plain invitation to the field:

Washington, December 29th, 1819

Sir,—

Your communication of the 30th ultimo reached me as I was

on the eve of my departure for the north; whence I did not return until the 22d instant. It was my determination, on the receipt of your letter, not to notice it; but upon more mature reflection, I conceive, that as I have suffered myself to be drawn into this unprofitable discussion, I ought not to leave the false coloring and calumnies, which you have introduced into your letter, unanswered. You state that a much more laconic reply to your letter of the 23d of October would have served your purpose. Of this I have no doubt; and to have insured such an answer, you had only to make a laconic call. I had already informed you of the course I had felt myself bound to pursue respecting you, and of the reasons which induced my conduct, and that, if you require it, I would overcome my own disinclination, and fight you. Instead of calling me out for injuries, which you chose to insist that I have heaped upon you, you have thought fit to enter upon this war of words.

I reiterated to you, that I have not challenged, nor do I intend to challenge you. I do not consider it essential to my reputation that I should notice anything which may come from you, the more particularly, when you declare your sole object, in wishing to draw the challenge from me, is, that you may avail yourself of the advantages which rest with the challenged. It is evident that you think, or your friends for you, that a fight will help you; but, in fighting, you wish to incur the least possible risk. Now, Sir, not believing that a fight of this nature will raise me at all in public estimation, but may even have a contrary effect, I do not feel at all disposed to remove the difficulties that lie in our way. If we fight, it must be of your seeking; and you must take all the risk and all the inconvenience, which usually attend the challenger in such cases.

You deny having made the communication to the British Consul at Pernambuco, which Captain Lewis and Mr. Goodwin have represented. The man capable of making such a communication would not hesitate in denying it; and, until you can bring forward some testimony, other than your own, you ought not to expect that the testimony of those gentlemen will be discredited. As to the veracity of the British Consul, I can prove, if necessary, that you have yourself vouched for that.

You offer, as your excuse for not returning to your country, during our war with England, that you had not been invited home by the then secretary, notwithstanding you had written him, expressive of your wishes to be employed. You state, that, if you "had received the slightest intimation from the department, that you would have been employed on your return, you would have considered no sacrifice too great, no exertion within your power should have been omitted, to obtain so desirable an object." From this I would infer, that, in consequence of not receiving this intimation, you did not make the exertions in your power to return; and this I hold to be an insufficient excuse. You do not appear to have made any attempt, except by the way of the cartel, the *John Adams*. You cannot believe, that reporting yourself to the department, at the distance of four thousand miles, when the same conveyance which brought your letter would have brought yourself, will be received as evincing sufficient zeal to join the arms of your country; and, besides, you say it was not believed, for a considerable time after the news of war arrived in Denmark, that it would last six months.

With those impressions, you must have known, that it would have occupied at least that time for your letter to have arrived at the department, you to receive an answer, and then repair to America. You deny that the opportunities of returning were frequent. The custom house entries at Baltimore and New York alone, from the single port of Bourdeaux, will show nearly a hundred arrivals; and it is well known, that it required only a few days to perform the journey from Copenhagen to Bour-deaux, by the ordinary course or post. You deny having been advised to return to this country, by your friends, during the war. Mr. Cook, of Norfolk, your relative, says he wrote to you to that effect; and Mr. Forbes, then our Consul at Copenhagen, who is now at this place, says he urged you in person to do so.

You have charged the officers, who concur with me in opinion respecting your claims to service, as being my satellites. I think I am not mistaken, when I inform you, that all the officers of our grade, your superiors as well as inferiors, with the exception of one, who is your junior, concur in the opinion, you ought not to be employed again, whilst the imputations, which now lie against you, remain; nor have they been less backward than myself in expressing their opinions.

Your charge of my wishing to obtain your rank will apply to all, who are your juniors, with as much force as to myself. You never have interfered with me in the service, and, at the risk of being esteemed by you a little vain, I must say, I do not think you ever will. Were I disposed to kill out of my way, as you have been pleased to insinuate, those who interfere with my advancement, there are others my superiors, whom I consider fairly barring my pretensions; and it would serve such purpose better to begin with them. You say, you were the means of obtaining me the first command I ever had in the service. I deny it. I feel that I owe my standing in the service to my own exertions only.

Your statement, that your advice prevented me from resigning on a former occasion, is equally unfounded. I have never, since my first admission into the navy, contemplated resigning; and instead of being ordered, as you state, from the first lieutenancy of the *New York* to the second of the *Chesapeake,* Commodore Chauncey, who was then flag captain, can testify, that I was solicited to remain as first lieutenant of the flagship; and I should have remained as such, had it not been for the demand which the government of Malta made for the delivery of the persons, who had been concerned in the affair of honor, which led to the death of a British officer. It was deemed necessary to send all the persons implicated in that affair out of the way; and I went home in the *Chesapeake* as a passenger.

You have been pleased to allude to my having received the hospitality of your family. The only time I recollect being at your house was on my arrival from the Mediterranean in the *Congress,* fourteen years past. You came on board, and dined with me, and invited the Tunisian Ambassador and myself to spend the evening with you at Hampton. I accepted your invitation. Your having now reminded me of it tends very much towards removing the weight of obligation I might otherwise have felt on this score.

You speak of the good conduct of your ancestors. As your own conduct is under discussion, and not theirs, I can not see how their former good character can serve at all your present purpose. Fortunately for our country, every man stands upon his own merit.

You state that the "Virginia delegation in Congress" had presented a memorial in your favor. I would infer from this, that all, or the greater part of the Virginia delegation, had interposed in your behalf. This, Sir, is not the fact. A few of them, I am informed, did take an interest in your case; but, being informed of the charges existing against you, of which they were before unapprized, they did not press further your claims. From the knowledge I have of the high-minded gentlemen that compose the Virginia delegation, if they would take the trouble to examine your case, I should, for my own part, be entirely satisfied to place the honor of the service upon their decision.

You offer, as your excuse for permitting four months to intervene between our June correspondence, (with which, from your letter, you appeared to be satisfied,) and your letter of the 23d of October, your indisposition. I am authorized in saying, that, for the greater part of the four months, you were out attending to your usual occupations.

Your offering your life to me would be quite affecting, and might (as you evidently intend) excite sympathy, if it were not ridiculous. It will not be lost sight of, that your jeopardizing your life depends upon yourself, and not upon me; and is done with a view of fighting your own character up. I have now to inform you, that I shall pay no further attention to any communication you may make to me, other than a direct call to the field.

> Your obedient servant,
> STEPHEN DECATUR

Barron's response was short:

> *Norfolk, January 16th, 1820*

SIR,—

Your letter of the 29th ultimo I have received. In it you say that you have now to inform me, that you shall pay no further attention to any communication that I may make to you, other than a direct call to the field; in answer to which, I have only to reply, that whenever you will consent to meet me on fair and equal grounds, that is, such as two honorable men may consider just and proper, you are at liberty to view this as that call. The whole tenor of your conduct to me justifies this course of proceeding on my part. As for your charges and remarks, I regard them not; particularly your sympathy. You know not such a feeling. I cannot be suspected of making the attempt to excite it.

> I am, Sir, yours, &c.
> JAMES BARRON

To this Decatur responded, on January 24, 1820, that he was "at a loss to know what your intention is. If you intend it as a challenge, I accept it, and refer you to my friend, Commodore Bainbridge, who is fully authorized by me to make any arrangement he pleases, as regards weapons, mode, or distance."

Decatur had asked John Rodgers to become his second in the affair. Rodgers had declined and sensibly advised his friend not to accept the challenge, as his reputation for courage did not require the endorsement of a duel. The foolish, gallant gentleman could not see it in that light, and took on Bainbridge, who proceeded accordingly.

Barron answered, on February 6, that an attack of bilious fever would delay his action, "but as soon as I am in a situation to write, you shall hear from me to the point." The formal challenge does not appear in the surviving correspondence, but Barron put his affairs in the hands of Jesse D. Elliott, who dealt thereafter with Bainbridge. To the latter Decatur laid down some stipulations. "The place we are to meet," he observed, "is entirely at our option. Their convenience will not be consulted. My preference to some point near this arises from the convenience of a man's lying wounded at a distance from his own house; and as both of us cannot be indulged in being near our homes, I should not like to yield to them on this point, unless you should find it inconvenient to come thus far. I leave you entirely the choice of weapons and distance, as also the time. I beg, however, unless it will inconvenience you very much, that Bladensburg, near the city of Washington, may be the point of meeting."

Bainbridge and Elliott got together at St. Mary's, on March 8, 1820, on board the frigate *Columbus,* which Bainbridge was fitting out. "It is agreed," they set down, "by the undersigned, as friends of Commodore Decatur and Commodore Barron, that the meeting shall take place at nine A. M., on the 22d instant, at Bladensburg, near the District of Columbia, and that the weapons shall be pistols; the distance, eight paces, or yards; that, previously to firing, the parties shall be directed to present, and shall not fire before the word 'one' is given, or after the word 'three'; and that the words, one, two, three, shall be given by Commodore Bainbridge."

In reporting their arrangement to Decatur, Bainbridge referred to it as "your unpleasant business with Commodore Barron," as indeed it was destined to be. He had, he said, prescribed the place, weapons, and distance. "Captain Elliott," he continued, "dwelt much upon Commodore Barron's defective sight; but that had no influence on my mind. . . . I observed to Captain Elliott, that I presumed Commodore Barron's sight had not failed since giving the challenge. Captain Elliott said Barron had not, and would not practice."

On the morning of March 22, 1820, agreeable to arrangement, Bainbridge and Samuel Hamilton, who had been selected as his associate, went to breakfast at Beale's Hotel, on Capitol Hill, Washington. They were joined there by Decatur, who ate with them. He had sat up late drawing up his will, which he sought to be witnessed. They then proceeded to Bladensburg by carriage, halting in a valley half a mile from Bladensburg village and there found Barron, Elliott, and John Latimer. The ground was paced by Bainbridge nearly North and South, crosswise with the sun. He then notified the duellists that he should give the word quickly: "Present. One, two, three," and that they may not, at their peril, fire before the word "one" or after "three."

Barron asked Bainbridge if he would informally repeat the words as he intended to give them. This he did. Bainbridge won the choice of positions, so Decatur took the North ground, that being a little lower. As they parted to take their positions, Barron expressed the hope to Decatur that "on meeting in another world, they would be better friends than in this."

Decatur answered: "I have never been your enemy, sir."

They fired so closely at the word "two" that but one report was heard. Both fell, Barron wounded in the thigh and Decatur through the abdomen. "I am mortally wounded," said the latter to his attending friends; "at least, I believe so, and wish that I had fallen in defense of my country."

Despite his refusal to act as a second, John Rodgers appears to have witnessed the affray. "In about five minutes after the affair," Barron wrote Commodore Richard Dale, "Commodore R. rode up and hung his horse about fifteen feet from me and stood and looked me full in the face for seven or eight seconds, then passed by me and went to Commodore Decatur; and made kind inquiries and gave such assistance as was there necessary. After which, he came back to me, and in a tone of voice that irritated me extremely, said, 'Are you much hurt?' I answered: 'The last time I saw you I touched my hat to you; you did not return the compliment, and you must apologize for that, before any question of yours will receive an answer from me.' Commodore Porter interferred and here ended the conversation."

Barron also told Dale: "I have been informed that he (Decatur) was advised not to push the affair to extremities. There have been some cruel, meddling men engaged in this affair for a long time past."

Decatur was carried at once to his home in Lafayette Square, Washington. Here he died twelve hours later, to the great grief of the nation, which continued to keep Barron on its black books, but did not deny him his rank in the service.

Barron's name stood next on the naval list to that of John Rodgers until 1838, when the latter died, and Barron, by the rule of fate, became senior commodore of the navy. He never saw serious service, spending his time in charge of various navy yards, and the Naval Asylum at Philadelphia. Yet he survived nearly all his old comrades, though reconciled to but few. One of these was Charles Morris. The handshake was brought about at Norfolk by Captain David Glasgow Farragut. Soon after Barron died at this station, April 21, 1851.

Decatur fell at the age of forty-one, having been born January 5, 1779. His biographer, Alexander Slidell Mackenzie, thus describes his person: "The erectness of his figure, adding to the appearance of his height, harmonized with the towering arrangement of his head, which, inclining upwards, gave him a spirited and noble air, and contributed to the graceful stateliness of his carriage. His hair and beard were black and curling, his brow lofty and calm, terminating in dark and well-arched brows; his eyes large; black, and lustrous, habitually soft and gentle in their expression, but of piercing brightness in moments of excitement. They had that rare brilliancy, which is recorded as having given such an air of majesty to the Macedonian

Alexander and Pompey, the Great. His nose, rather large than small, was slightly aquiline, on the Grecian, more than the Roman model; mouth of moderate size and elegantly curved. The expression of his countenance, when in repose, was calm, contemplative, and benignant; in conversation, complaisant and persuasive; in scenes of excitement, spirited, stirring, and commanding."

CHAPTER XII

Henry Clay *vs.* John Randolph

IN 1825, at the instance of the Liberator, Simon Bolivar, the Latin American Republics, then young and yet under the ban of Spain, called a Congress to meet at Panama the next year to consider their relationships with each other in their common interest. It is possible that the Liberator conceived some notion of a union of republics against the monarchies of Europe. President Monroe had already proclaimed his celebrated Doctrine, but John Quincy Adams had become President, thanks to a combination with Henry Clay, whom he made his Secretary of State. After following Jefferson for two decades, Adams's New England Federalism broke out into extreme Nationalism and the Republicanism of Jefferson underwent a split, which developed into the Democracy of Andrew Jackson and the Whig Party of Adams, Webster, and Clay.

To this conference the United States was asked to send two ministers. Oddly, it was a little more than one hundred years after that a similar Congress, and the only one since 1826, met at Havana, to be attended by President Calvin Coolidge and an imposing retinue. Adams had alarmed the believers in States Rights by his Federal program. When he now added to this a proposition to coöperate with Mexico and South

America, the criticism was severe and found its chief voice in the Senate through the eccentric but able John Randolph of Roanoke, Virginia, a descendent in the sixth generation from Pocahontas, daughter of the Indian chief, Powhatan. Randolph had inherited but little of the mild qualities belonging to his amiable ancestress. Indeed, he had in his mentality much of the vengeful qualities of the red man, varied by occasional evidences of the maternal traits. He liked to torture Clay, who was easily goaded to fury, though one of the most generous of men and always an honorable antagonist. The invitation to the Congress had come through Señor Salazar, the Mexican Minister at Washington, with whom Clay was intimate. Then, as now, the terms under which the great republic would consent to deal with the lesser ones was a matter involving wide differences of opinion. Among Southern statesmen the presence of much colored blood had forbidden the recognition of Haiti, which had freed itself from Bonaparte and was ruled by a black emperor. There were many mixed complexions south of the Rio Grande, that made questions of equality delicate. No adjustment had been made—or for that matter ever was—when, on November 5, 1825, Clay wrote the several Latin-American ministers in Washington that to avoid delay, President Adams proposed to lay the problems before the Senate, which was soon to meet. In his message Adams informed the Congress that "the invitation has been accepted, and ministers on the part of the United States will be commanded to attend at these deliberations." He accordingly nominated Richard C. Anderson, of Kentucky, and John Sargent,

HENRY CLAY

From the painting by Samuel Morse

of Pennsylvania, to be "Envoys Extraordinary and Ministers Plenipotentiary to the Assembly of American Nations at Panama."

The Senate felt outraged that their "advice and consent" had not been called for in accepting the invitation. The President was asked for further information. He doled it out sparingly. On February 15, 1826, Martin Van Buren, Senator from New York, moved: "That upon the question whether the United States shall be represented in the Congress of Panama, the Senate ought to act with open doors; unless it shall appear that the publication of documents necessary to be referred to in debate will be prejudicial to existing negotiations."

He added a request to the President as to whether or not this would be the case. Randolph objected to the open doors. He held it to be the duty of the President to lay before the Senate the information upon which it was expected to act. If he did not, no more attention should be paid him. So far he was standing by Adams. The President, however, did not respond frankly, deeming it his "indispensable duty" to let the Senate decide the conditions under which it chose to perform. This Randolph regarded as an affront and took ground accordingly. He assailed the Administration in a bitter speech, the effect of which was to charge that Clay had concocted the invitations through Salazar, and that the surface evidence to that effect was "sufficiently presumptive" to "satisfy a Charlotte County jury" that the letters were manufactured under the same hand.

"I did maintain," said he, "the rights of the President; but from the moment he sent us this message, from that moment did my tone and manner to him change; from that moment I was an altered man, and, I am afraid, not altered for the better.

"Sir, if he would leave to the Senate the decision of the question, I would agree with him; but the evil genius of the American house of Stuart prevailed. He goes on to say that the question 'involves a departure, hitherto, so far as I am informed, without example, from that usage, and upon the motives for which, not being informed of them, I do not feel myself competent to decide.' If this had been presented for a libel, what jury would have failed to have found a verdict on such an innuendo—that we were breaking from our own usages to gratify personal spleen? I say nothing of them. The innuendo was that our motives were black and bad. That moment did I put, like Hannibal, my hand on the altar and swear eternal enmity against him and his, politically. From that moment I would do anything within the limits of the Constitution and the law; for, as Chatham said of Wilkes, 'I would not, in the person of the worst of men, violate those sanctions and privileges which are the safeguard of the rights and liberties of the best; but, within the limits of the Constitution and the law, if I don't carry on the war, whether in the Peninsula or anywhere else, it shall be for want of resources.'

"Who made him (the President) a judge of our usages?" he went on. "Who constituted him? He has been a Professor, I understand. I wish he had left off his pedagogue when he got into the Executive chair. Who made him the *censor morium* of this body? Will anyone answer this question? Yes, or no? Who? Name the person, above all, who made him the searcher of hearts and gave him the right by innuendo, black as hell, to blacken our motives? Blacken our motives! I did not use such strong language. I said, if he could borrow the eyes of Omniscience himself, and look into every bosom here; if he could look into that most awful, calamitous and tremendous of all possible gulfs, the naked, unveiled human heart, stripped of all its covering of self-love, exposed naked, to the eye of God —I said if he could do that, he was not, as President of the United States, entitled to pass upon our motives, although he saw and knew them to be bad. I said if he had converted us to the Catholic religion, and was our father confessor, and every man in this House at the foot-stool of the confessional had confessed a bad motive to him by the laws of his church, as by this Constitution, above the law and above the church, he, as President of the United States, could not pass on our motives, though we had told him with our own lips our motives, though we had told him bad. I said this then, and I say it now. Here I plant my foot; here I fling defiance right into his teeth before the American people; here I throw down the gauntlet to him and the bravest of his compeers, to come forward and defend these miserable lines: 'Involving a departure, hitherto, so far as I am informed, without example, from that usage, and upon the motives for which, not being informed of them, I do not feel myself competent to decide!' Amiable modesty! I wonder we did not at once fall in love with him, and agree *vive voce* to publish our proceedings, except myself, for I quitted the Senate ten minutes before the vote was taken. I saw what was to follow: I knew the thing would not be done at all, or would be done unanimously. Therefore, in spite of the remonstrances of friends, I went away, not fearing that any one would doubt what my vote would have been if I had staid. After twenty-six hours' exertions, it was time to give in. I was defeated, horse, foot, and dragoons—cut up and clean broke down by the coalition of Blifil and Black George—by the combination, unheard of until then, of the Puritan and the blackleg."

This invidious use of two chief characters in Fielding's *Tom Jones* made a decided uproar. Adams, of course, was the "Puritan" and Clay the "blackleg."

"Mr. Clay," wrote H. A. Garland, Randolph's biographer, "was not a man of such forbearance and Christian virtue as to permit a gross imputation on his motives to pass unnoticed. He was compelled to act. Randolph . . . had been the evil genius that from the beginning stood in the way of his aspirations." Accordingly, the Secretary of State determined to challenge his vindictive foe to mortal combat, selecting General Thomas S. Jesup, of the Regular Army, to bear his message.

Well versed in the customs under the Code, Jesup took pains to find out whether Randolph would hide behind his Senatorial prerogative. He was at once relieved of this anxiety. "Mr. Randolph replied," Jesup narrates, "that the Constitution did protect him, but he should never shield himself under such a subterfuge, as the pleading of his privilege as a Senator from Virginia; that he did hold himself accountable to Mr. Clay; but, he said, that gentleman had first two pledges to redeem; one that he had bound himself to fight any member of the House of Representatives, who should acknowledge himself the author of a certain publication in a Philadelphia paper; and the other, that he stood pledged to establish certain facts in regard to a great man whom he would not name; but, he added, he could receive no verbal message from Mr. Clay—that any message must be in writing."

At this point Jesup presented the challenge in its written form.

Jesup continues: "I remarked that I knew nothing of Mr. Clay's pledges; but if they existed as he (Mr. Randolph) understood them, and he was aware of them when he made the attack complained of, he could not avail himself of them—that by making the attack I thought he had waived them himself. He said he had not the remotest intention of taking advantage of the pledges referred to. That he had mentioned them merely to remind me that he was waiving his privilege not only as a Senator from Virginia, but as a private gentleman; that he was ready to respond to Mr. Clay and would be obliged to me if I would bear his note in reply; and that he would in the course of the day look out for a friend."

Jesup then declined to be bearer of the reply, partly for propriety's sake and partly because he thought the eccentric Randolph ought to consult his friends before concluding so important an engagement. Expressing this in words, Randolph seized his hand and exclaimed:

"You are right, Sir, I thank you for the suggestion; but as you do not take my note you must not be impatient if you should not hear from me today. I now think of only two friends, and there are circumstances connected with one of them which may deprive me of his services, and the other is in bad health—he was such yesterday and may not be out to-day."

Jesup promised patience and bowed himself out, recording: "It is due to his memory to say that his bearing was, throughout the interview, that of a high-toned, chivalrous gentleman of the Old South."

This was in the forenoon of Saturday, April 1, 1826. Let Thomas H. Benton now take up the tale:

"Towards noon, the Senate not being that day in session, Mr. Randolph came to my room at Brown's Hotel, and (without explaining the reason of the question) asked me if I was a blood relation of Mrs. Clay? I answered that I was, and he immediately replied that that put an end to a request he had wished to make of me, and then went on to tell me that he had just received a challenge from Mr. Clay, had accepted it, was going out, and would apply to Colonel Tatnall to be his second. Before leaving, he told me he would make my bosom the depository of a secret which he should impart to no other person; it was that he did not intend to fire at Mr. Clay. He told it to me because he wanted a witness to his intention, and did not mean to tell his second or anybody else; and enjoined inviolable secrecy until the duel was over."

Randolph's determination not to fire on his antagonist, Benton explains, "rested on two grounds; first an entire unwillingness to hurt Mr. Clay; and, next, a conviction that to return the fire would be to answer, and would be an implied acknowledgement of Mr. Clay's right to make him answer. This he would do, neither by implication nor in words. He denied the right of any person to question him out of the Senate for words spoken within it. He took a distinction between man and Senator. As Senator he had a Constitutional immunity, given for a wise purpose, and which he would neither surrender nor compromise; as an individual he was willing to give satisfaction for what was deemed an injury. He would receive but not return a fire. It was as much as to say, Mr. Clay may fire at me for what has offended him; I will not, by returning the fire, admit his right to do so. This was a subtle distinction, and that in case of life and death, and not very clear to the common intellect, but to Mr. Randolph both clear and convincing. His allusion to the 'two pledges unredeemed,' which he might have plead in bar to Mr. Clay's challenge and would not, was another sarcastic cut at Mr. Adams and Mr. Clay, while rendering satisfaction for cuts already given."

Benton explains that the member of the House alluded to was George Kremer, of Pennsylvania, who, at the time when the Presidential election was pending before that body, had admitted the authorship of the anonymous letter for which Clay had threatened to call him to account, but had not done so. The "great man" was no less person than John Quincy Adams himself, with whom Clay had carried on a controversy in the press, involving a question of fact. It had become more important for Clay to beat Jackson than to continue a dispute with Adams, so this had faded out of the situation. It was probably in Randolph's mind that if Clay could overlook these things, he need not bother about being called a blackleg.

Benton accounts for all of Randolph's sarcasm and the keen personality of the Panama speech by the fact that Clay had stirred up the newspapers to keep up a fire on "the Virginian, whose eccentricities afforded ample material." The Senator from Missouri being ineligible because of his relationship to Mrs. Clay, Mr. Randolph now selected Colonel Tatnall as his representative. With no further delay Colonel Tatnall conveyed this response to General Jesup:

Mr. Randolph accepts the challenge of Mr. Clay. At the same time he protests against the right of any Minister of the Executive Government of the United States to hold him responsible for words spoken in debate, as a Senator from Virginia, incrimination of such Minister, or the Administration under which he shall have taken office. Colonel Tatnall, of Georgia, the bearer of this letter, is authorized to arrange with General Jesup (the bearer of Mr. Clay's challenge) the terms of the meeting to which Mr. Randolph is invited by that note.

To accept a challenge to mortal combat under protest was a novelty and not without humor. "This protest," Benton continues, "led to an explanation between their mutual friends on that delicate point—a point which concerned the independence of debate, the privileges of the Senate, the immunity of a member and the sanctity of the Constitution. It was a point which Mr. Clay felt; and the explanation which was made between mutual friends presented an excuse, if not a justification for his proceeding. He had been informed that Mr. Randolph in his speech had avowed responsibility to Mr. Clay, and waived his privilege—a thing which, if it had been done, would have been a defiance, and stood for an invitation to Mr. Clay to send a challenge. Mr. Randolph, through Colonel Tatnall, disavowed that imputed avowal, and confined his waiver of privilege to the time of the delivery of the challenge, and in answer to an inquiry before it was delivered."

In formal reply, General Jesup wrote Colonel Tatnall:

> In regard to the protest with which Mr. Randolph's note concludes, it is due to Mr. Clay to say that he had been informed Mr. Randolph did and would hold himself responsible to him for any observations he might make in relation to him; and that I distinctly understood from Mr. Randolph before I delivered the note of Mr. Clay, that he waived his privilege as a Senator.

This was putting the question squarely up. Colonel Tatnall had to do some wriggling in his reply, which read:

> As this expression (did and would hold himself responsible, &c.) may be construed to mean that Mr. Randolph had given this intimation not only before called upon, but in such a manner as to throw out to Mr. Clay something like an invitation to make such a call, I have, on the part of Mr. Randolph, to disavow any disposition, when expressing his readiness to waive his privilege as a Senator from Virginia, to invite, in any case, a call upon him for personal satisfaction. The concluding paragraph of your note, I presume, is intended to show merely that you did not present a note, such as that of Mr. Clay to Mr. Randolph, until you had ascertained his willingness to waive his privilege as a Senator. This, I infer, as it was in your recollection that the expression of such a readiness on the part

of Mr. Randolph was in reply to an inquiry on that point made by yourself.

Although Jesup, in first calling upon Randolph, carried to him what purported to be his remarks involving a waiver of privilege as a Senator, Benton observes: "For my part I do not believe that Mr. Randolph used such language in his speech. I have no recollection of having heard it. The published report of the speech as taken down by the reporters and not revised by the speaker contains nothing of it. Such gasconade was foreign to Mr. Randolph's character. The occasion was not one in which those sort of defiances are thrown out, which are either to purchase a cheap reputation when it is known they will be disregarded or to get an advantage in extracting a challenge, when there is a design to kill. Mr. Randolph had none of these views with respect to Mr. Clay. He had no desire to fight him, or hurt him, or gain cheap character by appearing to bully him. He was above all that, and had settled accounts with him in his speech and wanted no more."

But Randolph had said in his speech: "Here I plant my foot; here I throw the gauntlet to him and the bravest of his compeers, to come forward and defend these lines." The term "Pickwickian" had not then been invented, so it was easy to twist this verbal defiance into a willingness to face a "compeer" on the field after the custom of the day.

Neither Jesup nor Tatnall wished their principals to fight and on one pretext or another delayed the meeting for a week, taking Benton into their confidence, with the idea that his influence might prevail. In fur-

ther correspondence Jesup stated his principal's griev-
ance thus:

The injury of which Mr. Clay complains consists in this,
that Mr. Randolph has charged him with having forged or
manufactured a paper connected with the Panama Mission;
also, that he has applied to him in debate the epithet "blackleg."
The explanation which I consider necessary is that Mr. Randolph declare that he had no intention of charging Mr. Clay,
either in his public or private capacity, with forging or falsify-
ing any paper, or misrepresenting any fact; and also that the
term "blackleg" was not meant to apply to him.

Tatnall responded:

Mr. Randolph informed me that the words used by him in
debate were as follows: "That I thought it would be in my
power to show evidence sufficiently presumptive to satisfy a
Charlotte County jury that this invitation was manufactured
here—that Salazar's letter struck me as bearing a strong like-
ness in point of style to the other papers. I did not undertake
to prove this, but expressed my suspicion that the fact was so. I
applied to the Administration the epithet, puritanic, diplomatic,
black-legged, and Mr. Randolph, in giving these words as those
uttered by him in debate, is unwilling to afford any explanation
as to their meaning and application."

Benton thought in this statement Randolph had gone
far enough. "The speech" he comments, "was a bitter
phillipic and intended to be so, taking for its point the
alleged coalition between Mr. Clay and Mr. Adams,
with respect to the election and their efforts to get up
a popular question contrary to our policy of non-
enlistment with foreign nations, in sending ministers to
the Congress of American States of Spanish origin at

the Isthmus of Panama. I heard it all, and, though sharp and cutting, I think it might have been heard, had he been present, without any manifestation of resentment, by Mr. Clay. The part he took so seriously to heart, that of having the Panama invitations manufactured in his office, was to my mind nothing more than attributing to him a diplomatic superiority which enabled him to obtain from the South American ministers the invitations that he wanted; and not at all that they were spurious fabrications. As to the expression blackleg and Puritan, it was merely a sarcasm to strike by antithesis, and which, being without foundation, might have been disregarded. I presented these views to the parties, and if they had come from Mr. Randolph, they might have been sufficient; but he was inexorable, and would not authorize a word to be said beyond what he had written."

This ended all efforts at adjustment and the seconds proceeded to arrange details. They settled upon the afternoon of Saturday, April 8, 1826, as the time for the encounter. Mr. Randolph insisted upon fighting in Virginia, that if he fell, it might be upon his native soil and in defense of its honor, while its earth would receive his blood. To all this solemn highfalutin preparation, Clay soberly agreed. A spot above the Little Falls bridge, on the right bank of the Potomac, was selected as the field. Randolph chose pistols as weapons. The distance was short—ten paces. Two seconds, a surgeon and Thomas H. Benton as a mutual friend, were to constitute the party. There was to be no preliminary pistol practice. "One, two, three, fire, stop," were the words to be used. The last was in case anyone delayed beyond "fire"; and, to give chance all the range possible, the numbers and "fire" were to be ejaculated rapidly.

Virginia had a law prohibiting duelling. This was pointed out to Randolph by Benton. Randolph replied that as Clay would be the only one to shoot, the statute could have no personal application to himself. Benton was much concerned. On Friday night, before the duel, he called on Clay. "There had been some alienation between us," he narrates, "since the time of the Presidential election in the House of Representatives, and I wished to give evidence that there was nothing personal in it. The family were in the parlor—company present —and some of it staid late. The youngest child, I believe, James, went to sleep on the sofa—a circumstance which availed me for a purpose the next day. Mrs. Clay was, as always since the death of her daughters, the picture of desolation, but calm, conversable, and without the slightest apparent consciousness of the impending event. When all were gone, and she also had left the parlor, I did what I came for and said to Mr. Clay, that, notwithstanding our late political differences, my personal feelings toward him were the same as formerly, and that, in whatever concerned his life or honor, my best wishes were with him. He expressed his gratification at the visit and the declaration and said it was what he would have expected of me. We parted at midnight."

While Benton was calling upon the Clays, Colonel James Hamilton, of North Carolina, visited Randolph. He found the descendant of Pocahontas calmly reading Milton's *Paradise Lost*. In greeting, Randolph remarked, "Hamilton, I have determined to receive without returning Clay's fire; nothing shall induce me to harm a hair of his head; I will not make his wife a widow or his children orphans. Their tears would be shed over his grave; but when the sod of Virginia rests on my bosom, there is not in this wide world one individual to pay this tribute upon mine."

Hamilton was much disturbed at this determination and wished, on being permitted, to inform Tatnall. This request was granted. He hurried off and at midnight returned with Tatnall, to find Randolph still reading *Paradise Lost*. Tatnall remonstrated. "I must say to you, my dear sir," was his comment, "if I am only to go out to see you shot down, you must find some other friend." Randolph was firm, and Hamilton begged Tatnall not to withdraw because of the bad impression that might result. Reluctantly, he consented to continue. "Well, Tatnall," said Randolph at this, "I promise you one thing. If I see the devil in Clay's eye and that with malice prepense he means to take my life, I may change my mind."

The hour set for the meeting was half-past four. Randolph lived in Georgetown, not far from the ground chosen for the conflict. Benton called upon him *en route,* with the idea of clinching Randolph's determination not to fire at Clay, knowing his erratic temperament. Not daring to put the direct question, instead, he related his call at the Clay home, pictured the little James asleep on the sofa, Mrs. Clay's unconscious calmness, and added: "I could not help reflecting how different all that might be the next night. He understood me perfectly, and immediately said, with a quietude of look and expression which seemed to rebuke an unworthy doubt: 'I shall not disturb the sleep of the child or the repose of the mother.' "

Randolph was making elaborate preparations for the worst. His seconds were in another room attending to some of his final wishes, which included adding codicils to his will in scattering remembrances. He sent his personal attendant to the local branch of the United States Bank for some gold coins. Johnny came back with the word that they had none. "Liars!" exclaimed Randolph, calling at the same time for his horse. When the animal arrived, followed by Johnny, he rode to the bank. Benton reports what followed:

"Mr. Randolph asked for the state of his account, was shown it, and found to be some four thousand dollars in his favor. He asked for it. The teller took up a package of bills, and civilly asked in what sized notes he would have it. 'I want money,' said Mr. Randolph, putting emphasis on the word; and at that time it required a bold man to intimate that the United States Bank notes were not money. The teller, beginning to understand him and willing to make sure, said inquiringly: 'You want silver?' 'I want my money,' was the reply. Then the teller, lifting boxes to the counter, said politely, 'Have you a cart, Mr. Randolph, to put it in?' 'That is my business, Sir,' said he. By that time the attention of the cashier, Mr. Richard Smith, was attracted to what was going on. He came up, and understanding the question and its cause, told Mr. Randolph there was a mistake in the answer given to his servant; that they had gold, and he should have what he wanted."

Mollified, the statesman took a pocketful of gold

pieces and a check for his balance on New York. Benton, who awaited his return, was then given a sealed paper, to be opened in the event of death, otherwise to be returned; further, a slip to be read before reaching the field. This carried a request to feel in Randolph's pocket and take therefrom nine gold pieces, three for himself, three for Tatnall, and three for Colonel Hamilton, the other second. This attended to, Randolph and his seconds proceeded to Virginia in a carriage, Benton following on horseback.

Randolph, having no intention of firing at Clay, was indifferent as to the method of giving word. Not so Clay. According to General Jesup: "When I repeated to Mr. Clay the 'word' in the manner in which it would be given, he expressed some apprehension that, as he was not accustomed to the use of the pistol, he might not be able to fire within the time, and for that reason alone desired that it might be prolonged. I mentioned to Colonel Tatnall the desire of Mr. Clay. He replied: 'If you insist upon it, the time must be prolonged, but I should very much regret it. I informed him I did not insist upon prolonging the time, and I was sure Mr. Clay would acquiesce. The original agreement was carried out."

Benton reached the rendezvous a little late and was called to the carriage by Randolph, who said: "Colonel, since I saw you, and since I have been in this carriage, I have heard something which may make me change my determination. (That is, not to fire at Clay.) Colonel Hamilton will give you a note, which will explain it."

Colonel Hamilton wrote afterwards of the coming

JOHN RANDOLPH OF ROANOKE

together: "I shall never forget the scene as long as I live. It has been my fortune to witness several duels, but I never saw one, at least in its sequel, so deeply affecting. The sun was just setting behind the hills of Randolph's own Virginia. Here were two of the most extraordinary men our country in its prodigality had produced, about to meet in mortal combat. Whilst Tatnall was loading Randolph's pistols, I approached my friend, I believed for the last time; I took his hand; there was not in its touch the quivering of one pulsation. He turned to me and said, 'Clay is calm, but not vindictive—I hold to my purpose, Hamilton, in any event, remember this."

The affair now proceeded. Benton and Randolph's faithful Johnny, who were the sole spectators, took their places on a knoll, from which they could see and hear all that transpired. The "field" was a little depression of open ground thickly shut in by trees. Clay saluted Randolph courteously, who returned in kind. Tatnall won the toss for position, which left it for Jesup to give the word. "They stood on a line East and West" relates Benton, "a small stump just behind Mr. Clay's; a low, gravelly bank rose just behind Mr. Randolph. The latter asked General Jesup to repeat the word as he would give it; and while in the act of doing so, and Mr. Randolph adjusting the butt of his pistol to his hand, the muzzle pointing downward and almost to the ground, it fired. Instantly, Mr. Randolph turned to Colonel Tatnall and said: 'I protested against that hair trigger.' Colonel Tatnall took the blame on himself for having sprung the hair.

"Mr. Clay had not then received his pistol. Senator

Josiah Johnson, of Louisana, one of his seconds, was carrying it to him and still several steps from him. This untimely fire, though clearly an accident, necessarily gave rise to some remarks, and a species of inquiry, which was conducted with the utmost delicacy, but which, in itself, was of a nature to be inexpressibly painful to a gentleman's feelings. Mr. Clay stopped it with the generous remark that the fire was clearly an accident; and it was so unanimously declared.

"Another pistol was immediately furnished; and an exchange of shots took place, and, happily, without effect upon the persons. Mr. Randolph's bullet struck the stump behind Mr. Clay, and Mr. Clay's knocked up the earth and gravel behind Mr. Randolph, and in a line with the level of his hips, both bullets having gone so true and close that it was a marvel how they missed."

Benton now thought it was time to intervene, feeling that all the honor involved in the affray was now satisfied. The effort was futile. "Mr. Clay said, with that wave of the hand with which he was accustomed to put away trifles, 'This is child's play,' and demanded another fire."

To this Mr. Randolph assented. While the seconds were recharging the weapons, Benton took Randolph aside and begged him "to yield some accommodation" but "found him more determined than I had ever seen him, and for the first time impatient and seemingly annoyed and dissatisfied at what I was doing."

There was reason for this. The accidental discharge of his pistol laid Randolph open to an unfair imputation, and this led him to fire at Clay; besides, as he told Benton during the interlude, he had been informed by Tatnall that it was proposed to prolong the giving of the word, to give better opportunity to take aim and raised the thought in his mind which he had observed in the note Benton was to receive from Hamilton, which read:

Information received from Colonel Tatnall since I got into the carriage may induce me to change my mind, of not returning Mr. Clay's fire. I seek not his death. I would not have his blood on my hands—it will not be upon my soul if shed in self-defense—for the world. He has determined, by the use of a long, preparatory course of words, to get time to kill me; may I not then disable him? Yes, if I please."

This was a misapprehension, as the previous request of Jesup shows, but had the effect of risking Clay's person at the first fire, though Randolph had not leveled above the knee, having in mind only to disable his opponent. "I would not," he said to Benton during their conversation, "have seen him fall mortally, or even doubtfully wounded, for all the land that is watered by the King of Floods and all his tributary streams." With this he went back to his post "utterly refusing to explain out of the Senate anything that he had said in it, and with the positive declaration that he would not return the next fire."

Benton decorously withdrew a little way in the woods and kept his eyes on Randolph, whom he then knew to be the only one in danger. When the word was given, Clay fired, his ball lodging in the gravel, as before, but perforating the skirt of Randolph's coat *en route.*

Randolph fired in the air and called out: "I do not fire at you, Mr. Clay!" At this he stepped forward and offered his hand. They met halfway and shook hands, Randolph remarking "jocosely," as Benton relates it, "You owe me a coat, Mr. Clay." "I am glad the debt is no greater," was the hearty response. Hamilton, however, reports: "The moment Mr. Clay saw that Mr. Randolph had thrown away his fire, with a gush of sensibility, he instantly approached Mr. Randolph, and said with an emotion I never can forget: "I trust in God, my dear Sir, you are untouched; after what has occurred, I would not have harmed you for a thousand worlds."

The ball had cut close to Randolph's thigh. He had a narrow escape from at least a serious wound. "The joy of all was extreme at the happy termination of this most critical affair," records Benton, who went with the Randolph party to supper at his residence. They found a messenger from the bank to say that in withdrawing his funds Randolph had been overpaid $150. The only satisfaction he got was: "I believe it is your rule not to correct mistakes, except at the time and at your counter."

To the company he remarked that he would adjust the difference on Monday. He then asked Benton for the sealed envelope. Opened, it contained a check to Benton's order for $1,000, with which, had Randolph been killed, he was to have him buried in Virginia "under his patrimonial oaks," specifically forbidding his interment in Washington. He prescribed that one hundred hacks should follow his body to the grave. The gold pieces were designed to turn into seals for their recipients. "Gentlemen," he said, "Clay's bad shooting shan't rob you of your seals. I am going to London and will have them made for you."

This promise was kept. He even went to the Herald's office and looked up the arms of the English Benton's, which he adorned those designed for that personage, appending a motto: *Factis non verbis,* though he afterwards would remark that *et* should have replaced *non.*

The windup was highly dignified. "On Monday," Benton writes in concluding his account, "the parties exchanged cards, and social relations were formally and courteously resumed. It was about the last high-toned duel I have witnessed, and among the highest-toned I have ever witnessed, and so happily conducted to a fortunate issue—a result due to the noble character of the seconds, as well as to the generous and heroic character of the principals. Certainly, duelling is bad, and has been put down, but not quite so bad as its substitute—revolvers, bowie-knives, blackguarding, and street assassination under the pretext of self-defense."

Randolph had been out before when an eighteen-year-old student at the College of William and Mary. He exchanged shots with Robert B. Taylor, of Norfolk, who was wounded. He also had an opportunity to meet Major-General James Wilkinson, had he so desired. Randolph was the foreman of the Grand Jury which indicted Aaron Burr and Comfort Tyler for treason at Richmond, in 1807. The General, who was at the time Governor of Louisana, had been summoned as a witness and appeared in the jury room adorned with the full paraphernalia of his rank, including side-arms. He was a big, vain, showy man. "Disarm James Wilkinson!" commanded Randolph to the United States Marshal in attendance. This was done, to the deep umbrage of the General, who had to endure some pointed questions from the distinguished foreman. On December 24, 1807, he wrote Randolph an insulting letter designed to provoke a challenge. Randolph replied that he knew of no reason why Burr would not have an equal right to call him out, concluding: "I cannot descend to your level." Wilkinson did a deal of blustering, but the matter went no farther.

Despite this particularity, Randolph, worsted in debate by Daniel Webster when both were serving in Congress during 1816, challenged the latter to mortal combat. Webster countered cleverly in his reply:

This demand for an explanation, you, in my judgment, as a matter of right, were not entitled to make on me; nor were the temper and style of your own reply to my objections to the sugar tax of a character to induce me to accord it as a matter of courtesy. Neither can I, under the circumstances of the case, recognize in you a right to call me to the field to answer what you are pleased to consider an insult to your feelings. It is unnecessary for me to state other and obvious considerations growing out of this case. It is enough that I do not feel myself bound, at all times and under any circumstances, to accept from any man, who shall choose to risk his own life, an invitation of this sort; although I shall always be prepared to repel in a suitable manner the aggression of any man who may presume upon such a refusal.

Having failed to keep a copy of this note, Webster later wrote Randolph, courteously requesting one. The Virginian sent it with expressions of high esteem.

CHAPTER XIII

WILLIAM J. GRAVES *vs.* JONATHAN CILLEY

ON February 21, 1838, Daniel Webster, senator from Massachusetts gave a dinner in Washington to a distinguished party of Whigs, among whom were fourteen guests from New York, including Philip Hone and Colonel James Watson Webb, editor of the New York *Courier and Enquirer,* the foremost organ of the Whigs in that day. Webb was a man of large stature and bullying manner, who had been one of Jackson's chief supporters, until his course was changed by the president's war on the United States Bank. Webb had been a borrower at that institution, as well as at other banks in New York. His associate editor was James Gordon Bennett, later founder of the New York *Herald,* who wrote leaders supporting Jackson, the effect of which was to turn the money-lending screws on Webb, who was compelled to abandon the President. His advertisers were mainly Whigs, and the *Courier and Enquirer* became their mouthpiece in the metropolis.

The Webster dinner was a very jolly affair and was supplemented the next day by another, which the visiting New Yorkers gave to the Whig delegation from their state. Hone presided. Henry Clay sat on his right and Daniel Webster on his left. In all, forty attended. Events of such social and political magnitude naturally excited interest. Colonel Webb shone on both occasions and was naturally much in evidence otherwise. His presence led to the duel of which this is the chronicle.

Mr. Hone recites in his diary: "Mr. Webb, the editor of the *Courier and Enquirer,* was attacked with great violence in the House of Representatives by Mr. Cilley, of Maine, who took part in the debate on the subject of the charge made by Mrs. Davis (author of *The Spy in Washington*) against Mr. Ruggles, of the Senate (John, from Maine) of corrupt and dishonest conduct in relation to a patent. Mr. Cilley, in debate, asserted that (Mrs.) Davis was employed by Webb, a scoundrel editor, who had been bribed by the president of the Bank of the United States, etc. Webb was of our party in Washington, and soon after his arrival, took measures, it appears, to obtain satisfaction. He applied to Mr. Curtis and Mr. Draper to bear his challenge, both of whom very properly refused. He then called upon Mr. Graves, of Kentucky, a very fine fellow, who has been with us almost constantly, and he, unfortunately, consented. He called upon Mr. Cilley, who refused to accept the challenge, on the ground that Webb was not a gentleman, and, moreover, he was not bound to account for words spoken in debate; upon which, Mr. Graves, according to the ridiculous code of honor which governs these gentlemen, insisted upon his fighting him, and after some negotiation it was agreed that they should fight this day (March 24, 1838). The first suspicion I had of what was going on arose from my meeting Webb in the passage at Gadsby's, about eleven

JONATHAN CILLEY

o'clock, when I told him I was going to take leave of Mr. Clay, who lives in the same house with Mr. Graves, on which he said that Mr. Clay, not knowing of the extra train of cars at noon, had gone to Baltimore early in the morning. I went, however, to their lodgings, inquired for Mr. Graves, and was told by a servant that he had gone to Baltimore, but on inquiry I found that Mr. Clay was at home, and went to his room, where I saw and took leave of him. This circumstance, together with the mysterious appearance of things at our lodgings, caused me to make inquiry, and I found that Graves and Cilley had gone out to fight with rifles at eighty yards distance, the former with Mr. Wise (Henry A., of Virginia) and the latter, with General George W. Jones, of Wisconsin, as seconds; both adepts in this damnable practice, who would carry things to the utmost extremity, and who are said to have gone armed for the purpose of shooting any person who might come upon the ground to prevent this most unnatural combat.

"The friends of Graves, who is a gallant and amiable gentleman," continues Hone, who wrote the foregoing in Baltimore, whither he went on the noon train, "who has his wife here and his children at home, are doing everything to prevent the meeting and bring about a reconciliation; and Webb is much distressed at being the cause of his engaging in this quarrel, which he had nothing to do with, and much reason, I think, he has. This unhappy affair has caused a gloom among our friends, and prevented the members of Congress from coming to the public dinner prepared for us in Baltimore. We came, however, (all but Webb), in the extra car, after twelve o'clock and arrived here at three. The party consisted of King, Blatchford, Firaud, Ward, Blunt, Hoxie, Patterson, Draper, Ketchum, and myself. The car on our arrival was surrounded by the populace, who expected to see Webster and Clay."

The dinner came off without the great men and gave Hone a chance to shine, which he apparently improved despite the shadow of gloom. Meanwhile, this was being justified by events. The letter borne to Cilley by Mr. Graves was as follows:

Gadsby's Hotel, Washington, Feb. 21, 1838

TO THE HON. JONATHAN CILLEY,—

Sir: In the Washington *Globe* of the 12th inst. you are reported as having said in the course of the debate which took place in the House of Representatives of that day, growing out of a publication in the New York *Courier and Enquirer:* "He (you) knew nothing about this Editor; but if it was the same editor who had once made grave charges against an institution of this country, and afterwards was said to have received facilities to the amount of $52,000 from the same institution, and gave it hearty support, he did not think his charges were entitled to much credit in an American Congress."

I deem it my duty to apprise you, Sir, that I am the editor of the paper in which the letter from "The Spy in Washington," charging a Member of Congress with corruption, was first published; and the object of this communication is to enquire of you whether I am the editor to whom you alluded, and if so, to ask the explanation which the character of your remarks renders necessary.

Very respectfully, your ob't serv't,

J. WATSON WEBB

The *Courier and Enquirer's* account of what next occurred ought to be authentic. It reads:

"Mr. Cilley, after taking the note in his hand and being apprised of its contents, declined receiving it, and, as an eye-witness of the transaction states, threw it somewhat contemptuously into the hat of Mr. Graves, which Mr. G. held in his hand. Mr. Graves again tendered it and said: 'If you do not receive this note from Mr. Webb, you will place me in an unpleasant predicament, and compel me to tender you one from myself.' Mr. Cilley replied that he hoped not— Mr. Graves said it would be unavoidable—whereupon Mr. Cilley asked for half an hour for consideration. At the expiration of this time Mr. Cilley said to Mr. Graves, 'I have determined not to receive the note of Colonel Webb, because I will not hold myself responsible to any conductor of a public press for words spoken in debate on this floor.'

"Mr. Graves answered: 'Then I am to understand that you do not place the rejection of Colonel Webb's note on the ground that you do not consider him a gentleman?' To which Mr. Cilley responded: 'Certainly not—I do not know Colonel Webb even by sight, and know nothing against his character as a gentleman.' Mr. Graves said that he believed this would be sufficient, but he would take a few moments to reflect upon it.

"Immediately after this conversation Mr. Graves addressed a letter to Mr. Cilley, recapitulating the substance of the conversation, and requesting him to reduce it to writing. Hereupon, a consultation took place between Mr. Cilley, Mr. Duncan of the House (Alexander Duncan of Ohio), Mr. Benton of the Senate (Thomas H., of Missouri), and several others—the result of which was a reply late in the evening, wherein Mr. Cilley refused to recognize as much of Mr. Graves's report of their conversation as related to Colonel Webb, and said he had neither admitted nor denied his claim to be considered a gentleman."

This was not considered satisfactory by the Kentuckian, who again made a demand on Cilley to put in writing the remarks which he made disclaiming any impeachment of Colonel Webb's character as a gentleman. Cilley consulted his friends anew and then replied "that he neither affirmed nor denied in regard to his (Webb's) character, but did not intend any disrespect to Mr. Graves." Upon this Graves asked peremptorily whether Mr. Cilley declined to receive Colonel Webb's communication "on the ground of any personal exceptions to him as a gentleman or a man of honor."

Mr. Cilley's answer was a refusal to admit the right of Mr. Graves to ask him such a question. Upon receipt of this reply Graves sent a challenge to Cilley by the hands of Henry A. Wise, then a member of Congress from Virginia and a fervent upholder of the Code. This was accepted by Cilley through George W. Jones, territorial delegate from Wisconsin. Where was Webb all this time? Mrs. Mathew L. Davis, his "Spy in Washington," sent off this hectic message that tells:

"Washington, 24th Feb. 1838
"To the Editor of the *Courier and Enquirer*:
"It is with great reluctance that I ever notice in my

letters the collisions or contests of gentlemen, but cases do occur which seem to be imperative in their character, and one has recently occurred which I cannot pass unnoticed.

"It is within your knowledge that Mr. Cilley, of Maine, on the floor of the House, made an attack upon Colonel J. W. Webb. That gentleman arrived here a few days since and through Mr. Graves of Kentucky, called upon Mr. Cilley, in courteous terms, for an explanation of his language. It is my wish to state the facts correctly, and if an error is committed it shall be promptly acknowledged.

"On Mr. Graves presenting the communication of Colonel Webb to Mr. Cilley, he demurred as to receiving it, but took time to consider. Shortly after, Mr. Cilley declined to receive it, and assumed the ground, in conversation with Mr. Graves, that he did not hold himself responsible for language used in debate, &c., that he intended no discourtesy to Mr. Graves, and as Mr. Graves understood him, made no objections to Mr. Webb's character or standing as a gentleman.

"On separating, Mr. Graves addressed a note to Mr. Cilley, requesting him to commit to writing the substance of their conversation, which as he understood it, he repeated in his note. Mr. Cilley replied, admitting all the points except that which refers to Colonel Webb's character or standing, which he neither *admits* nor *denies*. Mr. Graves considered this equivocal, if not impeaching his own statement of the conversation, as contained in his note to Mr. Cilley, and so writes him requesting further explanation.

"Mr. Cilley adheres to the course he had adopted,

and adds, that he cannot permit himself to be catechised on that point, whereupon Mr. Graves, through
Mr. Wise, demanded satisfaction, which demand Mr.
Cilley agreed to grant, and proposed to meet this day
with rifles, provided the distance of one hundred yards
is also acceptable. Mr. Graves joins issue; and the
parties went out this morning with their respective
friends to a place unknown to me, for the purpose of
terminating the affair with rifles.

"The facts, as they are given above, I believe to be
substantially correct, but it is possible that they may
vary in some unimportant point; and I fear that, because they are not derived from the parties in direct
controversy, but through a channel I consider correct.

"While I am writing I am interrupted by a gentleman entering my room, and informing me that the
body of Mr. Cilley had just been conveyed to his
lodgings; that he fell and expired immediately after,
on the third fire; and that Mr. Graves had returned
unhurt.

"The city has been filled with rumors respecting
Colonel Webb, arising no doubt, out of the fact that he
had determined to prevent the fight between Mr. Cilley
and Mr. Graves; but he was kept in ignorance as to
time and place; and had no suspicion that they would
meet to-day or for some days to come, until about ten
o'clock this morning, when accompanied by two friends,
each of them armed, he proceeded to Bladensburg, in
search of the hostile party with a fixed resolution that
Mr. Cilley should permit him to take the place of Mr.
Graves. In this decision his friends would have

sustained him at all hazards, regardless of consequences. Not finding the combatants, Mr. Webb returned to Washington, and having received information that they might be found in another direction,
with the same friends he renewed the attempt to discover the place of meeting; but this was alike unsuc-
cessful. Returning to the city they made a third attempt
with the like result, and, I think most fortunately, for
no man can tell what would have been the termination
of such a meeting, supported as Colonel Webb was by
two chivalric and resolute friends.

"The movements, however, during the morning,
produced rumors that Colonel Webb was himself em-
barked in the conflict. They were without foundation.
Colonel Webb has neither given nor received any
challenge, except in the case of Mr. Cilley, since he
arrived in Washington.

"The Spy in Washington"

Webb was, of course, seeking to save Graves from
possible death or injury. He was not expert with the
rifle; Cilley was. The doughty Colonel was not alone in
his search for the field of action. Henry Clay and John
J. Crittenden, learning of the proposed duel, started
to head it off, but were unable to locate the meeting
place. The Marshal of the District of Columbia, too,
armed with a warrant, joined in the search, but without
result.

Matters had been proceeding rapidly, despite some
delay caused by difficulty on Mr. Graves' part in
procuring a proper rifle. Jones, advised of this, sent a

rifle to Wise, together with powder and balls, along with a polite note, offering their use. They then proceeded to the ground selected.

In addition to General Jones, the Cilley party included Congressmen Jesse D. Bynum, of North Carolina, and Senator Alexander Duncan, of Ohio; also Col. H. W. Schaumborg, of the Dragoons. Henry A. Wise, Congressmen John Calhoun and Richard H. Menifee, of Kentucky, attended Graves. Dr. J. M. Folz was his surgeon.

It was exceedingly cold, and the wind blew almost a gale. For exact details, it is well to repeat the formal statement drawn up and signed by the two seconds, Wise and Jones. It reads:

"After the reception of this note from Mr. Jones, Mr. Wise called upon him at Dr. Reilley's, and informed Mr. Jones that Mr. Graves had procured a rifle other than that left at his room by Dr. Duncan, and would be ready for the meeting at 3 o'clock P. M. It was then agreed that the parties would meet at the Anacostia bridge, on the road to Marlboro, in Maryland between the hours of 1½ and 2½ o'clock P. M. and if either got there first, he should wait for the other; and that they would thence proceed out of the District. Accordingly, the parties met at the bridge, Mr. Cilley and his party arriving first, and all proceeding about 2 o'clock P. M. to the place of meeting. On arriving at the place, Mr. Jones and Mr. Wise immediately proceeded to mark off the ground. They then decided the choice of positions. Mr. Wise won the positions and Mr. Jones consequently had the

giving of the word. At the time Mr. Wise was informed by Mr. Jones that two gentlemen (Mr. Calhoun of Kentucky and Mr. Hawes of Kentucky) were
at some distance off, spectators, but they should not
approach the ground. Mr. Jones replied that he
objected to their coming on the ground, as it was
against the articles of the meeting, but he entertained
for them the highest respect. Mr. Wise also informed
Mr. Jones that, contrary to the terms he had brought
on the ground two rifles; that if he (Mr. Jones) requested him to do so, he would immediately send one
of them away. Upon Mr. Jones finding that the rifle
was unloaded, he consented that it should remain in
one of the carriages. There were, it is proper to remark, several persons on the ground (beside the hack
drivers, and the two gentlemen before mentioned at
a distance) who were there without the authority or
consent of either party or their friends, as far as it is
known to either Mr. Jones or Mr. Wise, and one of
these persons was supposed to be the owner of the
field. Shortly after the hour of 3 o'clock P. M. the
rifles were loaded in the presence of the seconds; the
parties were called together—they were fully instructed by Mr. Jones as to their positions and the
words twice repeated to them, as they would be and
as they were, delivered to them in exchange of shots.
After this they were ordered to their respective
positions, the seconds assumed their positions, and
the friends accompanying the seconds were disposed
of along the line of fire to observe that each obeyed the
terms of meeting. Mr. Jones gave the word distinctly

audible, and in regular succession, and the parties exchanged shots without violating in the least a single instruction. They both missed.

"After which Mr. Wise called upon the friends generally, to assemble and hear what was to be said. Upon the assembling of the friends, Mr. Jones inquired of Mr. Wise whether his friend, (Mr. Graves) was satisfied? Mr. Wise immediately said in substance, 'Mr. Jones, these gentlemen have met here without animosity towards each other; they are fighting merely upon a point of honor. Cannot Mr. Cilley assign some reason for not receiving at Mr. Graves' hands, Colonel Webb's communication, or make some disclaimer which will relieve Mr. Graves from his position?' Mr. Jones replied in substance, 'While the challenge is impending Mr. Cilley can make no explanations.' Mr. Wise said in substance, 'The exchange of shots suspends the challenge and the challenge is suspended for the purpose of explanation.' Mr. Jones thereupon said he would see Mr. Cilley, and did go to him. He returned and asked Mr. Wise again: 'Mr. Wise, do I understand aright that the challenge is suspended?' Mr. Wise answered: 'It is.' Mr. Jones was then about to proceed when Mr. Wise suggested it was best to give the explanation or reason in writing. Mr. Jones then said in substance: 'Mr. Wise, if you require me to put what I have to say in writing, I shall require you to put what you have said and may say, in writing.' Mr. Wise replied, 'Well, let us have the explanation beforehand, as it may not be necessary to put it in writing.'

"Mr. Jones then proceeded, as he now thinks, substantially to say 'I am authorized to say that, in declining to receive the note from Mr. Graves, purporting to be from Colonel Webb, he meant no disrespect to Mr. Graves, because he entertained for him then, as he now does, the highest respect and most kind feelings; but he declined the note because he chose not to be drawn into a controversy with Colonel Webb.' Mr. Wise thinks the answer of Mr. Jones was, in substance, as follows: 'I am authorized by my friend Mr. Cilley, to say that, in declining to receive the note from Mr. Graves, purporting to be from Colonel Webb, he meant no disrespect to Mr. Graves, because he entertained for him then, as he does now, the highest respect and most kind feelings; but my friend refused to disclaim disrespect for Colonel Webb, because he does not choose to be drawn into an expression of opinion as to him.' Such is the substantial difference now between the two seconds, as to the answer of Mr. Jones. The friends on each side, with the seconds, then retired from each other, to consult upon this explanation. After consultation Mr. Wise returned to Mr. Jones and said: 'Mr. Jones, this answer leaves Mr. Graves precisely in the position in which he stood when the challenge was sent.' Much conversation then ensued between the seconds and their friends, but no nearer approach to conciliation being made, the challenge was renewed and another shot was exchanged in a manner perfectly fair and honorable to all parties. After this the seconds and their friends again assembled, and the challenge was again withdrawn, and a very similar conversation to that after the first exchange of shots again ensued. Mr. Jones then remarked: 'Mr. Wise, my friend in coming to the ground, and exchanging shots with Mr. Graves, has shown the world that, in declining to receive the note of Col. Webb, he did not do so because he dreaded a controversy. He has shown himself a brave man, and disposed to render satisfaction to Mr. Graves. I do think that he has done so, and that the matter should end here.'

"To this Mr. Wise replied in substance: 'Mr. Jones, Mr. Cilley has already expressed his respect for Mr. Graves in the written correspondence, and Mr. Graves does not require of Mr. Cilley a certificate of character for Colonel Webb; he considers himself bound not only to preserve the respect due himself, but to defend the honor of his friend Colonel Webb.' These words of Mr. Wise, Mr. Jones recollects, and Mr. Wise thinks he added the words: 'Mr. Graves only insists that he has not borne the note of a man who is not a man of honor and not a gentleman.'

"After much more conversation, and ineffectual attempts to adjust the matter, the challenge was again renewed; and whilst the friends were again loading the rifles for the third exchange of shots, Mr. Jones and Mr. Wise walked apart, and each proposed to the other anxiously to settle the affair. Mr. Wise asked Mr. Jones, 'If Mr. Cilley could not assign the reason for declining to receive the note of Colonel Webb, that he (Mr. Cilley) did not hold himself accountable to Mr. Webb for words spoken in debate?' Mr. Jones replied that 'Mr. Cilley would not assign that reason, because he did not wish to be understood as expressing the opinion whether he was or was not accountable for words spoken in debate.'

"Mr. Wise then, according to his recollection, asked Mr. Jones whether Mr. Cilley would not say that, in declining to receive the note of Mr. Webb, he meant no disrespect to Mr. Graves either directly or indirectly. To which Mr. Jones replied affirmatively, adding: 'Mr. Cilley entertains the highest respect for Mr. Graves, but declined to receive the note, because he chose to be drawn into no controversy with Mr. Webb.' After further explanatory conversation, the parties then exchanged the third shot, fairly and honorably, as in every instance. Immediately previous to the last exchange of shot, Mr. Wise said to Mr. Jones: 'If this matter is not terminated with this shot and is not settled, I will propose to shorten the distance. 'To which Mr. Jones replied, 'After this shot without effect, I will entertain the proposition.'

"After Mr. Cilley fell, Mr. Wise, for Mr. Graves, expressed a desire to Mr. Jones, to see Mr. Cilley. Mr. Jones replied to Mr. Wise: 'My friend is dead,' and went over to Mr. Graves, and told him there was no objection to his request to see Mr. Cilley. When Mr. Jones approached Mr. Graves, and informed him that his request should be granted, Mr. Graves inquired: 'How is he?' The reply was, 'My friend is dead, Sir.'

"Mr. Graves then went to his carriage. Mr. Wise inquired of Mr. Jones, before leaving the ground, whether he could render any service, and tendered all the aid in his power. Mr. Wise and Mr. Jones concur that three shots were exchanged.

"Such is the naked statement of all the material facts and circumstances attending this unfortunate affair of honor, which we make in justice to our friends, to ourselves, to all concerned, to the living, and to the dead; and it is made for the only purpose of allaying excitement in the public mind, and to prevent any and all further controversy upon a subject which is already full enough of woe. We have fully and substantially stated wherein we agree and disagree. We cordially agree, at all events, in bearing unqualified testimony to the fair and honorable manner in which this duel was conducted. We have endeavored to discharge our duties according to the code under which the parties met, regulated by magnanimous principles and the laws of humanity. Neither of us has taken the least exception to the course of the other, and we sincerely hope that here all controversy whatever may cease. We especially desire our respective friends to make no publication on the subject. None can regret the termination of the affair more than ourselves, and we hope again that the last of it will be the signature of our names to this paper, which we now affix.

GEO. W. JONES
HENRY A. WISE

The outcry was immediate and poignant from the public standpoint. The Washington correspondent of the New York *Evening Post,* in describing the event to his paper, wrote: "Mr. Cilley of Maine was murdered this afternoon by Mr. Graves of Kentucky. The murder was committed according to the approved rules of the code of honor, but it was nevertheless a cold-blooded, deliberate murder. The miserable being who prompted it has escaped, in this, as in every 'affair of honor' in which he has been concerned, either through failure of his own valor, or from the contempt with which he has been regarded by gentlemen. He was the original challenger of Mr. Cilley, Mr. Graves being the bearer of the message. Mr. C. declined to fight on the same ground which other gentlemen have taken in reference to this contemptible person. You, of course, understand I allude to James Watson Webb, of your city."

The *Evening Post* said editorially: "He has fallen a victim to a false and bloody code in a wretched quarrel. The dispute was whether James Watson Webb was a gentleman and a man of honor. A citizen, a legislator surrounded with the love and respect of his friends, has fallen. The hands of his challenger are stained with his blood; yet will it be said that any new light has been thrown upon this controversy? Has Mr. Graves done anything to whiten the reputation of his friend? Has any infamy been washed away by the blood that has been shed? Has the load of contempt been lightened by the deductions that have been made from human life?"

Hone's diary, under date of February 25, 1838, deals further with the affair: "I heard early this morning of the fatal termination of this savage *rencontre*. Mr. Cilley was killed in the third fire. It was reported that Webb and Mr. Duncan, of Ohio, were to fight to-day, but it is contradicted by a letter which I received this evening from Charles King, of which the following is an extract: 'The fatal issue of the duel

yesterday has caused a deep sensation. There will not
be, however, in my opinion, any more fighting. Webb
is truly and deeply distressed. He will remain here till
Tuesday, rather so as to appear not to avoid any consequences, than because there are any consequences to
be apprehended. Graves is, of course, sobered and
saddened, though with the consciousness that he had
done all that could have been done to avoid fighting.
They fought about five o'clock, on the Annapolis road,
and fired three times, the third shot from Graves passing into the cavity of Mr. Cilley's stomach. He placed
his hand on the wound, made a convulsive movement
to his second, fell, and died without uttering a word.
"It is singular that Cilley who, in practicing the day
before, had shot eleven balls in succession into a space
not bigger than your hand, did not hit Graves at all.
So confident were Mr. Cilley's political friends that
Graves would be killed, that in the House, during the
day, there was, it is said, manifest exultation at the
idea. Some washerwoman or servant told Mr. Crittenden, in the hearing of Mrs. Graves, that Mr. Graves
had gone out to fight, and she had to pass five mortal
hours in all the agony of suspense. Mr. Clay, whom I
saw in bed this morning, told me he had an interview
with her, so fearful that it had absolutely kept him
awake all night, and made him so sick and nervous
this morning from the mere recollection of it, that he
cannot get up. The event of Mr. Cilley's death will be
announced to-morrow. The funeral will then take
place, and, of course, both Houses will adjourn. It is
not impossible that after the death is announced some
discussion may arise upon the manner of the death,

and some attempt be made to censure the practice generally, and perhaps in this particular case, even."

Despite outward appearances, the Whigs of the inner circle rejoiced at what to them was a Whig victory over the Jacksonians. There being no telegraph, the tidings spread slowly by mail. "The papers are filled with this painful subject," noted Hone, on March 10th. "Some of the vile supporters of the administration attempt to give it political bearing. These men, who have always supported Jackson and made him the standard of their religion, morals, and politics, are now loud in their condemnation of the practice of duelling, although the wooden god of their idolatry was known as one of the most notorious duellists in the United States, and even had a *rencontre* of the most savage and sanguinary character with another of their oracles, Mr. Benton, of the Senate. The Supreme Court of the United States, consistently with the dignity of its high station, put the seal of condemnation on the practice of duelling, by refusing to attend officially the funeral of Mr. Cilley, and declaring the determination of the court not to unite hereafter in the funeral obsequies of any person who shall have fallen in a duel."

There was an effort made to connect Clay with the duel. He was charged with having written the draft of the challenge sent by Graves and with saying, in response to the warning that Cilley knew how to use a rifle while Graves did not, "Graves is a Kentuckian and no Kentuckian can back out for a rifle." Sounds likely, but there is other evidence that Clay feared the consequences for Graves—not Cilley. He refused to be catechised on the subject and escaped odium. Not so Henry A. Wise.

On all sides, save that of the better Whigs, the affair was widely denounced. "The wretches who put up and perpetrated this tragedy are execrated by every honorable man" wrote the Washington correspondent of the New York *Journal of Commerce.* The reporter for the New York *Gazette* wrote "There is not an honorable man living, who knows all of the circumstances, that would not at this moment prefer the situation of Mr. Cilley, stiff and cold as he is, to that of his antagonist, and of his antagonist's seconds, who perpetrated his murder," He added: "A Southern gentleman of high rank, technically acquainted with duelling, told me just now, that he did not blame Webb for challenging Cilley, nor did he blame Graves; but, said he, in such a quarrel, the seconds who allowed a second fire, ought to be hanged for murder."

Horace Greeley wrote in the *New Yorker:* "Our caption of this account is 'Murder,' and murder we believe the whole affair to be—clear, unequivocal, downright murder. It can be softened down to nothing else. It was conducted in opposition to all the known laws of the duel, let the seconds call it as 'fair' and 'honorable' as they may. Mr. Graves's share seems to be hardly greater than the weapon he held in his hand. He could not, of course, after having given the challenge, refuse to do anything that the seconds determined upon. And it seems clear as light that the seconds, had they possessed the slightest inclination to do so, might have terminated the affair without any bloody issue. . . . We regard the whole affair, from beginning to ending, with the utmost detestation and abhorrence. Holding as we do duelling to be nothing better than authorized murder, we should have condemned the affair had it been instigated by enmity between the parties. We have here, however, a refinement of barbarity. Two persons, with the most friendly feeling towards one another, committed this great sin to satisfy a most ridiculous punctilio, which might have been adjusted had not their respective friends acted without the least show of reason or humanity."

At this time, Greeley was conducting, in the interest of the New York Whigs, a campaign sheet called, curiously enough, the *Jeffersonian*. In its columns he unburdened himself further to the following effect:

"The reader . . . can lay the blame where he chooses. We blame only the accursed spirit of false honor which required this bloody sacrifice—the horrid custom of duelling, which exacts and palliates this atrocity. It appears evident that Mr. Cilley's course must have been based on the determination that Colonel Webb was not entitled to be regarded as a gentleman; and, if so, there was hardly an escape from a bloody conclusion after Mr. Graves had once consented, however unconsciously, to bear the note of Colonel Webb. Each of the parties, doubtless, acted as he considered due his own character; each was right in the view of the duellist's code of honor, but fearfully wrong in the eye of reason, of morality, of humanity, and the imperative laws of man and God. Of the principals, one sleeps cold and stiff beneath the icy pall of winter and the clods of the valley; the other, far more to be pitied, lives to execrate through years of anguish and remorse the hour when he was impelled to imbue his hands in the blood of a fellow being.

"Mr. Graves we know personally, and a milder and more amiable gentleman is rarely to be met with. He has for the last two years been a representative from the Louisville district, Kentucky, and is universally esteemed and beloved. Mr. Cilley was a young man of one of the best families of New Hampshire; his grandfather was a colonel, and afterwards a general, in the Revolution. His brother was a captain in the last war with Great Britain, and a leader of the desperate bayonet charge at Bridgewater. Mr. Cilley himself, though quite a young man, has been for two years Speaker of the House of Representatives of Maine, and was last year elected to Congress from the Lincoln district, which is decidedly opposed to him in politics, and which recently gave a 1,200 majority for the other side. Young as he was, he had acquired a wide popularity and influence in his own State, and was laying the foundation of a brilliant career in the national councils. And this man with so many ties to bind him to life, with the sky of his future bright with hope, without an enemy on earth, and with a wife and three children of tender age, whom his death must drive to the verge of madness—has perished miserably in a combat forbidden by God, growing out of a difference so pitiful in itself, so direful in its consequences.

"Could we add anything to render the moral more terribly impressive?"

They brought Cilley's body back to his home in

Washington. "I have just returned from a horrid and harrowing spectacle," wrote the *Evening Post* correspondent. "Lying on the floor of his own room, wrapped in a blanket smeared with his blood, lay the ghastly corpse of Jonathan Cilley, one of the members of Congress from Maine, and in all respects one of the most promising public men in the House."

On the 26th of February, 1838, Senator Ruel Williams, of Maine, announced the outcome of the duel to the Senate, and Congressman John Fairfield, of the same state, informed the House of the demise of his colleague, without detailing the cause, predicting that his "sudden and deplorable death would produce a deep sensation in Maine . . . indeed, throughout the country," as it did. In hiding the cause, Fairfield bore out the remark of the correspondent of the New York *Journal of Commerce,* to wit: "But notwithstanding all the meanness, connivance, and atrocity that marked this affair, I do not believe there is a man in Congress who dares to announce the event in a proper manner."

The funeral was attended by President Van Buren and Vice-President Richard M. Johnson, together with the members of both Houses and the foreign ministers, and a great throng of citizens. The body was placed in a vault in the Congressional cemetery, to be transferred later to Thomaston, Maine, where it was buried on May 3, 1838.

If Mr. Fairfield did not recite the cause of Mr. Cilley's demise at the moment of announcing it, he made up for the lapse after the funeral by moving the appointment of a committee to investigate the duel and its cause. William Cust Johnson, of Maryland, in opposing the resolution, threatened the personal safety of any one who might presume to investigate an affair between gentlemen. The motion was passed, however, as was a resolution by Matthias Morris, of Pennsylvania, reading:

"*Resolved,* that the selected Committee this day ordered be instructed to enquire into the means more effectually to suppress the practice of duelling, and report a bill for this purpose as early as practicable."

This won by a vote of 107 to 68. James K. Polk, of Tennessee, afterwards President, who was Speaker, named seven members of the House for the task. They were Isaac Toucey, of Connecticut; A. D. W. Bruyn, of New York; George N. Briggs, of Massachusetts; F. H. Elmore, of South Carolina; James Rariden, of Indiana; Albert G. Harrison, of Missouri, and William W. Potter, of Pennsylvania. Briggs and Harrison asked to be excused because of other duties, and their places were filled by George Grinnell, Jr., of Massachusetts and Seaton Grantland, of Georgia. The committee reported on April 21, 1838, splitting into three opinions. The majority report was signed by Toucey, Potter, Bruyn, and Grantland; the minority by Rariden and Grinnell. Elmore made an independent statement. The majority report summed up as to Graves thus:

"The Committee . . . viewing the breach of the rights and privileges of the House on the part of Mr. Graves, to have been an offense of this high character against the vital principle of deliberative assembly and of representative government, feel constrained by a

sense of duty to present to the House a resolution that
he be expelled therefrom." They found Henry A.
Wise "deeply involved" and as "deserving the decided censure of the House." Jones was also sentenced to censure for his share in "the breach of
privilege."

James Watson Webb and two accessories (Major
William M. Morrell and Daniel Jackson) whose
names do not appear on the report were dismissed as
unworthy of further notice, and left "to the chastisement of the course of law and public opinion." The
latter was very much against the three men. The law
did nothing.

The disapproving Philip Hone wrote in his diary,
on May 4:

"To the disgrace of the administration party, instead of making this lamentable case the occasion of
correcting the popular code of morals in relation to
these personal encounters, and thereby removing as
far as practicable this stain of blood-guiltiness from
our land, they seized it with avidity, and endeavored
to turn it into part of their detestable party capital.
The Speaker appointed on the Committee of Seven, a
chairman and three other whole-hog men, political
enemies of Mr. Graves and his second in the duel, Mr.
Wise—fellows who would sell their souls for their
party, and have no more notion of political honesty
than they have of the refined feelings of gentlemen.
This committee has brought in a report, recommending that Mr. Graves be expelled and Mr. Wise
reprimanded by the House—the most outrageous proceeding I have ever known in a legislative body,—a

grand jury trying the accused, convicting them, and awarding their punishment; a greater violation, as Mr. Adams (John Quincy) told them, of the privileges of the House, than the offense itself, which the committee were appointed to investigate.

"This report has been before the House several days, and occasioned a warm debate. Some high-minded gentlemen of the Administration (Van Buren) party cannot be made to swallow it. Mr. Adams made a great speech, in which he placed the unworthy conduct of the majority in such a point of view as would have made them blush, if their instructions had permitted. On Monday last Mr. Graves and Mr. Wise both addressed the House, protesting against the unparliamentary course of proceedings, which would constitute four political adversaries their proper judges and condemn them unheard.

"Mr. Graves closed his speech with the following touching remarks, which, while they depict his sensibility and distress of mind for the part which he had taken in that unhappy affair, portray in glowing colors the absurdity of the tyranny which is exercised by public opinion over the minds and consciences of the people of this country in all things relating to affairs of honor, as we mostly unwisely call them. Who that read them would venture to decide that the lot of the survivor in this duel is better than that of the victim? And who that knows, as I do, this amiable and high-minded gentleman (Graves), would not desire to pour the balm of consolation into his afflicted bosom, rather than seek to make the event which he, in common with all good men, so deeply deplores, a

subject for the display of personal hostility and a
weapon of political warfare? 'Sir,' said Mr. Graves,
'I was involved in the commencement of this unfortunate affair innocently. I never conceived that such consequences would have developed upon me when I
consented to become the bearer of that ill-fated note.
Otherwise, I would never have taken upon myself
the task. I am not, and never have been, the advocate
of the anti-social and unchristian practice of duelling.
I have never up to this day fired a duelling pistol, and,
until the day when I went to the field, I never took
any weapon in my hand in view of a duel. Public
opinion is practically the paramount law of the land;
every other law, both human and divine, ceases to be
observed, yea, withers and perishes, in contact with
it. It was this paramount law of this nation and of
this House that forced me under the penalty of dishonor, to submit myself to the code which impelled me
unwillingly into this tragical affair. Upon the heads
of this nation and at the doors of this House rests the
blood with which my unfortunate hands have been
stained.' "

The poor young man spoke truly enough, but for-
got that he stood in the shoes of James Watson Webb,
not his own, Wise objected to "the sudden and arbitrary assumption of a despotic judicial Power" by a
House committee. "When the House shall be duly and
properly informed that I am implicated in a breach of
its privileges," he declared, "I shall demand a trial at
its bar by the judgment of my peers."

The full report of the Committee failed of acceptance, and Graves remained a member of the House

until 1841. A resolution of censure was, however, passed, 102 to 76. Wise never lived down his share in the tragedy, though the Whigs sustained him as far as voting went so late as 1842. John Quincy Adams, once President, then a Member of the House, denounced him as "a man who came to the House with his hands and face dripping with the blood of murder," and held him, not Graves, to be the guilty man.

Maine was deeply stirred. "The proprietors of the Bath Reading Room," reported the Portland *Transcript,* on March 10, "have struck Webb's paper from their list, resolved not to countenance a man whose hands are stained with the blood of a citizen of this State. From all quarters we hear expressions of condemnation and execration on the parties concerned in this affair. Congress has chosen an investigating committee. Our Legislature has taken the matter in hand, rather tamely, to be sure. Town meetings have been called in various parts of the State. The press has universally spoken out, and from a number of our pulpits last Sabbath, sermons were preached appropriate to the subject. One universal burst of indignation—from every quarter—every party—every class—seems to have been poured upon the aiders and abettors of this cold-blooded murder. Never, perhaps, in the history of the world, was there another instance of individuals on whom the concentrated scorn and contempt of a nation was more fully and deservedly fastened."

The Legislature had taken up the matter tamely

enough, passing, on March 5, these perfunctory resolutions:

"*Resolved,* that the intelligence of the sudden death of the Hon. Jonathan Cilley, a Representative in Congress, from this State, has been received with unfeigned grief.

"*Resolved,* that the People of this State hold in high estimation the distinguished talents and public services of the deceased, and feel the deepest sympathy for his afflicted widow, children and friends."

On April 2, 1838, a special election was held in the Lincoln, Maine, District, represented by Mr. Cilley. The candidates were John D. McCrate, of Wiscasset, Democrat, and Edward Robinson, of Thomaston, Whig. The latter won with a vote of 4,113 to 3,420 for McCrate. One Farley, a bolting Whig, polled 497 votes. The panic of 1837 was more potent in filling the vacancy then sentiment for Cilley. Naturally, the Whigs again rejoiced. When the Democrats of Thomaston proposed to raise a monument to Cilley's memory, Horace Greeley, in his *New Yorker,* of April 28, 1838, remarked: "The partisan character of the call is not in good taste."

In the *Democratic Review* for September, Nathaniel Hawthorne, who had been a fellow student with Cilley in Bowdoin College, printed a sympathetic account of his friend. Hawthorne, by the way, was a Democrat.

The Morris resolution produced the desired prohibition of duelling in the District of Columbia, Senator Prentiss of Vermont introducing a measure to prevent

affairs of honor in the District of Columbia. Ten
years in prison were to punish all persons concerned
in sending a challenge, and a sentence of death
awaited the victor should his opponent die. The anti-
duelling act became a fact in 1839, modified to the
extent of five years in prison instead of ten for giving
or accepting a challenge. Senator Thomas H. Benton
did not regard the law with favor. He had fought
often, formally and informally, and was inclined to
think the abolition of the field of honor would lead to
worse things—the carrying of concealed weapons,
and substituting brutal encounters for gentlemanly
meetings under a meticulous code. "The act should
have pursued the homicidal intent into whatever form
it might assume; and, therefore, should have been to
include all unjustifiable homicides,"—meaning thereby,
murderers who were too respectable to be hanged by
a vulgar sheriff. The act, as he put it "was, therefore,
defective in not pursuing the homicidal offense into all
the new forms it might assume; in not giving dam-
ages to a bereaved family—and not punishing the
carrying of weapons whether used or not—only accommodating the degree of punishment to the more
or less use that had been made of it." He would have
had offenders in the halls of Congress subjected to all
the penalties of high misdemeanor—removal from
office—disqualification to hold any office of trust or
profit under the United States—and indictment at law
besides.

Some states passed anti-duelling laws, partly to
pander to the moral sentiment of the community, and
partly because the rising Whigs had produced so good

a marksman. New York was one of these. Oddly enough, and justly, the only person ever convicted under it was Colonel James Watson Webb. But of that in its place.

It was given out that Cilley was the first member of either House to be killed in a duel. This was not correct. On February 6, 1819, General Armistead T. Mason, Senator in Congress from Virginia, lost his life in an encounter with John McCartey, from the same state. The pair fought with muskets, each carrying a charge of three balls, at the distance of six paces. Mason's death was never formally announced in the Senate and so the affair escaped official recording.

Cilley was young and possessed of many agreeable characteristics. He was born in Nottingham, New Hampshire, February 2, 1802, grandson of Major-General Joseph Cilley, a distinguished officer in the Revolution. Graduating from the Bowdoin College in the celebrated class of 1825, he studied law, was admitted to the bar, and set up practice in Thomaston, Maine, in 1829. He also took on the editorship of the Thomaston *Register,* which he retained from 1829 to 1831. He was elected to the State Legislature and served from 1835 to 1837, inclusive. For two years he held the post of Speaker. A follower of Martin Van Buren, he was elected a member of the Twenty-fifth Congress, taking his seat March 4, 1837. The dead Congressman left a widow, who had been Deborah Prince, and three small children. His home had been at Thomaston, Maine. One of the three orphans grew up to be a distinguished citizen of Maine, Jonathan

Prince Cilley, born in 1835, and surviving far into the twentieth century. He became a brigadier-general in the Civil War, and after its close practiced law at Rockland.

William J. Graves, though also young, was a veteran, having been a member of the Twenty-fourth Congress as well as of the Twenty-fifth. He was reelected to the Twenty-sixth in the Whig sweep of 1838. A son of Mr. Graves, William Preston Graves, became a major in the Second Artillery, of the Regular Army, dying at Little Rock, in 1890.

Of the two seconds, General George W. Jones was the last delegate in Congress from the Michigan territory, the Wolverines securing statehood. He subsequently removed to Iowa. Henry A. Wise continued in politics, became minister to Brazil under Tyler, Governor of Virginia at the time of the John Brown raid, and served with distinction in the Confederate Army. It was he who first blocked Grant at Petersburg. His son, John S. Wise, became a Republican leader in Virginia, and his grandson, another Henry A. Wise, was United States District Attorney in New York.

CHAPTER XIV

THOMAS F. MARSHALL *vs.* JAMES WATSON WEBB

IN 1840 "Tippecanoe and Tyler, Too" placed the Whig party in power for the first time, and it took over the national government with an exultation that bore hard upon the discomfited Democrats. William Henry Harrison's death, after a month in office, put John Tyler in the White House. In policy he was more of a Democrat than a Whig, but Whigs got the offices, and they crowed prodigiously. The chief chanticleer was Colonel James Watson Webb, editor of the New York *Courier and Enquirer.* Horace Greeley had begun to chirp in his newly established New York *Tribune,* but had not yet found his full voice. Webb was the Big Noise in the party.

Besides being on top in the nation, the Whigs had captured the great state of New York, electing William H. Seward governor. Webb was hardly to Seward's taste, but he was "in" with the wealthy Whigs, who constituted respectable society in New York City and had to be considered carefully. Indeed, it was Webb who gave the organization its name. When John Quincy Adams and Henry Clay, at the beginning of the Jacksonian period cut loose from the Jeffersonian Republicans, they called their schism the Republican-Democratic party. Webb, taking title from the Liberals of England who had followed the two

Pitts, selected "Whig" which became the name of his party.

From 1827 to 1842 Webb was the exemplar of personal journalism in the United States. Above the shooting belt which ran coterminous with Mason and Dixon's famous line, he was immune from consequences and did about as he pleased. Angered at the impudence of a former employee James Gordon Bennett, in starting the New York *Herald* right under his noble nose, he not only continually villified that enterprising journalist, but "beat him up" on several occasions, the lesser editor taking his thrashings meekly, though publishing sprightly accounts of them in his paper. Towards other editors Webb was equally bellicose, and his part in the politics of the day was, to say the least, muscular. Burly in person and truculent in manner, he was always in evidence, and he managed to make himself master of men and things about him. Once a Jacksonian Democrat, like most men who change their faith, he was fearfully zealous for his adopted cause, and as such provocative to the highest degree.

To start with, the Colonel was proud of himself and his family line. He was born at Claverack, New York, February 8, 1802, the son of Samuel Blatchford Webb, hailing from Weathersfield, Connecticut, whither his forbears had followed the Rev. Thomas Hooker in his revolt against extreme Puritanism. His mother, a second wife, was Catherine Hogeboom, of Claverack, Columbia County, New York, daughter of an old Holland Dutch family, prominent along the upper Hudson. Samuel Blatchford Webb, an aide-de-camp of General George Washington, was wounded at White Plains and active at Trenton. He became colonel of the Third Connecticut regiment, and finally a brigadier-general. His stepmother, by the way, was a daughter of Silas Deane, of diplomatic fame—or ill-fame, according to view—who bothered Benjamin Franklin in France. The elder Webb was also one of the sixteen founders of the Society of the Cincinnati, which Thomas Jefferson and many others feared was to become the foundation for a military aristocracy. It was he who held the Bible on which Washington took the oath as first President of the United States.

In addition to his pedigree, Colonel Webb inherited the gout, which was to plague him for half a century and undoubtedly had as much to do with his touchiness as a superlative sense of honor. Much pleasure may be had in acquiring the gout, but none at all comes with its inheritance.

Because of his lineage, Colonel Webb was able to hold his head high in the best circles, despite his foul pen and his despotic ways. The close-up to Washington was one of his greatest joys. He often adverted with pride to the effect that the General first met Rochambeau at the Webb homestead in Weathersfield. Close contact with the War of 1812 bred military longings in young Webb's mind, and he entered the Regular Army in 1819, first as ensign in the Fourth Artillery and then as a lieutenant in the Third Infantry. He served on the frontier with his regiment at Detroit. In the meantime he increased his social status by marrying Helen Lispenard Stewart, the daughter in a family still distinguished in New York's society.

Finding army life too dull in peace for one of his spirit, Webb returned to New York, and in 1827 founded the New York *Courier,* which was consolidated in 1829 with the New York *Enquirer,* and so continued until 1860, when it was absorbed by the newly established *World.* He thundered from the beginning to the end of his career.

His first fracas of record appears on May 6, 1830, when he came into collision in Washington with Duff Green, editor of the Washington *Telegraph,* a Jackson organ that later shifted to John C. Calhoun. At this date Webb was a Jacksonian, wavering, however, on the issue of the United States Bank, which was soon to take him out of the fold and into Whiggery. Philip Hone records the encounter in these terms: "*Monday May 10.—* A singularly ridiculous article appears under the signature of Mr. James Watson Webb in the *Courier and Enquirer,* this morning, of which he is editor, relating an account of a fracas between him and Duff Green (editor of the Washington *Telegraph*) in Washington, on Thursday last. Webb went out to flog Green, and the latter armed himself with a pistol and was so unreasonable as to refuse his consent to let the other pull his nose and slap his face. The public might say with Iago in relation to this quarrel:

> Now, whether he kill Cassio,
> Or Cassio him, or each do kill the other
> Every way makes my gain."

January 20, 1836, Hone had occasion again to mention Webb invidiously: "There had been published in the newspapers a most disgraceful correspondence between James Watson Webb, editor of the *Courier and Enquirer*, and Henry Lynch, in relation to stock transactions, in which the softest words used by either party are 'liar,' 'swindler,' and 'scoundrel.' Lynch appears to have the best of the controversy, but it discloses a scene of unprincipled gambling in stocks, alike discreditable to the parties and disgraceful to the character of the city. Such things I have no doubt occur every day, but the moral sense of the community is not often insulted by so open an exposure of them. Webb lost by one transaction upwards of $50,000; that is, he would have lost it if he had had the means or the disposition to pay."

For commenting on this transaction in his New York *Herald,* Webb's former employee, James Gordon Bennett, had to undergo a castigation at his hands, being deemed unworthy of a call to the field of honor. Webb next caused a riot at the Park Theater, late in the following May, by his strictures on an opera company performing there. His attacks caused "the rabble" to gather at the house and force the withdrawal of Mr. and Mrs. Wood, chief performers, by Simpson, the manager.

None of these things appear to have disturbed the editor's social status. Indeed, Hone visited at his place in Whitestone, Long Island, one unpleasant spring day as one "of a pleasant party," which enjoyed "a good dinner, and excellent wine." Mr. Webb's place he found "most beautifully situated on the Sound, opposite Throgg's Neck, and presents fine views of Westchester and a great distance up the Sound. He has a comfortable house, a fine greenhouse, and his grounds are uncommonly beautiful."

Webb's share in the Cilley-Graves duel, and Hone's relation of it have been previously described. He was now to be given a dose of his own medicine. Thomas F. Marshall, of Kentucky, was a brilliant Democratic member of Congress, distinguished about equally for his eloquence and excesses. "The lion of the day," Hone describes him, on May 10, 1842; "a member of the House of Representatives from Kentucky, a man of talents, undoubtedly, a fierce, impassioned declaimer, and, as he is proud of declaring to the world, a 'reformed drunkard.' He is now in the city for the purpose of attending the temperance meetings and going about from place to place to tabernacles and taverns, churches and fire engine houses, all of which overflow when it is announced he is to speak, inveighing against the use of all liquors from wine down to whisky, and extolling water as the only panacea for soul and body. His strongest argument is his own case."

Temperance talking was not the sole cause of Marshall's coming to the city. He became one of the counsel for a Kentucky "Colonel"—Monroe Edwards, a swindler of singular merit, who had separated some $50,000 from New York merchants with plausible schemes, and engaged a formidable body of counsel in his defense, which included, besides Marshall, Senator J. J. Crittenden, also of Kentucky, William M. Evarts, then a rising young attorney, Thomas Addis Emmett, and others of lesser note.

Webb announced Marshall's prospective appearance

in the *Courier and Enquirer,* of June 1, 1842, in these snappy terms:

"We learn from the *Tribune* that the Hon T. F. Marshall, after wandering about the country for some thirty days lecturing on temperance and giving his experience as a devotee of the Bottle, has returned to this city to defend the notorious Monroe Edwards. When he gets back to Washington, he will have been absent about forty days, for which he will doubtless draw from the Treasury, with the sanction of his brother members, three hundred and twenty dollars. Now, while the editor of the *Tribune* was advocating the reduction of the Army and Navy, why did he not gently hint to Congress the necessity of reducing their own pay, and of not paying themselves anything from the public purse, while making mountebanks of themselves or devoting their time to the cause of notorious swindlers?"

The reason for this greeting soon came out. Marshall retaliated in court. On June 11 Webb told the whole story in the *Courier and Enquirer,* unburdening himself on "Hon. Thomas F. Marshall," as follows:

"This gentleman commenced summing up yesterday in behalf of Monroe Edwards and devoted the first thirty minutes of his speech to his personal difficulties with the editor of this paper, in which, if he did temporarily lay aside the character of a mountebank, it was only to assume that of the blustering bully. It becomes our duty, therefore, much as we regret the necessity of again alluding to Mr. Marshall in our columns, briefly to reply to his ill-timed attack upon us —an attack for which the public were prepared by an annunication in the world, and by Mr. M's. bar-room declarations.

"All that he said was in excessive bad taste; and prepared as it was for effect, it singularly failed in its object. We of the North have long since been satisfied with the truth of the old adage that barking dogs don't bite, and if we mistake not, those who heard Mr. Marshall yesterday proclaim his readiness to hold himself personally responsible when called upon for all he said in every situation in life, were irresistibly reminded of this ancient saw. His evident desire to assume a quality which he feared his audience doubted his possessing, apparently excited in his hearers no other feeling than that of surprise to hear a subject treated of in such a presence, and contempt for the individual who could thus indelicately intrude upon them his purely personal affairs; and that, too, in a tone of bravado assumed to cover a craven and shrinking spirit. It was the vaunting bully, asking for the pity and sympathy and protection of his auditory—a second edition of his 'dear mama' affair at the Tabernacle.

"Inasmuch, however, as Mr. Marshall has thus brought our personal difficulties before the jury impanelled to try Monroe Edwards, and a crowded audience, our readers will admit that we have no alternative, but very briefly and succinctly to remind them of the character and circumstances connected with our differences.

"Early in January last, Mr. Marshall, from his place in the House of Representatives, pronounced the *Courier and Enquirer* a 'Pensioned Press' and ourselves a 'Pensioned Editor.' This charge, we were satisfied, was founded upon a basely false publication in the infamous *Herald;* and instead of assailing Mr. M. in return, we calmly pointed out, through our columns, the source of his deception, and expressed our conviction that he was a high-minded gentlemanly man, and would take early occasion to do us justice. In the very same article we announced our determination to transmit him a file of the *Courier and Enquirer,* with a view of convincing him of his error and demonstrating the great injury he had done us.

"We accordingly, on the same day, addressed a private letter to Mr. Marshall, enclosing him a file of the *Courier and Enquirer,* and at the same time asking him to convince himself of the error into which he had fallen, with a view to do us justice from his seat in the House of Representatives. This was on the 26th of January. Day after day elapsed, but not the slightest notice was taken by Mr. Marshall of our public call upon him or of our private letter, except through the columns of the New York *Herald,* where it was announced that Mr. Marshall did not intend to retract his slanders. After the lapse of several weeks we again addressed Mr. Marshall a private letter, calling for a retraction of his charge; and as he had now become a member of the Temperance Society, and ceased to disgrace the hall of Congress by disgusting exhibitions of the most beastly character which the abandoned sot can perpetrate, we did not doubt but he would either make the *amende honorable*, or as it was the duty of a gentleman to do, quietly to apprise us that he did not intend to retract his allegation,

but held himself personally accountable for his conduct. But in this we were destined to disappointment.
It did not suit his purpose then to assume that responsibility into which he has since been whipped by public
opinion; but treated it with silent contempt; and had
we ventured to call him to account for his gross injustice, the public would have been favored with another Cilley affair.

"That we felt his conduct it would be idle to deny.
We had no remedy. But as we did not intend to abandon our profession or to suffer it to be degraded in our
person, we determined quietly to bide our time, and
when occasion offered, teach this honorable, and now,
forsooth, courageous member of Congress, that he
was not beyond the reach of a sound public opinion;
and that no gentleman would sustain him in an indis-
criminate abuse of the Press of the country merely because accident had made him a member of the House
of Representatives. Four long months passed without
the slightest notice of our appeals by Mr. Marshall,
and without our attempting to disturb him in his
vainly imagined security. He then came among us as
a laborer in the great and good cause of temperance;
and then, when he was in the very height of his glory
and followed by thousands of admiring friends, who
rejoiced with us in the reformation of a public and
notorious drunkard, we took occasion to show that
much as we admired the cause, how sincerely we des-
pised its most prominent advocate. It was now our
time to be felt. We openly and publicly arraigned him
at the bar of public opinion; held him up to the

merited scorn of all honorable men; and, that was
certainly the very reverse of his course—we proclaimed that for all we said and wrote, we held ourselves personally responsible.

"Well, we carried the war into Africa; as we are
happy to say, with so much effect, and so much in con-
sonance with an honest public opinion, that even
Thomas F. Marshall, the very honorable and courageous member of Congress, has all at once discovered
that we are not quite so insignificant as he supposed,
and would now fain retrace his steps and occupy the
position in which we first found him."

There followed much more sneering at Marshall's
courage, the diatribe ending with:

"We assuredly shall do nothing to disturb the public
peace; and we are quite certain that there is not a
female in the city who will read the speech of Mr.
Marshall in the *Herald* to-day, but will agree with all
those who heard it that he is 'as harmless as a sucking
dove.' "

The Edwards case went to the jury on June 13. The
jury, not at first agreeing, were held for a verdict.
Webb, in noting the fact, took a further fling at Marshall in his issue of June 14:

"We have frequently spoken of Mr. Marshall as
a man of admitted talents and eloquence, even when
censoring him. But we are now compelled to say that it
is the very general opinion of all who heard him that
he is considerably overrated and not entitled to the
reputation he enjoys. His voice is bad and his manners far from pleasing; and we do him no injustice

and do not overrate the New York bar when we say we have fifty lawyers in this city who are in every respect Mr. Marshall's equals."

Edwards was convicted the next day, and Marshall found time to deal with Webb. There was an interchange of correspondence, which the Colonel did not make public, that ended in an arrangement to meet. Rumors of the duel got about. On June 25, the New York *Herald* noted editorially:

"It was currently reported in the city yesterday that Marshall had challenged Webb and that the latter had accepted the challenge. We do not believe the story. We do not believe that Webb has the courage to fight Mr. Marshall. And we think that Mr. Marshall has too much good sense to send Webb a challenge after all that has passed. Still we have reason to believe that certain letters, or verbal communications, remotely connected with a fight, have passed between the parties, in which Mr. Marshall had the advantage."

The *Herald* had to recant its criticism on Monday, June 27, when it reported the occurrence of the duel on Saturday, the twenty-fifth, in its report from Wilmington, Delaware:

"The duel between Thomas F. Marshall and James Watson Webb was fought this morning at four o'clock, at the old duelling ground, just this side of the State line, about seven miles north of this city. Mr. Marshall was attended by Dr. Carr of Baltimore, as second, and Dr. Gibson, of the same place, as surgeon. Mr. Morrell, of your city, acted as Webb's friend.

"The parties exchanged one shot without injury. Marshall demanded immediately a second pistol, and wounded Webb upon that fire, in the fleshy part of the hip, sustaining no damage himself. Marshall, who came determined to fight it out, demanded a third shot, but Webb could not stand it and the matter was made up.

"It is the general opinion that Webb was anxious to be arrested before the fight, and his conduct really seemed to indicate it. He arrived here on the boat about nine o'clock yesterday (Friday) morning, and before twelve it was known all over the city that he had come to fight a duel. Marshall arrived in the city at two, but by that time the affair had obtained such publicity, that crowds assembled to see them start for the ground, and they were followed by at least one hundred and fifty persons in carriages and on horseback. Our authorities being disposed not to baulk the sport after the honorable gentlemen had travelled one hundred miles for the purpose of the interview, made no effectual interference; but when the parties arrived at the designated place, there were found to be too many spectators present, in case the meeting terminated fatally, and an adjournment of the matter was made till this morning.

"Mr. Marshall was the challenger, but there is a universal regret expressed that by so doing he has at last made Webb a gentleman."

This the *Herald* followed with another account, reading:

"The anticipated duel between the Hon. Thomas F. Marshall, of Kentucky, and James Watson Webb, of the New York *Courier and Enquirer,* came off Saturday morning about daylight at Naaman's Creek, near the Delaware and Pennsylvania state lines, about three miles from Marcus Hook, in the presence of several gentlemen from this city (Wilmington), and a number of laborers from the vicinity.

"Dr. Carr, of Baltimore, was the second of Mr. Marshall, and Mr. Morrell, of Missouri, the second of Mr. Webb. After arranging the preliminaries, the choice of ground and the order to fire, being won by Mr. Webb, the parties proceeded to the spot selected, both of the principals manifesting the utmost coolness and decision. They fought with pistols at the distance of ten paces, and exchanged two shots. The first took no effect, the balls striking the ground a short distance from the feet of the principals. On the second fire Mr. Webb was shot in the back part of the left leg, just below the knee joint, and fell, his fire taking no effect on his opponent.

"He was caught as he was falling by the second of Mr. Marshall, and conveyed from the scene of conflict, and arrived at the U. S. Hotel, in Philadelphia, about nine o'clock Saturday morning. We learn from a gentleman who witnessed the affair that the parties had arranged to meet Friday afternoon, but that in consequence of an excitement among the citizens of Wilmington, it was deferred, the parties remaining in the vicinity all night, Colonel Webb and his friends in a carriage near the ground, and Mr. Marshall and friends putting up at a hotel at Marcus Hook, and by arrangement proceeded to the ground before daylight Saturday morning.

"There was no intercourse between the principals either before or after the duel, and as a matter of course no reconciliation took place between them. Mr. Marshall manifested much feeling for feeding fat the grudge he bore his antagonist; yet throughout the whole affair he demeaned himself with magnanimity, coolness, and courage. After Webb had fallen and it was ascertained that he was only wounded in the leg, Mr. Marshall expressed determination that a third fire should take place. This was protested against by Webb's surgeon, and upon further consideration and advisement on the part of Mr. Marshall and his friend, the latter expressed himself satisfied and seemed to regret that he had demanded a further shot.

"Mr. Marshall's brother was near the ground and after learning the result 'Thanked God that it had not a more serious termination.' From all we can learn, the duel was fought according to the 'Code of Honor,' the parties having agreed upon the terms of conflict which were read aloud before the pistols were handed to them by their seconds and which were mutually assented to in the presence of the company, and when asked by the seconds, both said, 'We are ready.' The wound inflicted on Webb's left leg is the result of the position in which he stood, the left being thrown forward, he standing with his side exposed to the fire of his antagonist.

"Mr. Marshall left the grounds with his friends and proceeded to Washington. The wound of Colonel Webb is not considered serious."

The Baltimore *American's* account asserted that Marshall's pistol went off before he raised it to take aim, and Webb's went off in about the same fashion, which accounts for both bullets striking the ground at their feet. It appears that Dr. Carr acted as Webb's surgeon, and that Josiah Randall and several others of Webb's Philadelphia Whig friends attended the meeting.

June 28th the New York *Herald* contained a letter from Baltimore, signed "Roderick," dated the twenty-seventh, with this comment on the duel: "The Hon. T. F. Marshall, late victor over Colonel Webb, in honorable combat, left here for Washington yesterday afternoon. He appeared altogether unconcerned, and, I presume, had the glorious satisfaction within that he had redressed what is dearer than life—his honor. There is, let the world say what it will, satisfaction in standing forth to defend a gem, so bright, so beautiful, when a tarnish is attempted upon it by some craven scoundrel. It is fortunate for Mr. Marshall that his antagonist sustained the qualities of a gentleman, otherwise his grievances must have gone unredressed.

"There are in the world those so contemptible, so nearly allied to filth, that they cannot insult decency, and were they to attempt it, to hold them responsible at the point of honor would be descending from proper dignity. Such things are only fit to spit upon. Their blood is not worth drawing, being much less precious than that of a sick pig."

Philip Hone took note of the affair under the date of Tuesday, June 29, 1842. "*Duel*—A duel was fought on Saturday (May 26th) morning at sunrise, near Marcus Hook, in the State of Delaware, by

James Watson Webb, editor of the *Courier and Enquirer,* and Thomas F. Marshall, member of Congress. . . . There has been a quarrel of some standing between these parties. Webb accused Marshall
rather indecorously in his paper, and the latter took
an unwarranted advantage of his situation in summing
up in the Court of Oyer and Terminer, where he was
employed as counsel for Monroe Edwards, to retort
upon Webb in a scurrilous attack whilst he was sitting
by, and, of course, precluded from making any reply.
. . . To this attack Webb replied bitterly in his paper,
and the controversy ended in a challenge from Marshall, which was accepted and the parties met as above
stated. At the first fire both missed, and at the second
Webb was wounded in the left leg, the ball passing
through just below the knee and severing the tendons.
Marshall, who, it appears, was savagely bent on
blood, demanded another shot, but Webb's second and
surgeon declared him unable to stand."

Marshall went back to Kentucky much acclaimed by
Democrats, and equally belittled by Whigs. Finding
Louisville much in need of a temperance revival, he
plunged into one with his usual eloquence and success.
No one could picture the horrors of a drunkard's life
better than he. He knew all the details from nausea to
delirium tremens.

The *Herald's* Philadelphia correspondent reported
on July 1: "Colonel Webb has determined to return
home on the 2d. His veal is duly improving." This
was a delicate allusion to the wound in the calf of his
leg. His return does not seem to have been noted and
must have been at a day later than July 2.

After the first day's news was spent, the duel received little attention in the metropolitan press, probably from a desire not to advertise Webb. Dorr's War in Rhode Island was filling the scanty space in the New York papers and the Fourth of July celebration took up much room also, Colonel Samuel P. Colt, inventor of the revolver, having given the nation's natal day an extra enlivenment by testing out off the Battery a submarine idea he had developed. It performed in the presence of the British man of war, *Warspite,* and a large crowd, destroying the hulk at which its efforts were aimed.

No mention of the affair appeared in the *Courier and Enquirer* until July 16, and then only by inference in a hotel puff, reading:

"Having been detained some days in Philadelphia—though not exactly from inclination—we are enabled to do the travelling public a favor by calling their attention to the United States Hotel, under the management and personal supervison of the Proprietors. It has been newly fitted up and newly furnished in very neat and appropriate style; the rooms are large and airy; the attendance prompt and good, and the public ordinary, both for gentlemen and ladies the very best of the size we ever met with. The cooking department is in good hands and one doubts whether seventy or eighty persons ever sat down at the same table with as little noise and confusion as at this admirably kept public house."

It is to be presumed that this item paid the Colonel's hotel bill, after the manner of editors in his day—and much later. He was quiet in his columns for a time, but the constant criticism set him going again. The sly *Herald* noted his umbrage thus:

"The last act of Folly: Poor Webb, writing an account of his late ridiculous duel, an attempt to impose on the chivalry of Tom Marshall, and the correct conduct of Lieutenant Duke for the part he took in the matter. Poor Webb must be getting childish! There is a letter from Wilmington, in possession of one of the parties concerned, which, if published, would make poor Webb look very, very small indeed."

Effort was made to stir up some action in Delaware and to remove the Colonel to that state for trial, but it came to nothing. In New York, however, there was a law against duelling that punished a citizen of the state for leaving it to take part in a duel. The Democratic District Attorney, James F. Whiting, laid a complaint before the Grand Jury. This body returned an indictment, which was found defective. A second one held. Under this Colonel Webb was arraigned in the Court of Sessions on November 19, 1842. He pleaded guilty to the charge and was remanded to a cell in the Tombs Prison to await sentence.

James Gordon Bennett, owner of the New York *Herald,* and Webb's former employee, made merry over the Colonel's plight. "Colonel Webb—His Condition of Mind in Prison," he headed a leader, on November 23, 1843. It read:

"We are afraid that an old friend and fellow-sufferer, Colonel Webb, of the Regular Army, is hardly in the right frame of mind to receive acts of kindness, mercy, or pardon. The Rev. Dr. Anthon should by all means visit him, for since his confinement he has established some strange aberrations of temper. Let us unfold our budget.

"As soon as the Colonel was imprisoned, notwithstanding all he has said and done against us, I felt softened to the heart at his melancholy condition—wounded and in prison in such an affair. I accordingly got up a petition on Sunday last, and by Monday night had it signed by nearly five hundred as respectable names as there are in New York. I sent it up to the Governor as fast as possible, so as to throw my little mite of sympathy into his case, and aid his pardon and liberation as much as possible.

"In addition to all this I sent a note to Mr. Gilbert Davis, corner of William and Pine Street, who keeps a famous wine cellar there, ordering a half-dozen of champagne to be sent to Webb's apartments in the Tombs—also a similar order to Henriques, 51 William Street, an equally famous segar store, to send a box of his best Regalias. The following contains the order for the latter:

ORDER

DEAR SIR: A man called on us and requested us to send up to Colonel Webb, 100 good Regalias. Do you mean it? If so, please acquaint the bearer, and it shall be promptly done—say so in writing. One hundred Regalias cost $5, but we have a good article for $3 the 100.

Your obedient servant,
HENRIQUES, 51 William St.

Monday Afternoon

JAMES WATSON WEBB

J. G. BENNETT

"By some mistake the wine was not sent—but on Monday afternoon the segars reached Webb's apartments. On the young man entering, he found Webb attended by four friends, a black servant waiting behind. He presented the box of segars and stated the message. What was Webb's reply? Anything but what we expected. Colonel Webb looked at him like an old-fashioned thunder cloud, saying, 'I have nothing to say to you, but tell Henriques that had he brought them himself, and dared to offer them, I would have kicked him out.' The messenger, astonished, retreated precipitately, while the four persons present laughed outright. He returned to 51 William Street, segars, reply, and all in the one general box of astonishment. A further correspondence, verbal and written, has passed between Colonel Webb and Mr. Henriques, in relation to this unnecessary insult, but what is its tenor, we do not yet know. Henriques has spunk and will hardly brook it.

"Now, really. This affair seems strange, and positively indicates that Colonel Webb wants advice and prayers of no ordinary kind. Hence, we have been getting up petitions, aiding him in his difficulties and doing everything we could with propriety and delicacy to increase his comfort in prison, till the pardon is procured—till the veto on the sentence is certain. Acting on such motives, and in such a way, the Colonel certainly behaved very unhandsomely to Henriques, who had nothing further to do with the matter than we have related. Instead of wine and segars, our old friend seems to require in a greater degree, the pious prayers of some clergyman.

"We shall therefore endeavor to procure the Rev. Mr. Miller (The Adventist) or the Prophet Joe Smith, or some other eminent and pious person, to call upon him (the Rev. Mr. Anthon hardly has power enough) to put him by prayers and other devotions, into a right frame of mind, while we follow out the petition till he gets released. The wine and segars, we shall send to the poor prize-fighters of White Plains, who are in pretty much the same predicament with the gallant Colonel, and who will soon be in as much need of a pardon. Will they refuse them and insult the messenger? We hope not.

"In the meantime we call upon every humane person in New York, within the reach of our words, who have not signed the petition in favor of poor God-forsaken Webb, to come to the *Herald,* at the corner of Nassau and Fulton Streets, and put down their names forthwith. Come in—come in—come in. We have now well on to a thousand, and we mean to make it five thousand, if we can, before Friday, next, the last day of grace. On Saturday the Colonel receives his sentence. Although he behaves badly, we shall not."

The prize-fight alluded to had been fought at Hastings-on-the-Hudson, between Messrs. Lilley and McCoy. The latter stood up for 119 rounds and then dropped dead in the ring. Lilley and sundry abettors were on trial at White Plains for manslaughter, which gave a little point to Bennett's jest.

The next day Bennett found the Colonel still in an unregenerate frame of mind. Also, while names were being fast added to the *Herald's* petition, many signers noted a proviso that they must also go forward to aid the prize-fighters, if convicted. He put Webb on the *Herald's* free list so he might learn what was going on. Bennett also offered the Colonel the services of his barber, Jean Grant. Further than this he "knew not what to do," as "what with pardons and duellists, and the devil and David Hale [of the *Journal of Commerce*] and prize-fighters, and Archbishop Hughes [with whom he was quarreling] and the governor and the sheriff, and the clergymen, and the burning of the city prison and the burning of the world, we have so much on our hands that we really wish Father Miller would postpone the end of the world, as Felix said to Paul, to a 'more convenient season.' "

The sentence was pronounced by the Recorder on Saturday, November 26, Webb having been "convicted by confession of a felony, in leaving the state for the purpose of giving or receiving a challenge to fight a duel with the Hon. Thomas. F. Marshall, a member of Congress from the State of Kentucky," as the record runs.

The courtroom was crowded. James F. Whiting, the District Attorney who had prosecuted Webb, moved for his sentence. Asked what he had to say for himself, the Colonel responded that he might argue much against the constitutionality of the law, also much more upon the prosecution and malignity of those persons who had pressed the indictment against him; but as it could avail nothing at the moment to alter the state of the matter, he should say nothing and content himself with bowing to the sentence of the court. The Recorder called the Colonel's attention to the fact that he was liable to be punished twice, as the state of Maryland had also a law prohibiting duelling, which he had also violated. He noted that it was the first case of the kind that had been prosecuted, and then, desiring to spare the feelings of the convict, sentenced him to be confined in the State prison for two years.

Commenting on this, Mr. Bennett observed: "We really think this business has gone far enough. We owe no favors or good feeling to Webb for seven years past, but we think the Governor ought to put an end to the suspense and pardon the poor fellow at once. We could give reasons enough for it, but there is no necessity. Webb has now a wound in his leg that he will carry to the grave. Is not this, in the name of all that is called justice, quite enough of punishment?"

Philip Hone wrote in his diary on November 26, 1842:

"James Watson Webb was brought up in the Court of Sessions this day, and sentenced by the Recorder, on his plea of guilty of the charge of leaving the State to fight a duel, and fighting a duel with Thomas Marshall. The sentence was two years imprisonment in the State prison—the shortest term prescribed by the statute. There is very little doubt that the sentence will be followed immediately by an unconditional pardon from Governor Seward, to whom petitions to that effect have been forwarded, signed by fourteen thousand citizens of New York. In this large number are included most of the leading men in the party in politics opposed to Colonel Webb, fourteen of the seventeen members of the Grand Jury who found the bill, every Alderman and assistant of the city except one, a great many of the clergy, judges of the several courts, and members of the bar. The roll was upward of four hundred feet in length. This is all very flattering to the delinquent, who has fallen into the law's danger; but there is good reason to believe that Governor Seward did not require this strong appeal to incline him to exercise the most agreeable prerogative of executive power. The pardon is, no doubt, prepared already, and all reasonable men will justify it on the present occasion. "

Webb was taken back to his cell "looking nervous and careworn," having escaped a maximum penalty of seven years. The petition went at once to the Whig governor, William H. Seward. He lost no time in acceding to the "popular" demands, filing a lengthy "pardon" on the Monday following the sentence, November 28, and before the Colonel could start for Sing Sing, citing that the judges, grand jurors, and jurors, as well as citizens too numerous to mention, had joined in the appeal, and in consideration of which he acted, "but upon the express condition that the said James Watson Webb shall not, while he remains a citizen of this State, violate any of the laws to prevent duelling, nor by any act aid, assist or abet any such violation, nor print nor publish any justification or defense of the practice of duelling, or any paper with intent to advocate or uphold the same."

Upon this the doughty Colonel was allowed to go

free, amid much rejoicing on the part of himself and
friends. The *Evening Post* quite disapproved of the
pardon, feeling that Webb had earned the right to
spend two years in prison for his sins.

All of the *Herald's* sympathy was, of course,
mockery. When Webb was released it expressed its
real feelings thus:

"The more we reflect on the pardon given Webb,
the more we are satisfied that all pardons to criminals
are useless. In that particular instance it has only in
creased the impudence, pomposity, and mischievous pro-
pensities of the Regular Army. We shall go for no
more pardons. Let the law in every case have its course.
Webb is a worse man and a worse editor—more
abusive and unprincipled than ever."

The luckless prize-ring culprits were convicted of
manslaughter in the fourth degree, and not pardoned.
Even the *Post* gave twenty times as much space to their
troubles as it gave Webb. There was a deal of news,
besides, to drown the event—the mystery of the death
of Mary C. Rogers, John Anderson's beautiful tobacco
seller; the murder of Samuel Adams by John C. Colt,
besides Dorr's War in Rhode Island, were all under
way at the moment.

Webb has been charged with expectorating into the
face of James Gordon Bennett. He had himself to
undergo this extremity of insult at the instance of
one Leconte, agent for the French Transatlantic Company, who had fallen under his displeasure. This was
on Friday, August 20, 1847. "The Frenchman," Hone
noted, "spat in Webb's face, who, of course, struck
him, and several blows passed, but I did not learn in

the imperfect account I had of the affray, who had the advantage in the conflict. I do not care what is the origin of such an attack, or who is in the right, but I hold any man justified (and so I should, if I was a grand juryman in the case) who kills on the spot, if he had a deadly weapon, the filthy brute who voids his rheum in his adversary's face."

In 1848 Zachary Taylor, Whig, was elected President. In 1849 Webb was appointed Minister to Austria. The Senate refused to confirm. The Whig party dying, Webb became a supporter of the Republicans. To his other prowess the Colonel added that of a mighty hunter. He made a memorable trip to the Rocky Mountains in the fifties after big game and bagged it in large quantities, writing an account of his adventures after returning. It was called "Tarowan."

In 1861, after the *Courier and Enquirer* had been consolidated with the *World,* President Lincoln offered the Colonel the mission to Turkey. This he declined as not being to his taste, and accepted instead, that to Brazil. He had a good deal of temperamental trouble there, but performed some important services, and was later useful, through his personal friendship with Napoleon III, in inducing that monarch to withdraw his troops from Mexico, to the relief of his friend, William H. Seward, then Secretary of State.

Despite his many brawls and the gout, Webb lived to number eighty-two years, dying in 1884. Philip Hone once summed him up thus sententiously, in contrast with William B. Astor, "who thinks twice before he speaks once," as one "who speaks a good deal and does not think at all."

CHAPTER XV

Thomas L. Clingman vs. William L. Yancey

IN antebellum days two famous fire-eaters were Thomas L. Clingman, of North Carolina, and William L. Yancey, of Alabama. Both were members of Congress in 1845, when the conflict occurred, of which this is the chronicle. The two became engaged in a fierce debate in the House on January 7, at the close of which day Mr. Clingman, after conferring with Congressman Artemas Burt of South Carolina, sat himself down and indited the following note to Yancey:

SIR,—

In the course of your remarks today you declared that you wished to have nothing to say with one possessed of the head and heart of the gentleman from North Carolina, alluding, as I understand, to me, personally.

I desire to know of you whether, by the use of that expression, you intended toward me any disrespect, or to be understood that I was deficient in integrity, honor, or any other quality requisite to the character of a gentleman.

Yancey replied the next day in these terms:

SIR,—

I do not recognize as mine the language attributed to me in your note of yesterday.

I send you, extracted from the *Globe,* of the 7th, with my

THOMAS L. CLINGMAN

corrections, an accurate report of my remarks concerning yourself. Of the language I did use, or of my motives, I have no explanation to make.

This reply called forth a further query from Clingman, dated January 10, 1845:

SIR,—

The language furnished me as having been used by you, being different from that attributed to you in my first note, I deem it proper to inquire if I am to understand you as having finally declined to give me any satisfactory explanation of it?

The affair had now reached the state where both parties turned matters over to representatives. Mr. Yancey had taken himself to Baltimore with John M. Huger, his second, to be free from the law against duelling that prevailed in the District of Columbia. Here he was waited upon by Congressman J. M. S. Causin of Maryland, to be informed by that gentleman that Mr. Charles Lee Jones of Baltimore would continue the formalities on behalf of Mr. Clingman. Mr. Jones was the bearer of the note above quoted. To this Mr. Huger bore the following response under the same date:

SIR,—

The language of your note today appears to me to be indefinite. My note of the 8th corrects the misapprehension under which you seem to labor in attributing to me language different from that (which) was really used by me in the political discussion which took place in the House of Representatives on the 7th, and for which you desired an explanation. That you may be put in possession of my remarks as regarded yourself at the earliest possible moment, I enclosed in my note of the 8th a corrected copy. I deem any explanation superfluous.

Mr. Jones came back with this:

SIR,—

I am happy to perceive in your reply to my note of this date, what appears to be a disposition for an amicable adjustment of the difficulty between us. I presume that you will now state whether, in the report of your speech, as furnished by you to me, you intended any personal disrespect, or to intimate that I was deficient in integrity, honor, or any other quality requisite to the character of a gentleman.

This was a large order. That night, at ten o'clock, Huger deposited with Jones an uncompromising retort:

SIR,—

In reply to your note of this afternoon, suggesting that I might now reply to the inquiry which you substantially made in your note of the 7th inst., I have to say that, a perusal of the remarks, which I furnished you on the 8th, will enable you to determine whether they imputed to you "any deficiency in integrity, honor, or any other quality requisite to the character of a gentleman," or whether they characterize your conduct as a Representative in Congress; and I must repeat in relation to them that I deem any explanation superfluous.

This tart reply convinced Jones that further correspondence would be useless; but after consultation with Clingman, it was decided to defer till dawn any further proceeding. Accordingly Jones went to Barnum's Hotel at ten o'clock the next morning and found Huger awaiting him. They reviewed the situation on behalf of the several principles, but found no middle ground upon which they could compromise without a withdrawal of the entire correspondence. With polite formality it was accordingly agreed to treat the condition as *de novo,* but in reality the controversy began where it left off with a renewal on the part of Jones of Clingman's demand in this form:

I hope you will now state whether, in making the remarks as published in the *Globe* newspaper, which are understood to have been revised and corrected by yourself, you intended any disrespect to me, or to cast any reflection on my honor or character as a gentleman?"

To this Huger could only bring himself to say, on behalf of Yancey:

The remarks in reference to yourself, and substantially reported in the *Globe* of the 8th sprung from, and received their tone, almost entirely from the imputations cast upon the motives and character of the great body of the Southern representatives in the House of Representatives on the 6th inst. by yourself. The only construction which I, in common with the great body of those gentlemen could place upon them, demanded and elicited that portion of mine which bore upon you. Mr. C. will at once perceive that he is not entitled to, and must understand me as refusing to give, any explanation of language elicited by his own imputations upon the character of my brother representatives.

Jones would not accept this, quite naturally, and was asked to write out what would suffice. He responded with this rather reasonable draft:

SIR,—

In reply to your note of this date (the 11th), I have only to say that the language applied to you in my speech, was made in the heat of a political debate and not intended to be personal.

Mr. Huger regarded this as "entirely inadmissible," and the correspondence returned to its original status. Such being the case, Mr. Clingman favored Yancey with a formal demand for· satisfaction in these terms, under the date of January 11:

SIR,—

Having failed in all my efforts for an amiable adjustment of the difficulty between us, nothing remains for me but to demand of you the satisfaction usual among gentlemen.

To this Mr. Jones brought a verbal assent and the seconds proceeded to arrange the details. Huger selected pistols on behalf of his principal. After some dispute the time of meeting was set for Monday, January 13, at a spot between Beltsville, Maryland, and the District of Columbia line on the Washington turnpike. The hour agreed upon was three o'clock in the afternoon. The following rules and regulations were assented to and formally put into writing by the seconds:

1.—Weapons to be used, smooth-bore pistols of the usual duelling length.

2.—Distance ten paces (thirty feet).

3.—Pistols to be held perpendicular, the muzzles up or down, at their selection.

4.—The word to be given in a clear, loud, distinct tone, as follows, "Gentlemen, are you ready? Fire—one—two—three—halt!" at intervals of one second each.

5.—The wind and sun to be equally divided.

6.—The giving of the word and the choice of positions to be decided by the toss of a dollar.

7.—The pistols to be loaded by the seconds with powder and single ball, in the presence of all parties.

8.—Each party to be permitted to have on the ground a surgeon and three friends, all of whom must be unarmed.

9.—The seconds to be armed with pistols, loaded with powder and single ball.

10.—The seconds to be permitted to examine the person and dress of each principal.

11.—Neither principal to commence lowering or raising his pistol before the word "fire" nor after the word "halt."

Yancey, Huger, and Mr. Buchanan left Baltimore in a hack on Saturday night and drove to the vicinity of the ground chosen. They passed Sunday at a wayside tavern, registering under assumed names. Buchanan left the party and returned to Washington by train Sunday afternoon. The other two were discovered by a friend, who, learning their errand and fearing arrest, took them to his home and harbored them over night. The next morning they proceeded to Brown's Hotel, a mile west of Beltsville, where Jones joined them, and, in company with Huger, located the ground, half a mile west of the inn. Huger won the choice and decided to give the word. A group of Yancey's friends, led by Buchanan, now arrived from Washington. They included Congressman Artemas Burt of South Carolina, James E. Belser and Reuben Chapman of Alabama, R. M. Saunders of North Carolina, A. B. Meek of Alabama, Dr. Gwyn of Mississippi, and Dr. Tate of the same hot-blooded state. Word had got about, and a force of police invaded the hotel. Chapman and Meek were arrested and bound over, but Yancey and Huger, slipping out of the back door, made their way on foot through the woods to the ground. Here Clingman and Jones awaited them. The men were hurriedly placed, in anticipation of interruption by the police, who rushed upon the scene just as Huger gave the word. Both fired and missed. The presence of the police assisted in settling the dispute without further use of ammunition, though formal terms were drawn up and signed by the seconds, reading:

"After a first and ineffectual fire, a consulation followed between the friends of the parties; and upon a suggestion of Hon. Mr. (Kenneth) Rayner, of North Carolina, that Mr. Yancey might now retract his personally offensive remarks applicable to Mr. Clingman, Mr. Huger suggested that this difficulty existed: That Mr. Yancey considered Mr. Clingman's speech as casting personal and offensive imputations on Southern Democrats. Upon which Mr. Jones, as Mr. Clingman's friend, at once disclaimed such construction, and declared that the speech was purely political, and that Mr. C. intended no personal imputation upon any member of the House of Representatives. Whereupon, Mr. Yancey made the suggested retraction."

So ended the only duel that grew out of the proposition to extend slavery to Texas under the annexation treaty that was then pending, and this between two Southern statesmen, Clingman being opposed to the proposition and Yancey favoring it. Violent talk of secession had been indulged in on the part of the proslavery members of Congress, led by Yancey, who never changed his attitude and was a leading factor in the organization of the Southern Confederacy when the movement took final shape in 1860-1861.

A photograph of an oil painting in the State Capitol at Montgomery, Alabama.

CHAPTER XVI

DAVID S. TERRY *vs.* DAVID C. BRODERICK

ONE day, in 1849, David S. Terry, born in Tennessee, but then in the garb of a Texas Ranger, rode into the village of Yerba Buena, which later became San Francisco, California. Here he was destined to have an amazing career. Devoted to all things Southern, he arrived when the great company of adventurers gathered at the Golden Gate were intent upon statehood. He joined those who wished California to become a Southern adjunct and permit the ownership of slaves. North and South met in fierce contention on the Pacific coast.

The leadership of the anti-slavery forces fell to David C. Broderick, son of an Irish stone-cutter, who had carved the capitals on the columns supporting the portico of the Capitol at Washington, where he was born. Taken to New York, he grew up in that city and became an active member of Tammany Hall. The call of gold took him to California, where he was soon a political power. He did not go into the mines, but made money speculating in claims and real estate. He also acquired one of the surest ways of getting into trouble that then existed—the ownership of a newspaper, the San Francisco *Herald*. For an editor, he picked a slim young chap of twenty-eight, William Walker from Nashville, Tennessee, via New Orleans.

317

Walker had a long head, strong chin, wide mouth, and optics that led him in due time to be famous as "The Gray-eyed Man of Destiny"—the Fillibuster who was to conquer Nicaragua, and to die there before a file of soldiers. Walker made the *Herald* a pungent paper. His pen got him into a duel with William Hix Graham, a former Philadelphian. They used pistols and Walker was hit. He did not let this be known, but his second caught sight of a blood spot on the sand and prevented further proceedings.

Walker then retired from the *Herald,* but the paper continued to make enemies for Broderick. Among these was a California character of the day, William Smith, of Virginia, whose father had been governor of the Old Dominion. He held a judgeship in San Francisco, administering the office in free and easy fashion, such as became one who had earned the sobriquet of "Extra Billy" Smith. Smith called Broderick to account for some strictures in the *Herald.* The two fought on the Eastern shore of San Francisco Bay in 1852. Navy revolvers were the weapons used; the distance, ten paces. Each man emptied the six barrels on his pistol. Smith was not touched, but one Colt bullet struck Broderick's chest. It encountered a thick watch case and so only effected a bruise. At this, honor was satisfied.

David S. Terry was the next person to cross Broderick's path. He had taken up the practice of law and reached a judgeship. California voted to come into the Union as a Free State and was so admitted. Terry was soon prominent in the anti-Broderick faction, which had an organ in the *Bulletin,* edited by a Virginian, who called himself James King of William, after the County in which he was born.

King made Broderick a target for many of his fiercest attacks. He dubbed him "David Cataline Broderick", accusing him of jobbery in land sales to the city, of exacting a price for nominations in cases where election was sure, of ballot-box stuffing, and general corruption. "We have every confidence," he wrote, in concluding one conspicuous attack, "that the people will stand by us in this contest; and, if we can only escape David C. Broderick's hired bullies a little longer, we will turn this city inside out."

Broderick's "bullies" existed, but they did not harm King. Neither was he sued for libel. Much that King charged was true enough in that every-man-for-himself welter, but it rolled off Broderick's back in the larger contention. Delay in hanging a gambler, named Cora, who had killed a rival, led King to an aggressive assault upon James P. Casey, supervisor, who had served a term in Sing Sing. For this Casey killed King in May 1856.

As a result, the old Vigilance Committee of 1851 reformed and hanged both Cora and Casey. They took over the government of the town. A law-and-order party was formed to bring back legal authority. In this both Broderick and Terry joined, without, however, becoming friendly. Terry had come to the defense of Cora and Casey, and the Vigilantes determined to arrest him. This he resisted, and carved one of the posse with a bowie knife. He had a narrow escape from sharing the fate of Cora and Casey. Indeed, the Vigilantes would probably have hanged him but for the interference of Captain David G. Farragut, U. S. N., who brought a warship down from the Mare Island navy yard, where he was stationed, and interrupted the program. There was no popular ill-feeling, however, against Broderick, though he stood by Terry, who was placed on the Supreme Court bench in 1855, by vote of the so-called American party, as Chief Justice, while Broderick went to Washington as a Senator.

Broderick had been a member of the state convention that framed the anti-slavery Constitution. On the floor at Sacramento he was vigilant in support of free labor. Dr. Stephen W. Gwin, one of the state's two Senators in Congress, was a Southerner and pro-slavery. The two men clashed, but Broderick, being on the ground, won out and the pair came to terms. When Gwin was up for reëlection, he conceded to Broderick, who was also a Democrat, the parceling out of the United States patronage, which James Buchanan, then President of the United States refused to deliver, Broderick being an open antagonist to the Lecompton Constitution in Kansas, which Buchanan had recognized and which made the territory slave.

Broderick had grown in size in the fresh atmosphere of the coast. He had been "one of the roughs," as Walt Whitman described them in New York—keeper of a saloon, foreman of a volunteer fire company, and kept pretty tough political company. In California he became studious and an able statesman; in the United States Senate he speedily grew into a man of importance, though outlawed, along with Stephen A. Douglas, by the Administration. Yet, according to James Ford Rhodes: "The purity of his life and his scrupulous honesty, associated with pride, energy, and ambition, commanded respect from men of both sections and of all parties. Fearless and frank, the serious and reflective cast of mind of this man, alone in the world, without relatives or family, was an added charm for those who knew best his early circumstances. One cannot but wonder whether, had fortune bestowed upon him opportunities of refining influence, his career might not have been an unalloyed benefaction to his country."

In the Lecompton debate in the Senate, Broderick, Stewart of Michigan, and Pugh of Ohio, were the only Democrats to sustain Douglas. All men beholden to them for office were turned out, and warning went forth that to vote against the measure meant political extermination. The four stood undauntedly against the measure. Kansas reversed the verdict against it, voted to reject the Constitution on a recall, and stood outside of statehood. So it was that, in 1859, there was little political excitement. But in California, Gwin raised an issue. It was that southern California be set off from the northern part and be given the right of human bondage.

Gwin had permitted Broderick to come to the Senate under a sort of sufferance to save himself. He was now openly arrayed against his colleague on the slavery issue. A spirited campaign resulted. The fight was one of faction. Broderick's friends in Washington, where he had many, begged him to keep out of it and take a trip to Europe in the interest of his personal safety. His office was not at stake and he might well have taken this advice, but refused to do so. Yet he went back to California with forebodings. To

Colonel John W. Forney, clerk of the House, he said, on departing: "I feel, my dear friend, that we shall never meet again. I go home to die. I shall be challenged, I shall fight, and I shall be killed."

He felt that as a leader he should not forsake his following even to secure personal safety. Besides, he believed in his cause. His return was greeted with a fusillade of abuse. After an effort to conduct the campaign on something like a decent level, he was compelled to use the language employed by his enemies. Pro-slavery was rampant. Gwin ceased to be a submissive colleague and became an open enemy. Broderick met his utterances with those of equal bitterness. Aware that the issue was to be fought to a finish, he used all the weapons at hand, scandalous and otherwise. Ill, with a wasting affection, he became desperately aware that his career was to be cut short.

Thus it was that he denounced Gwin mercilessly and charged that he was "dripping with corruption." Gwin had been the first Senator elected by the new state, along with John C. Frémont, who had drawn the short term. The State election was due on September 7. From the first of July to that date, Broderick was in the thickest of the fight, with Gwin actively against him and Terry equally in evidence. His strictures on Broderick smarted. Soon after the contest began, the Senator, while dining in a mixed company at the International Hotel, publicly expressed the opinion that Terry was a corrupt man. One Perley, who was present, a friend of Terry's, urged that he be less open in his strictures, whereat Broderick repeated the charge with emphasis. Upon this Perley

DAVID C. BRODERICK

challenged him to a duel. Broderick, perhaps sensing
the fate he had foretold to Forney, declined—first,
on the ground that Perley was an Englishman; second,
that the challenger was not his political equal; and
third, that his duty to his supporters would not permit
him to risk his life before the election. Perley did not
persist, and the campaign went on with increasing in-
tensity.

In the course of the campaigning, Terry, still on the
Supreme Court bench, had alluded in a speech to Broderick as "a follower of the Black Douglass, whose
name is Frederick, not Stephen"—referring to the
noted colored orator who was an ex-slave. Broderick
made no public retort; but to an acquaintance remarked that he had once considered Terry the only
honest man on the Supreme bench, "but now I take
it all back." This was carried to Terry by a tale
bearer. Neither remark would be remembered ordinarily, but there was a purpose behind the pursuit of
Broderick. "Between the 1st of July and the 7th of
September," wrote a reporter, "the political campaign
was accompanied by the bitterest personalities, and
Broderick in his speeches did not spare the name
of Terry. The latter was ultra-Southern in his morality as well as his politics. On the morning of the 8th,
the day after election, before breakfast, while Broderick was still in the height of his rage on the first
news of the overwhelming defeat of his party, he received a polite little note from Terry, to which none
of the objections made to Perley's challenge would
apply."

Indeed the Judge had resigned from the bench at

the same time, to free himself from possible criticism, and was vindictively preparing for eventualities. He was a practiced hand with the pistol, and in his prime —about forty years of age. Broderick knew nothing of firearms, and the state of his health was such that he could have declined with propriety, even under the code. He was too proud to give this excuse, but delayed his response. When made, he accepted the challenge. It was arranged that the meeting should take place on the beach of the Pacific Ocean, nine miles south of the city, at six o'clock on the morning of September 12. Its impendency became known and set San Francisco agog with excitement. As a result there was a great crowd at the appointed ground to see the show. Some arrests were made, and the duel was delayed, but only till the morrow, though the San Francisco *Bulletin* announced that it had come off and that Terry had been severely wounded in the neck.

The ocean beach was abandoned as too public in favor of a small valley, ten miles from Merced Lake. Choice of weapons was left to lot. Terry won. He had, therefore, the advantage of a weapon with which he was thoroughly familiar, its trigger so delicately sprung that a breath would move it. He had fought more than once before and had the deliberate purpose to kill his man.

Broderick, by evil chance, got a pistol even more sensitive than that held by Terry. The distance was set at ten paces. Broderick was weak from illness, unnerved, and in no condition to fight for his life. Calhoun Benham and Thomas Hayes acted as seconds for Terry, while Hon. J. C. McKibben and Mr. Coulter acted in like capacity for Broderick. It took the seconds half an hour to arrange the details, during which time neither principal showed signs of nervousness or concern. Then ten paces were marked off and the combatants took their positions. The seconds divested them of their collars and outside coats, to make less of a mark, and took charge of their watches and coins. The terms of the duel were read and assented to by both. Then Coulter, who had to give the word, explained the manner in which he should do it—"One —two—fire—stop!"

All this while, according to an eye witness, the two men stood in positions with the utmost composure, pistols in hand, pointing to the ground. Each was dressed in black and wore a slouch hat. Broderick held his body erect, but his head down. Their attitudes were quite different when facing the fire. Terry maintained that of the practiced duellist, with his body poised to prevent exposure, while Broderick's pose was careless and afforded the better target. Unaccustomed to firearms, he held his pistol awkwardly and used his left hand to twist his right into place for action. He did not raise his eyes until the word came to fire; and once he shifted his foot beyond the line, for which he was corrected by McKibben. The bearing of Terry did not outdo in coolness that of the iron-nerved Broderick, who knew he had come there to die.

When the word was given Broderick touched the hair trigger before he took aim. The pistol fired, taking effect in the earth at Terry's feet. The latter deliberately took aim and fired after an instant's ghastly pause. Broderick clapped his hand to his side and moved slowly toward a canvas shelter that had been erected. He was a man of powerful physique, but before his seconds could reach him, his right leg crumpled beneath his body and he fell slowly to the ground. Dr. Locke, the surgeon, took him in hand. He found the bullet had entered Broderick's breast under his left arm. Terry had aimed for the heart. During the examination the latter stood with folded arms, pistol in hand. When Broderick had been removed to his carriage, Terry and his friends departed from the field, drove rapidly to San Francisco, and then took a boat across the bay to Benecia, thence to await the storm at Sacramento.

Broderick was borne to the home of his friend, Leonidas Haskell, at Black Point, on the Bay. Here hundreds called. He saw many and exchanged greetings, in murmuring voice. The wound, however, was fatal. He survived from Tuesday until nine-thirty on the morning of Friday, September 16.

San Francisco and all the state went into mourning. Flags were everywhere lowered to half-staff, with the Union down. The dead man had been so pure a patriot, so good a man, and so fine a figure that his death seemed a devil's deed. There were no wires across the continent then, and the evil news did not reach the outposts of the telegraph in Missouri until the middle of October. Then the North joined in the mourning. New York held memorial services.

The funeral took place in San Francisco on September 18. Ten thousand people gathered about Broderick's bier to listen to the funeral oration made by Colonel E. D. Baker, the best speaker in the state.

"Fellow citizens," said Baker, "the man who lies before you was your Senator. From the moment of his election his character has been maligned, his motives attacked, his courage impeached, his patriotism assailed. It has been a system tending to one end. And the end is here. What was his crime? Review his history, consider his public acts, weigh his private character—and before the grave encloses him forever, judge between him and his enemies. As a man to be judged by his private relations, who was his superior? It was his boast—and amid the general license of a new territory, it was a proud one—that his most scrutinizing enemy could fix no single act of immorality upon him. Temperate, decorous, self-restrained, he had passed through all the excitements of California unstained. No man could charge him with broken faith or violated trust. Of habits simple and inexpensive, he had no lust for gain. He overreached no man's weakness in a bargain and withheld from no man his just dues. Never in the history of the state has there been a citizen who has borne public relations more stainless in all respects than he.

"But it is not by this standard that he is to be judged. He was a public man and his memory demands a public judgment. What was his public crime? The answer is in his own words, 'They have killed me because I was opposed to the extension of slavery and a corrupt administration.' "

"The Code of Honor," said Baker, in further comment, "is a delusion and a snare; it palters with the hopes of a true courage and binds it at the feet of crafty, cruel skill. It substitutes cold and deliberate preparation for courageous and manly impulse. It makes the mere truth of the weapon superior to the noblest cause and the truest courage."

The vast concourse wept. Soon the dogs of war were loose, with the gallant Baker one of their earliest victims. And the cause for which Broderick fell triumphed. The Legislature had censured him for his free-soil attitude in the Senate, but in 1863 expunged the criticism and lauded him as a patriot.

Commenting on the outcome, the amiable George William Curtis wrote in *Harper's Weekly:*

"Most of the papers here characterized the event as a murder. It seems certain that many politicians, among whom Dr. Gwin occupied a conspicuous place, had determined to fight Broderick; had he escaped Terry, other duels awaited him, and in a country of marksmen he could hardly have escaped in the end. . . .

"There are parts of the United States where a politician must necessarily be prepared to fight duels. In the origin the practice is said to have risen from the want of some potent correction of the prevailing rudeness of customs among the early settlers. Men got into the way of fighting in order to anticipate insult, just as Texans carry bowie knives so as to ensure peace and order. Whether the method was sound, and whether it answered its purpose; whether duellists are more tender of each other's feelings than members of the Peace Society; whether turbulence is peculiar to the unarmed; and rare among the General Chotlops, it is now not worth while to inquire. However this may be, it is clear at the present day, as well in California as in every other state of the Union, that society could get on very well without duels. No person of repute will assent that the abolition of the duello would now involve injurious social consequences.

"Yet, it is undoubted, that in many states of the Union, a politician who will not fight must stand aside, and cannot command the popular suffrage. . . . Man is a carnivorous and bloody-minded creature. Civilization, even of the purest kind, only half tames him. Many of the best of men have a secret relish for blood, and slaughter, and horrors.

"Political duellists are the prize-fighters of their part of the country. . . . Jones and Smith, of Arkansas, may not like being shot at; but the people of Arkansas—like the rest of us—relish the excitement of a duel, and this is the price they set on their suffrages. . . . Candidates among them they require to be fighting men, just as Mrs. Potiphar required her footmen to have calves."

Gossip had it that a plot was laid for Broderick's life—that he was to be challenged in turn by Terry, his colleague Gwin, and General J. M. Denver, to be sure that one or the other "got him." Denver had killed Edward Gilbert, editor of the *Alta California*, in 1852, while he was Secretary of State. Gilbert had assailed Gov. Bigler, and Denver took up the quarrel. The enterprising capital of Colorado immortalizes his name.

What of Terry? There was a strong movement to revive the Vigilance Committee and hang him, but no one wanted to bell the cat. Finally he was indicted for murder, put under arrest, and released on $10,000 bail. He succeeded in securing a change of venue to another county and was acquitted on trial. He continued to live in San Francisco and held his head high, but people viewed him much as New Yorkers had viewed Aaron Burr. He lived a long and troubled life, which came at last to a violent end. Carrying on a suit against Senator William Sharon, in the interest of a notorious woman, Sarah Althea Hill, he married the woman, and in umbrage at the outcome of the suit, made threats against United States Judge Stephen J. Field, brother of Cyrus W. Field, layer of the Atlantic cable. The Judge went about thereafter under guard of a deputy marshal. August 14, 1889, Terry and Judge Field met on the platform of the railway station, in Lathrop, California. David Nagle, Field's bodyguard, took no chances, and killed the old man with a revolver shot. Public sentiment was shocked, but the marshal went free. So the fiery soul was unceremoniously snuffed out.

There was another anti-slavery duel in the same period that did not make so much noise. It occurred in Arizona, and was without fatalities. It was between Edward E. Cross, advocate of Free Statehood, and one Mowry, who had been delegated to represent the territory in Congress as a supporter of slavery. Both were excellent marksmen, and to render the result doubtful, their seconds placed the pair so that a strong prairie wind would blow across their stand and deflect the bullets. They fought with Burnside rifles at ten paces. On the first fire a ball grazed Mowry's ear; on the second Cross lost a lock of hair. On the third Mowry's rifle missed fire, while Cross failed to get Mowry. Mowry demanded the right to make another trial without a return. To this Cross's seconds demurred, as meaning nothing less than murder. Cross overruled them and, folding his arms, became a non-resisting target. Mowry had the wisdom to aim in the air. So the affair ended.

It did not close the career of Cross, which was rather remarkable. He had been a fellow apprentice with Charles F. Browne, better known as "Artemus Ward," in the *Democrat* office at Lancaster, New Hampshire, and was pretty wild. Growing up, he took to newspaper writing in Cincinnati, then served as a Colonel in the Mexican Army and worked as a miner in Arizona. When the Civil War broke, he returned to his native state and became Colonel of the Fifth New Hampshire volunteer regiment, which he led heroically on many fiields until a bullet ended his Odyssey at Gettysburg. He seldom went into battle without receiving wounds.

INDEX